Living in the Crossfire

to Paul,

Com carinho,

Maria Helena
Moreira Alves

Maria Helena Moreira Alves and Philip Evanson

Living in the Crossfire

Favela Residents, Drug Dealers, and Police Violence in Rio de Janeiro

With the assistance of
Cristina Pedroza de Faria (Kita Pedroza)
and José Valentin Palacios Vilches

TEMPLE UNIVERSITY PRESS
Philadelphia

TEMPLE UNIVERSITY PRESS
Philadelphia, Pennsylvania 19122
www.temple.edu/tempress

Library of Congress Cataloging-in-Publication Data

Alves, Maria Helena Moreira, 1944–
    Living in the crossfire : Favela residents, drug dealers, and police violence in
Rio de Janeiro / Maria Helena Moreira Alves and Philip Evanson ; with the
assistance of Cristina Pedroza de Faria (Kita Pedroza) and José Valentin
Palacios Vilches.
        p.   cm. — (Voices of Latin American life)
    Includes bibliographical references and index.
    ISBN 978-1-4399-0003-1 (cloth : alk. paper)
    ISBN 978-1-4399-0004-8 (pbk. : alk. paper)
    ISBN 978-1-4399-0005-5 (electronic)
    1. Violence—Brazil—Rio de Janeiro.   2. Drug traffic—Brazil—Rio de
Janeiro.   3. Squatter settlements—Brazil—Rio de Janeiro.   4. Slums—
Brazil—Rio de Janeiro.   I. Evanson, Philip.   II. Title.

    HN290.R5A48 2011
    303.6'2086942098153—dc22   2010030474

♾ The paper used in this publication meets the requirements of the American
National Standard for Information Sciences—Permanence of Paper for Printed
Library Materials, ANSI Z39.48-1992

Printed in the United States of America

2 4 6 8 9 7 5 3 1

We dedicate this book to the people who live and struggle in the favelas of Rio de Janeiro. We make special mention of the Mothers of Acari and all the mothers who have lost their children to violence in their communities, especially when that violence has been carried out by agents of the state, who have the duty to protect them. Like their counterpart, Mothers of the Plaza de Mayo, the Mothers of Acari spend their lives fighting for justice, often also struggling to determine the whereabouts of their disappeared children.

This book also belongs to all those who continue to be victimized by state-induced violence but, in spite of it all, continue to believe that the Brazilian system can be modified to provide security for all citizens, with respect for democratic and human rights.

Contents

Acknowledgments

We thank the Rio de Janeiro organization Rede de Comunidades e Movimentos contra a Violência (Network of Communities and Movements against Violence). Through members of the network, many of whom are from families that have been victims of police violence, we had direct access to communities and families deeply traumatized by conflict. The courage and persistence in pursuing justice for the victims of state and police violence demonstrated by the members of the network are truly admirable. We must also highlight the work of the human rights lawyer João Tancredo, who has put his life on the line to defend the human rights of others, and the work of the Institute of Defenders of Human Rights (IDDH), which he helped to establish in late 2007 at a time when the defense of human rights in Rio de Janeiro had virtually disappeared from the agenda of its public institutions.

We offer our deepest thanks to Ação Comunitária do Brasil Rio de Janeiro and to Viva Rio, two nongovernmental organizations (NGOs) that helped us get to know and admire the people of the communities where they have social and cultural projects. They showed us the energy, creativity, and generosity of the people who live there and provided guidance and contacts that were indispensable in undertaking the research and carrying out the interviews for this book. We also acknowledge the important work of the Observatório de Favelas and thank the students of the organization's project Imagens do Povo (Images of the People), who gave us permission to publish their photographs of daily life in Maré. In particular, we are grateful to A. F. Rodrigues, Elisangela Leite, and Rodrigues Moura for their photographs of community life. Rosinaldo Lourenço provided photographs of the death and funeral of the child Matheus. Carlos Latuff gave us free use of the photographs he took during the siege of the Alemão complex of favelas in 2007 and helped us understand better the tactics of the Rio de Janeiro police in siege operations and in incursions into the favelas. We also acknowledge the teachers at the schools we visited. We are in awe of their courage and dedication. The children who talked to us and shared their experiences through their drawings deserve a special thank-you.

We are grateful to the members of the Núcleo de Estudos da Violencia of the University of São Paulo, specifically Professor Paulo Sérgio Pinheiro and former Minister of Justice José Gregori, as well as the students and human rights activists who were present for the focus group discussion. And we thank all who shared their time and expertise during the interviews. Finally, we have not included—in some cases we do not even know—the names of many people who contributed directly to the making of this book by speaking with us along the way. A community leader urged us to talk to the "people," and we followed his advice.

In preparing and writing the manuscript, we received assistance from the following people: José Navarro, who translated several interviews; Ivan Drufovka, Ph.D., of the Bilingual Media Company, who helped prepare the photographs included in the book; Regina Coeli de Azevedo-Evanson, who assisted in transcribing and translating interviews and made useful suggestions to improve the text. We owe special thanks to James Green, our reader for Temple University Press, whose many helpful suggestions we took care to incorporate in revisions to the text. We also benefited from the comments of James Hilty, Joseph Arbena, Gary Wallin, and Francisca L. N. de Azevedo, who read parts of the manuscript in draft form. Finally, we acknowledge the help of Janet Francendese, editor in chief at Temple University Press, and Arthur Schmidt, editor of the *Voices of Latin American Life* series, for seeing better than we could what should and should not be in the book, for reminding us of deadlines, and for supporting and encouraging us in the preparation of the manuscript at various stages. Any errors and flaws that may remain are solely the responsibility of the co-authors.

Living in the Crossfire

Introduction

On May 2, 2007, the state government of Rio de Janeiro mounted a massive police operation in the Alemão complex of favelas in the Northern Zone of Rio de Janeiro. The Alemão complex consists of sixteen different communities with populations estimated at 80,000 to 180,000 people. The operation was a clear break with previous public security policies because it used techniques of war, including besieging the area for four months, until the Pan American Games ended in August. Governor Sérgio Cabral, who had recently taken office, described the operation as a declaration of war. The governor called on the federal government to send to Rio the recently established National Security Force (NSF) with the assignment to encircle all sixteen communities. The 1,280 men of the NSF carried out siege activities—encircling the area, carefully screening people who entered or left any of the communities, checking documents, looking for weapons, and the like. Residents of the communities and photographers, however, provided ample evidence that these special troops, trained to intervene directly in areas of conflict, also acted inside the residential areas. Besides the NSF, the government of the state of Rio de Janeiro employed its own troops—specifically, the State Military Police and the elite Special Police Operations Battalion (BOPE). During the period of siege, significant numbers of people were killed or wounded who were not proved to have been involved in criminal activities. It is known that at least nineteen children were killed by stray bullets, including a two-year-old who was being rocked to

sleep at home when he was struck in the head by a bullet. Also killed was a
three-year-old boy who was playing in front of his home. At least forty-three
people were killed from the time the operation began in May until it ended
in August, and eighty-five more were reported wounded.[1]

The police assault on the Alemão complex was the largest of its kind
using "war" and siege tactics. The military strategy of siege was unique and
was not repeated in other favelas of Rio de Janeiro. However, what continued and still occurs are mega-operations by the local forces of the State
Military Police that follow a pattern. First, the territory of a particular
favela is invaded by the BOPE and the Military Police using the *caveirão,* or
"Big Skull" armored vehicles.[2] Then the favela is occupied, with frequent
shootouts. Finally, the troops leave the area, sometimes, but not always,
having accomplished the mission of finding weapons and drugs and arresting *traficantes* (drug traffickers). It is important to state that whether or not
the troops find drugs, weapons, or *traficantes,* innocent people are killed or
wounded.

These mega-operations more often than not are aided and abetted by the
media that in effect have criminalized the favelas in the name of combating
the drug-trafficking gangs that have appeared in many of them. Outside
observers have called this an example of criminalizing poverty. The irony and
error of this perspective is found in the record of upward development of the
favelas during recent decades as residents have striven, with considerable
success, to improve both their lives and the quality of life in their communities. Although conditions vary widely in the more than 900 favelas of Rio de
Janeiro, anyone with firsthand knowledge of them knows the pattern in
which flimsy shacks are continually being replaced by brick-and-mortar
homes as favelas climb the steep hills or spread elsewhere in metropolitan
Rio, thus leaving behind the condition of shantytowns. These homes are
strong enough to support a cement slab roof, or *laje,* on which additional stories can be erected. The laje is a symbol of the strength and permanence of
the favelas.

The favelas have been under construction since the end of the nineteenth
century, and most have undergone extensive development in their urban
infrastructure, which can include systems for running water, electricity, and
sewage. In a series of reports in 2008, the daily newspaper *O Globo* noted
that only one-third of Rio's poor lived in the favelas and that the rising income
of the poor had lifted many *favelados* out of poverty. Certain durable goods
were a standard presence in favela homes. Ninety-seven percent of the population had television sets, 94 percent had refrigerators, 59 percent had DVD
players, and 55 percent had cell phones. Local area network Internet centers

are common. In Alemão itself, 94 percent of residents lived in houses that were more than 90 percent brick and mortar; 80 percent of these homes were occupied by their owners. In surveys, 60–90 percent of favela residents said they wished to remain. Among the reasons they cited were high levels of solidarity and community spirit, which interviews in this book confirm.[3]

At the time the Alemão complex was invaded, Maria Helena Moreira Alves was working with NGOs that have projects in many favelas. Alves knew the Alemão complex well, witnessed the military and police siege, and reacted sharply in two published documents. The first was an article that appeared on June 24 on the website of the Network of Communities and Movements against Violence. It provocatively asked whether the police invasion represented public security or genocide. The article told of the death of innocent residents, including children who were victims of stray bullets. It also reported on the violent disruption of community life caused by the State Military Police, especially the BOPE, which operated from the large armored *caveirão,* or "Big Skull," vans and entered communities shooting randomly. In fact, the Military Police act more like army infantry engaged in search-and-destroy missions than police, while the elite BOPE has characteristics of an armored unit. The article was republished several times.[4] The second document was titled "Open Letter to the National Executive of the PT [Workers' Party]" and published on July 7, 2007. The PT had been in power since 2003, following the election of its leader, Luis Inácio Lula da Silva, as president in 2002. For two months, the residents of the Alemão complex had been deprived of water, electricity, and trash collection. Schools had been closed, and children had been forcibly moved out of the community. Police had engaged in summary executions denounced by human rights organizations. The letter asked for an alternative program of public security. There had been proposals to invest in social programs in the favelas, especially in programs to rescue youth at risk. On the side of police work, there were proposals to upgrade intelligence work, and for better-paid and better-trained police who would know how to resist corruption. Finally, the letter made an appeal to lift the siege of Alemão by national and state police forces. Instead of following a policy of surrounding the Alemão complex, Alves wrote, it would be better to invest in infrastructure that Lula himself had noted was a way "to compete with the drug dealers."

The siege of the Alemão complex continued until the Pan American Games ended in late August 2007. By that time, we had discussed the idea of a book that would include testimony from residents who had lived through the siege period in the Alemão complex. We also sought testimony from residents of other favelas that had experienced mega-police operations. It was

Searching a resident in the Alemão complex. *(Photograph by Carlos Latuff.)*

important to hear what residents might say about living in this crossfire. Through Viva Rio, Ação Comunitária do Brasil Rio de Janeiro, and especially the Network of Communities and Movements against Violence, Alves had contacts with community leaders and could count on the trust of residents. Joining us as an interview assistant was Alves's husband, José Valentin Palacios Vilches, a Chilean trade union officer and human rights activist who had been part of the opposition to the dictatorship of Augusto Pinochet (1973–1990) and was a close observer of Brazil and Rio de Janeiro for more than two decades. His presence was indispensable in conducting several interviews in the communities and with authorities in Brasília. In addition, we were able to enlist the support of the photographer and anthropologist Cristina Pedroza de Faria. She has worked in the vast Maré complex of favelas for several years, which gave her access to many of the photographs we used. She also did several of the interviews.

The testimony of community residents was of paramount importance. Media reporting largely looks at warfare between police and drug gangs through a lens of the state repressing and killing *bandidos*. Favela residents have become double casualties in this story. First, they are literally casualties of the belligerents who fire powerful weapons at one another in densely populated favela communities. Second, they are casualties of media reporting that portrays favelas as territories occupied by bandidos. This had led to reductionist thinking that classifies favelas as areas of crime and virtually nothing else. In addition to being untrue, such thinking increases the dangers for residents and makes the task of gaining understanding and support from middle-class and upper-class communities more difficult. According to social science research, fewer than 1 percent of favela residents belong to drug gangs or engage in violent crime. The testimony was therefore important in combating perceptions that residents have somehow gone over to the side of the bandidos.

However, we also wanted to understand the making of security policy. Favela residents were on the receiving end of security policy. As far as we could see, that policy was being made without consulting them. At this moment, Brazil calls itself democratic; the present government even speaks of "participant democracy" as if the people are really allowed to participate in the making of government policies. If this were really the case—if the people of the favelas have participated in the making of government policy—one can duly ask: Where is their voice? Who pays attention to what they are trying to say? Where are the voices of those who are in the crossfire of this supposed "war"? To understand the making of public security policy,

Soldiers occupying the Alemão complex. *(Photograph by Carlos Latuff.)*

we wanted to interview authorities and representatives of the police. But would this be possible? Alves stood out as a critic of the policy of confrontation practiced by Governor Sérgio Cabral and Secretary of Public Security José Mariano Beltrame. Neither man seemed much given to dialogue. But there was also some hope. In 2007, at the same time police and members of the NSF were invading the Alemão complex, Minister of Justice Tarso Genro was in another Rio de Janeiro favela unveiling the National Program of Public Security with Citizenship (PRONASCI), a government initiative tying public security to the enhancement of citizenship. PRONASCI would be linked to the Program for the Acceleration of Growth (PAC), a vast public works program with funds for infrastructure projects in selected favelas, including the Alemão complex. At the same time, there was growing criticism of Brazil's human rights record, which would culminate in 2008 with a damning United Nations Human Rights Council report by Special Rapporteur on Extrajudicial, Summary, or Arbitrary Executions Philip Alston. Perhaps the authorities and representatives of the police would agree to be interviewed by us.

By June 2008, authorities in Brasília, including President Lula, indicated a willingness to be interviewed. The trip to Brasília in early July by Alves and José Valentin Palacios yielded interviews with President Lula; Minister of Justice Tarso Genro; National Secretary for Public Security Ricardo Brisolla Balestreri; Special Secretary for Human Rights Paulo de Tarso Vannuchi; and Congressman Raul Jungmann, president of the Chamber of Deputies' Commission on Public Security and Organized Crime. The trip also made possible the scheduling of meetings with Governor Cabral and Secretary Beltrame and discussions with police officers assigned to the PRONASCI office in Rio de Janeiro. Meanwhile, the interviews with community residents took place without incident, though some required anonymity. The interviews with police officers, public security experts, and Secretary of Public Security José Mariano Beltrame were done by Philip Evanson because we believed they would feel more at ease discussing such issues with an American scholar perceived as more sympathetic to their viewpoint. The interview with Governor Sérgio Cabral was done by Philip Evanson and Maria Helena Moreira Alves. All interviews and testimony published in this book were recorded between September 2007 and February 2009. We express our deepest thanks to the many individuals who met and spoke with us and allowed us to record their statements. Many others gave us their personal testimony, helping us to understand the complexity of living in the crossfire. Their ideas are reflected in this book even though we lacked the space to publish all of their accounts.

Our aim has been to contribute to the debate on human rights and public security in Brazil in the belief that there cannot be one without the other.

Note on Methodology

To prepare for this book, we researched public security policies in Brazil using national and international reports, government documents, releases and communications by different social movements, media reports, and academic research in books and articles available mostly in Portuguese, which had the most recent information.

Testimony and interviews. Identifying individuals to be interviewed and getting the testimony published in this book was the result of discussions among Maria Helena Moreira Alves, Philip Evanson, José Valentin Palacios, and Cristina Pedroza de Faria. However, Alves and Evanson have final responsibility for the content. Participant observation was important in eliciting testimony from community residents. A focus group discussion produced the testimony of four teachers. Interviews with authorities had a different quality: They were based on questions prepared in advance by Alves and Evanson and submitted to them. Certain official protocols were carefully followed; the interviews were audiotaped and, in the case of President Luis Inácio da Silva, recorded by a stenographer. However, the interviews themselves were almost always conducted in an atmosphere of free exchange allowing for spontaneity and for ranging beyond prepared questions. Interviews with authorities sometimes have a give-and-take quality because they were an opportunity for all concerned to question and think about certain security policies in which events can contradict expectations and planning. In the interviews with Tarso Genro and Paulo de Tarso Vannuchi, Alves and Palacios were both present, but Alves asked the questions.

Participant observation. To collect testimony and interview residents in conflict-ridden favelas, Maria Helena Moreira Alves and José Valentin Palacios lived in three different communities for a period of six months in 2007 and 2008. They conducted sixty-one interviews, many of which focused on the confrontation that began with the siege of the Alemão communities. They directly witnessed the violent environment. In addition to the interviews, they collected photographs taken by community photographers, as well as spent ammunition left behind after shootouts and by the firing of the Big Skulls. Cristina Pedroza de Faria has worked in favelas for many years, including those of the large Maré complex, where competing drug factions are present.

Focus groups. We held sessions with different groups to allow for discussion and dialogue that might provide a clearer picture of reality. This was the case of the focus group session with teachers at an elementary school that was particularly vulnerable to crossfire violence. We also held a focus group with lawyers who were working to defend the families of victims in search of justice. This was important to expand our understanding of the judicial system and the difficulties involved in obtaining justice. A focus group was also held with children in which we discussed their perspective and their experiences amid war. The methodology for conducting focus groups with community residents, who were highly vulnerable and traumatized (especially the children), was necessarily different from that used to conduct focus group discussions with lawyers and human rights activists. The first requires long preparation and a careful approach to establish a climate of trust and confidence that allows opinions to flow, whereas the second requires mainly a leadership role in guiding the discussion. Another valuable focus group was held around the presentation of photographs and video material at the Núcleo de Estudos da Violencia, University of São Paulo, in June 2008. It was organized by Professor Paulo Sérgio Pinheiro, who served as secretary of human rights in the government of President Fernando Henrique Cardoso, and included, among others, José Gregori, minister of justice in the Cardoso administration. Also present were students from the University of São Paulo who were working on public policy and violence and an officer of the São Paulo Military Police. This focus group discussion provided helpful academic and human rights perspectives.

Fieldwork. Alves did fieldwork in Rio de Janeiro from 2002 to 2009, with direct involvement with community leaders and residents in different projects of the NGOs Viva Rio and Ação Comunitária do Brasil Rio de Janeiro. Working directly with these NGOs provided an understanding of the reality of those who live in the many communities of metropolitan Rio de Janeiro and the problems that they face. Of particular importance was the contact with family members of victims of violence and police brutality, as well as with community leaders, who are active in the Network of Communities and Movements against Violence. Their participation in this book was important not only because their direct experience provided us with further material, but because they were a crucial channel to community residents who were not connected to other NGOs working in the favelas but who were key participants in the daily events where they lived. We are most grateful to all who spent their time instructing us about the realities of living in the crossfire.

Part I

Rio de Janeiro
The Marvelous City and Its Communities

Chapter 1

The Decline of Poverty and the Rise of Violence

The Marvelous City

Squeezed between the ocean and the mountains of Rio de Janeiro are beautiful, well-kept areas that are known throughout the world. They provide a spectacle of sandy beaches, deep-blue ocean waters, and impressive condominium complexes with carefully maintained garden plots and unforgettable views. These are the everyday delights for the wealthy residents of Barra da Tijuca, Botafogo, Copacabana, Gávea, Ipanema, Jardim Botânico, Lagoa, Laranjeiras, Leblon, Leme, and Urca, who live in the so-called bairros nobres (noble districts) of the Zona Sul (Southern Zone). The residents include some of the richest people in the world. Their children go to state-of-the-art private schools and may complete their university educations in Europe or the United States. They live in apartment buildings covered in marble, some with swimming pools and private sports areas and balcony gardens that call to mind the fabulous hanging gardens of Babylon. Of course, maintaining these marvels requires many invisible hands. They belong to the doormen, the drivers who care for the vehicles, the gardeners, and the building maintenance personnel. Each family also has an abundance of household help, from humble housecleaners, carefully picked nannies, cooks, and houseboys to serve at table to well-trained butlers who rival the British "gentleman's man," for discretion and propriety.

The topography of Rio is peculiar, indeed. There is very little land space between the blue ocean and the steep granite mountains that tower up in the

Zona Sul. This has led to the construction of ever higher residential and hotel buildings along the beach, despite some architects' and urban planners' wishes to set limits on the height of construction to keep the mountains visible from the beaches. Urban development in Rio de Janeiro has also involved large-scale destruction of mountain terrain. In the 1950s and early 1960s, an entire mountain was torn down to build the Aterro de Flamengo—a park built on filled land that buried a good part of Guanabara Bay. The enormous tract was then landscaped by the architect Roberto Burle Marx, who had gained fame for laying out the grounds around the Ministry of Education's building in downtown Rio de Janeiro and for landscaping Brasília. One of the interesting points of the vast park is that it contains only native Brazilian trees and is thus an important botanical garden. Leme, Copacabana, Ipanema, and Leblon were also transformed when reclamation projects extended the original beach areas farther into the Atlantic Ocean to provide room for new multilane highways, much to the detriment of swimmers, who can face strong ocean currents almost immediately when they enter the water. Barra da Tijuca was the biggest landfill engineering project of all. Originally an area occupied by numerous lakes and lagoons that joined the sea, this vast extension of land has probably been the largest urban development project for the middle and upper classes in Rio de Janeiro.

The development of Rio de Janeiro is closely associated with the enormous accumulation of wealth based on the export of coffee from the vast *fazendas* (plantations) of the aristocracy in the nineteenth century and the fact that the city was the national capital from 1763 until 1960. The social and economic contrasts can be seen in areas of the urban landscape. Different worlds exist side by side. One is rich and well educated; its people live in buildings with world-class architecture in neighborhoods with paved streets, sewage systems, electricity, cable television, and the most modern communication systems, including Internet and wireless satellite communications. Government services such as trash removal and street cleaning are provided, as are financial services and convenient access to legal documents in registry offices. The other world—that of the favelas—crawls up steep hills that look down on the middle-class and upper-class condominiums, beaches, restaurants, hotels, and shops that one sees in postcards of Rio de Janeiro. In this other world, the streets are not paved; in fact, some are not even streets but alleys. This is the reason residents of the hilltop favelas refer to those down below as the "people of the asphalt." Infrastructure and services have largely been left to favela residents themselves to provide. They did this by organizing into a tight community, with collective work being the norm. They built their own roads, collected garbage, and even distributed mail. Electricity arrived in homes by "hanging" cables—that is, connecting cables to larger electrical outlets of those residents who are better off and have electrical service. This is known as a *gato* (cat)," in reference, perhaps, to the animal's known ability to "hang" from anywhere. Water pipes are also interconnected down the hill in self-built systems that eventually connect to the city's potable water system down on the asphalt. Fuel for cooking is provided through the use of bottled gas. With the development of cable TV and broadband Internet, a new sort of *gato* arrived called "gatonet" or "gatocablenet." These "services" may be provided to "customers" by drug lords and, increasingly, by the members of militias—mostly police or former police officers—who are displacing the drug lords in many areas. They charge a fee to install their gatonet or gatocablenet, then also charge a fee per month for their use. Bottled gas is usually provided by the same people, and customers are charged both for the gas and for delivery up the hills. In the past few years, another service has become available to the favela residents in the form of alternative transportation by minibus vans that also are usually run by drug lords or members of local militias.[1]

Cariocas, or residents of Rio de Janeiro, 73 percent of whom said they were proud of their city in a survey conducted in 2008, are, of course, aware not only of Rio's many marvels, visual and otherwise, but also of its paradoxes. These paradoxes include some of the world's highest homicide rates in certain areas of a city that, *Forbes* magazine reported in September 2009, is nevertheless the world's "happiest," due mainly to the spectacular Carnival and the presence of a festive, communicative people.

The city of Rio is just one of twenty municipalities that officially make up metropolitan Rio de Janeiro, a region first recognized in 1974. Rio de Janeiro, with more than 6 million inhabitants, was the largest municipality in 2008, while Tanguá, with slightly more than 30,000 residents, was the smallest, according to estimates by the Brazilian Institute of Geography and Statistics. The population of the entire metropolitan region is more than 11 million. Two million people are said to live in favelas. The favela population grows at a much faster rate than the rest of the population. During the 1990s, it grew an estimated 2.4 percent annually, while the populations of other areas (which takes into account the middle and upper classes) grew by 0.4 percent. Also, while the state of Rio de Janeiro as a whole has had one of the lowest rates of economic growth since 1980 of any state in the Brazilian federation, there is a dynamic region of population and urban growth centered in the Baixada Fluminense, a flat interior area between the Zona Sul and the interior mountain towns of Petropolis, Teresopolis, and Nova Fiburgo.[2] The most important of the cities in the Baixada, and one that represents the new Rio economy, is Duque de Caxias. Rio de Janeiro and Duque de Caxias rank second and sixth, respectively, in economic output among Brazilian cities, making the metropolitan region second only to São Paulo in economic importance in Brazil and third in importance in South America. The Baixada is now the main area of economic and population growth in metropolitan Rio de Janeiro.

Economic Growth: The Decline of Poverty and the Rise of Violence in Rio de Janeiro

The diversified economy of metropolitan Rio de Janeiro and surrounding cities provides employment for a large working class while maintaining prosperous middle and upper classes. The region therefore continues to attract poor migrants from the Brazilian north and northeast and from the neighboring state of Minas Gerais. From the point of view of these migrants, Rio de Janeiro is always welcoming. It has communities in which to live with friends, relatives, and other migrants from the same region, as well as educational and employment opportunities that outstrip what they knew. The migrants' comparative youth, in turn, helps keep the region robust and attractive for investment, leading to the creation of jobs. Barra da Tijuca, Ipanema, Copacabana, Botofogo, Laranjeiras, and Gloria in the Zona Sul and downtown Rio contain highly mixed commercial and middle- and upper-class residential areas but depend heavily on the commercial activities and backyard production of working-class areas and favela populations.

Textiles, clothing, cosmetics, shoes, furniture and other products are important components of the growing economy in the Baixada Fluminense. Economic development is built on the idea of different growth poles and industrial clusters centered in different municipalities, each with at least a dozen factories or production units. Duque de Caxias is a gas, petrochemical, and plastics pole; it also has one of Brazil's largest refineries. Campo Grande has Brazil's largest shirtmaker, Fred Vic, which produces 35,000 shirts a month. The different municipalities in the Baixada have their own mayors, city assemblies, and govenment agencies. The 2010 census is expected to show that nearly 4 million people live in the municipalities of the Baixada Fluminense. The level of development and the industrial and commercial importance of the Baixada Fluminense are outstanding features of the socioeconomic reality of greater Rio de Janeiro. However, as in the history of urban development elsewhere in Brazil, extreme income concentration in the Baixada has generated low human development indices in terms of life expectancy, educational attainment, and income. Pockets of poverty in the Baixada contribute to the formation of many new favelas, following patterns originally set by the Zona Sul and center-city favelas. It is a largely silent and underpaid labor force that makes the accelerated rate of development of the industrial, service, and commercial sectors possible. Differences in income, education, and housing availability are present, as they have been in the Zona Sul favelas. However, public security is much worse in many areas of the Baixada. Statistical studies since 1991 show homicide rates for the Baixada run 20 percent to more than 40 percent higher than for the city of Rio de Janeiro.[3] Zona Sul residents enjoy a high human development index that has had the effect of raising standards of behavior of both police and drug-gang bandidos. As the police reporter Dimmi Amora has noted, the human development index in Zona Norte (Northern Zone) is much lower, and the level of violence is much higher. He observed how bandidos of the Zona Norte tend to live shuttered in favela ghettos, except when they emerge in early morning hours to rob people riding to work on buses. They burn people alive in what becomes an act of cremation using a technique called "microwaving," in which old tires are fit over an individual and then set on fire. They are known to have decapitated a police officer. The police in turn take revenge and kill many more people in proportion to the population in the Zona Norte than in the Zona Sul. Meanwhile, Zona Sul bandidos, having infiltrated the police, remain well informed about planned police actions and can act to protect themselves.[4] The homicidal and sadistic violence found in parts of the Baixada and some other areas of metropolitan Rio has largely been absent from the Zona Sul.

A Broken or Integrated City?

The dramatic rise of violent crime in the favelas coincided with the appearance of drug-trafficking gangs in the 1980s. Together with the police, the gangs disrupted community life that, in turn, led to a new era of stigmatizing favelas by the media and by many in the middle and upper classes. In the 1960s and 1970s, state policies had called for the removal of favelas to suburban areas. However, removal did not improve living conditions for the people who were resettled. Many could not afford the new public housing. At the same time, social protest grew. The restoration of democratic politics shifted government policy away from removal toward urbanization. When Leonel Brizola was elected governor of Rio de Janeiro State in 1982, he proclaimed that the favela was the solution, not the problem.

By the 1990s, the favelas were being identified with crime and violence almost to the exclusion of anything else. The media portrayed the violence of drug-trafficking gangs at war with one another, or with the police, as if homicide and drug dealing were endemic to favelas. This encouraged the public to draw sharp distinctions between the favelas on the hills and the middle-class and elite communities on the asphalt. At its simplest, this meant a media narrative of crime-infested favelas dominated by well-armed bandidos, in contrast to the rest of law-abiding society below. The police were seen as entering favelas to repress bandidos, which often involved gunfights that ended in deaths and casualties. However, the police themselves were not well regarded. Some reporters wrote about recurrent *chacinas* (police massacres), and well-informed people knew that the police also went into favelas to extort money from traffickers and that some police sold guns to bandidos. Thus, a perverse structure of crime involving drug traffickers and the state's police agents was being built. Casualties were high on both sides, although many more bandidos and innocent young men died than police officers. According to one news report in 2007, forty-one civilians were killed for every Rio de Janeiro police officer, four times the international average.

The media's pursuit of a narrative of police war against the drug gangs and other criminals seemed to satisfy the public, but it may also have contributed to escalating the violence. The Rio de Janeiro press has been faulted for giving excessive coverage to violence compared with the press in São Paulo and Belo Horizonte, two cities that also have suffered from drug gangs and violent police actions against them. It has been argued that such coverage increased the sense of public insecurity in Rio that, in turn, helped to establish conditions favoring greater state repression and leading to human rights violations and unnecessary loss of lives. A more sinister argument has it that police conduct these wars as part of a largely successful strategy to prevent police institutions themselves from being reformed. A frightened public applauds a police war against drug-trafficking bandidos in poor neighborhoods as long as the war does not extend into the middle- and upper-class bairros nobres.[5] It therefore was not surprising when Zuenir Ventura, a prominent journalist with *O Globo*, published *Cidade Partida* (*The Broken City*) in 1994, using the word "broken" to convey the idea of a city severed into two parts.

Ventura wrote the book in the wake of one of the most dramatic *chacinas* by the Military Police in a Rio de Janeiro favela. In retaliation for the murder of two of their colleagues by bandidos in 1993, several military policemen went into the Vigário Geral favela and shot to death twenty-one people who had never been shown to have any connection to drug trafficking. It was an act of savage reprisal against the entire community. Ventura was shocked by the event and decided to investigate. He spent several months in the favela interviewing residents. In the resulting book, he describes a community ignored by the state in which people live in the shadow of a powerful drug gang. At the same time, they do not despair or surrender. A majority of residents aspire to join the more affluent part of Rio. This, he found, was especially true of young people. He suggested that the city's elites could help by supporting urbanization and cultural projects, as well as the work of NGOs, in the favelas. *The Broken City* was part of a movement of the Rio de Janeiro elite that led to the establishment of the NGO Viva Rio in 1994 with its headquarters in the traditional Zona Sul area of Gloria. Viva Rio became a presence in Vigário Geral, and, to complete the circle, residents of Vigário Geral got involved in the work of the NGO.[6]

The concept of the "broken city" emphasizes the wide gap between the middle-class and upper-class bairros nobres and the more than 900 favelas of metropolitan Rio de Janeiro. The economic, sociological, and political realities of metropolitan Rio, however, suggest a far more integrated city. Much has been written that questions the broken city paradigm and argues that Rio is in fact integrated economically and socially—that is, the asphalt world and the favela world depend on the each other. The labor of the supposedly ignored and abandoned poor is crucial to the maintenance not only of the lifestyle of the rich but, more substantially, to the overall functioning of the economy of metropolitan Rio de Janeiro.

Social scientists who work directly with favela communities, such as Jailson de Souza e Silva, coordinator of the Observatório de Favelas, an NGO with many projects in Maré and other poor areas of the Baixada Fluminense, strongly defend this line of thought. His article "Adeus a Cidade Partida (Farewell to the Broken City)," published in 2003 on the NGO's website, defends the idea of an integrated city—the rich with the poor, the developed with the underdeveloped.[7] The article begins by recalling an event that shocked the city of Rio de Janeiro: On September 30, 2002, the drug-trafficking kingpin Fernandinho Beira-Mar, though in prison at the time, ordered Rio de Janeiro businessmen to close their establishments as a sign of obedience and "mourning" after the police killed some of his colleagues. Rio de Janeiro then witnessed something incredible: commercial activity ceased in as many as forty city neighborhoods, including in many bairros nobres. This demonstrated the drug traffickers' enormous capacity for intimidation and brought to the fore an old specter that supposedly haunted Rio's elite: that of people coming down the hills to demand compensation for the enormous social inequality and injustice that is part of daily life in the city. It fit the "broken city" idea that geographic, economic, and cultural distinctions marking the territories of different groups were sufficient to break the city apart. The media had endorsed and reinforced this idea. Souza e Silva then posed a question: How it is possible for a city to be broken when favela residents continue to produce in ways that, economically and culturally, are very much a part of the city's identity and development? In fact, Rio de Janeiro was pluralistic, not broken. Souza e Silva's analysis of 2003 remains relevant today.

Urbanization. From the 1950s to the 1970s, elite and expert opinion denigrated the favelas. In one extravagant metaphor, they were compared to sores on the body of a beautiful woman. The first census of the favelas in 1948 described them as having "infested" the city. The solution was removal, at least from the Zona Sul. This was tried in the 1960s and 1970s. However, by the late 1970s, perspectives had changed, and favelas started to be seen as occupied by people seeking to better themselves through hard work, thrift, and education.[8] Governor Leonel Brizola turned his government's attention to building schools in favelas and linking them to utilities that supplied water and electricity.[9] Urbanization continued in the 1990s, as the state developed sewer systems, day-care centers, health clinics, public squares, and leisure areas in the favelas. A growing number of favelas began to have access to some public services, and the issue of quality of services became important.

Commercial activity. Especially in the food, clothing, and entertainment sectors, commercial activity has grown in the favelas. Internet centers arrived in the late 1990s, a decade that also saw the development of social organizations founded by individuals and groups within and outside the favelas. NGOs and, in smaller measure, private enterprises flourished. The major exception to this progress was public safety which did not advance at all.

Land values. A housing shortage (800,000 units in 2009) and the relative lack of attention by urban planners to meeting the needs of the popular classes are two of the reasons that have caused buildings to grow upward in older favelas. Many of the small homes on the steep hillsides are built solidly enough to support heavy concrete-slab lajes, and additional stories that can be used to generate rental income. Renting rooms and houses has become a big favela business. Some community entrepreneurs built small efficiency-apartment buildings in better established favelas, such as the large and still growing Rocinha which overlooks the elite neighborhoods of São Conrado and Barra de Tijuca. As the owners of such properties have prospered, some have moved out of the favelas into upscale neighborhoods. The same process has accelerated occupation in other areas of the city, particularly in the Jacarepaguá flatlands, the Baixada Fluminense, and the Zona Oeste (Western Zone). As they have spread, and as incomes within them have grown, favela communities have become more visible in the general landscape of Rio de Janeiro. The investigative series by O *Globo* in 2008 estimated that the 2 million inhabitants of Rio's favelas earned 5 billion–10 billion *reais* (roughly $2.5 billion–$5 billion in early 2009) annually, and that $3 billion *reais* were spent in the favelas—enough to attract the interest of a wide range of businesses and investors. It was difficult to determine how many of the favelas' residents were truly poor. An estimated 8 percent (or one in twelve) had a middle-class income. In fact, the favelas have always included a small middle class. Finally, the series reconfirmed that a majority of favela residents—from 65 percent to 90 percent—did not want to leave. They wanted better security and urban services or, in other words, better favelas.[10]

Educational and cultural production. Community courses to prepare students for university entrance examinations have exploded in the favelas. Furthermore, theater, music and dance groups, courses in cinema and video, and computer and Internet courses became available to young people in the 1990s. The introduction of internationally popular music genres such as funk and hip hop brought on a silent revolution in the favelas of Rio. Taken together, this process formed new social attitudes, particularly among young people, who generally have become more critical of social inequality.

Residents' Associations. Residents' Associations have had an important historical role in the favelas as the institutions that articulate residents' demands. In the 1980s, however, their leaders began to develop strong ties to political parties and, in effect, became "professional" community leaders. In the 1990s, this leadership was forced to yield to the power of drug-trafficking gangs and formed other kinds of partnerships with municipal and state power structures. The Residents' Associations stopped holding elections, began to lose their legitimacy, and eventually became more like organizations that provide local services—functioning in some ways like NGOs.

Drug trafficking. The aspect of favela life that is most emphasized in the media is the influence of drug-trafficking groups, a result not only of the confrontation among different criminal gangs but also of police activity devoted exclusively to repression. The police are ineffective in the face of drug gangs that play complex roles within a favela, which can range from mediating community disputes and relations with state power to recruiting labor for public works projects, sponsoring public entertainment, mobilizing support for political candidates, and maintaining shadowy links with the police. There are many examples of accommodation, but little trust, between the drug gangs and corrupt police. The police are also ineffective when faced with the armed power of the criminal gangs. The police may enter favelas and fight gun battles, but they do not stay to win the war.

Militias. Since 2002, militias composed mostly of current and former police officers have grown dramatically in the favelas. This has introduced something the drug dealers never achieved: a structure of organized crime. The militias promise security and impose a stern regime of law and order on residents, and on the drug dealers by setting rules for the sale and use of drugs in the community. Militias are economically motivated. They bring a type of death-dealing security; monopolize certain economic activities, such as the distribution of bottled gas; become clandestine providers of cable television; and control transportation via fleets of vans. For all of this, residents must pay. In 2009, militias were said to dominate some two hundred of metropolitan Rio's more than nine hundred favelas, and their annual income was estimated at $140 million.[11] Their reach extended into politics, to elected representatives in the Rio state legislature and member of the City Council. In an interview for this book, Rio de Janeiro's Secretary of Public Security José Mariano Beltrame stated there was no organized crime in the favelas except for the militias. Sensing a growing threat, the Rio state government finally appeared to move in earnest against certain militias in 2008 and 2009. Claudio Ferraz, who headed the anti–organized crime unit of the Rio state police, has described the militias as ten times worse than narco-traffickers: They are embedded in party politics, control votes, and win elections. In 2009, Ferraz predicted that, if something were not done, "half of the legislative assembly [would] be members of militias. The political class already sees this happening."[12]

All of these arguments make evident that there have been changes in the favelas of Rio that go beyond the homogeneity implicit in old explanations that centered on poverty. Nor is it possible to understand favelas via a monolithic perception of the residents as potential criminals or passive victims. Criminal violence—in particular, that connected to drug trafficking and the militias—is not intrinsic to the favelas; it is a part of the social dynamic of the city and its political and police structures. Residents of the favelas are citizens of Brazil and must exercise their rights and duties as *cariocas*. In fact, the favelas make Rio de Janeiro ever more *carioca*.

Chapter 2

Living in the Favelas
in the Twenty-first Century

The strength of the favelas lies in their history of development by way of themselves. Because they are largely self-sufficient, they historically have placed almost no burden on the state, which, until recent decades, has been mostly absent or, at times, hostile. Since the rise of drug gangs in the 1980s, the state has not fulfilled its responsibility to provide security in the favelas, leaving them at the mercy of trafficking gangs, intimidating militias, or violent police. Despite this, the favelas continue to grow, and people are not moving out of them. For various reasons, they have become an optimal solution for 2 million people in metropolitan Rio de Janeiro whose way of life is based on self-help and who encounter in the favelas community solidarity and a rich cultural legacy. The favelas also have the advantage of relative youth: Fifty percent of the population is said to be younger than 25, while in the rest of metropolitan Rio, 50 percent are calculated to be younger than 37.[1] The people of the favelas bring an input of youthful energy to Rio de Janeiro where an aging population looms large.

Legacies and Traditions

The oldest Rio de Janeiro shantytown settlers appear to have been free blacks or runaway slaves who established *bairros Africanos* (African communities) in the nineteenth century. In the late 1890s, impoverished soldiers returning from the war against the followers of Antônio Conselheiro in the hinterlands city of Canudos, in northeastern Bahia State, settled the favela of Providencia on a hill in the center of Rio.[2] It is from that settlement that the name "favela" derives: the steep hill reminded some of the settlers of Mount Favela in the Canudos war. Providencia was thus the first favela to be established; its continuance today demonstrates that, once established, favelas do not disappear. Other people built new favelas on other hills overlooking Rio de Janeiro. In the first decade of the twentieth century, the city government forced thousands of poor people out of crowded neighborhoods that were being demolished around the downtown port area in an effort to eliminate yellow fever and turn Rio into a cosmopolitan capital city. The new Rio would have a broad boulevard heading away from the docks lined with Belle Époch architecture. Many poor individuals and families who were expelled took to the hills, and the favelas grew. Former slaves and African-descended *cariocas* were strongly represented in the favelas, but Portuguese and descendants of indigenous people were also present. They have been joined over time by a steady stream of migrants from neighboring Minas Gerais State and from the distant states of the northeast. In 2007, the population of the favelas was approximately 60 percent black or brown and 40 percent white—roughly the opposite of the rest of Rio de Janeiro.[3]

Resistance had been a strong part of Afro-Brazilian history and is present in the history of favelas. Resistance to slavery was both physical, with runaway slaves forming independent villages known as *quilombos,* and social, with the strengthening of community bonds among different tribal groups, creating a grassroots solidarity in community survival and collective work. The Brazilian government officially recognizes communities that descend directly from original quilombos, which are spread over the nation.[4] Urban movements have also sprung up inspired by the history of the quilombos' resistance, keeping their traditional artistic roots and incorporating contemporary international music and dance trends such as hip hop, rap, and graffiti. The strongest characteristic of such movements in Brazil is pride in their culture—especially in their art and music—and in their ability to adapt to adverse conditions and keep certain legacies intact. Both men and women consider themselves beautiful, and this is reflected in Brazilian culture in general.

The strong connection to cultural and historic roots is present in dance, in music, in painting and sculpture, and in Afro-Brazilian religions, such as Candomblé, Macumba, and Umbanda. The martial dance art of *capoeira* was developed for the self-defense of slaves and is recognized officially as part of the historical and artistic patrimony of Brazil. But most important, the legacy of working together as a people, of solving problems in solidarity with one

Mutirão. (Photograph by Rodrigues Moura/Imagens do Povo.)

another, is what characterizes the favela communities. Perhaps the most visible aspect of this legacy is the *mutirão,* in which people gather to build
houses, pave roads, install sewage systems, clean streets, or do any work that
is best done collectively. Neighbors help one another in this way and, at the
same time, strengthen the ties that bind them together and form the spirit
that they refer to as *"comunidade."* This fills the void left in a time of war
against the drug traffickers, when the state becomes most present as an agent
of violent repression. Even garbage collection has to be done by residents, as
organized by the Residents' Association.

Outsiders have often used the word "favela" pejoratively, associating it
with violence, crime, poverty, lack of order, and people of dark skin color.
However, for those who live in favelas, the term imparts a sense of history, of
connection to the past. In Rio de Janeiro, the residents say they are from
"Comunidade such and such" and ask one another, "Which comunidade do
you live in?" They also feel different from those who live in middle-class and
upper-class areas. This strong relationship to the community may be contrasted with the lack of community feeling in the middle-class and upper-
class districts of the city: One cannot, for example, say that one belongs to
the community of Ipanema, Leblon, or Barra da Tijuca. In these places, much
as in large modern cities around the world, neighbors often do not know one

Street scene. *(Photograph by Elisângela Leite/Imagens do Povo, 2008.)*

another and have a reduced collective sense of what a community is. The sense of community in the favela is one reason residents do not want to leave.

In the favelas, by contrast, the sense of community is reinforced by a strong local culture that includes rooting for certain soccer teams and creating a community-supported *escola de samba* (samba schools). Tourists who come to see the great spectacle of the Rio de Janeiro Carnival, the beautiful dancing opera of the *escolas de samba* down the avenue of the Sambódramo do not realize how deep the cultural and creative roots are that make possible such a magnificent display. The samba schools, founded in connection with communities' preparations for Carnival, run training sessions for children and adults year-round. They hold annual competitions to choose a theme song, the *samba enredo,* in which community residents participate. They are an enormous source of energy and creativity: for designers, for the seamstresses who make the costumes, for the sculptors who create the magnificent figures in the different allegoric cars, and for those who research and write the story that will be told by the *escolas de samba.* It is unlikely that the *escolas de samba* would exist without the historical legacy brought by the slaves, and they could not exist without the sense of community and collective work that is expressed in the tradition of *mutirão.* The traditional *escolas de samba* are always identified by the community that they represent—for

Cookout on the laje. *(Photograph by A. F. Rodrigues/Imagens do Povo, 2008.)*

example, the Estação Primeira de Mangueira from the favela of Mangueira. Rio de Janeiro did not have gangs before the drug traffickers appeared; instead, people joined Carnival groups and samba schools. They still do. So although one can say that people in the favelas have been shaped by a history of exclusion, exploitation, and resistance, one should also take note of these astonishing efforts of collective and individual creativity and the tenacious maintenance of community traditions. At their best, the favelas offer the rest of Brazil lessons in community spirit and the strength that comes from joining together with neighbors. They show people working together in a way that overcomes race and regional ties. They promote a feeling of joy and energy that is contagious and marks what many refer to as the "spirit of the *cariocas*."

Are the Favelas Becoming the *Senzalas* of the Twenty-first Century?

At the present moment, when many favelas are under stress produced by criminal groups and the police, it is sometimes said they have become twenty-first-century *senzalas*.[5] "*Senzala*," an African word that entered Brazil in the sixteenth century, describes the huts and dormitory spaces for slaves living under the domination of the *casa grande* (big plantation house). A whipping post, or *pelourinho,* was erected in front of each *senzala.* Slaves left the *senzala* to work on the sugar plantations but spent much of the rest of their time within it. When applied to the contemporary favela, the reference suggests crowded living quarters in dormitories and communities turned inward, with a structure of police repression mounted outside and ready to intimidate, beat, and even kill.

The idea that the favelas are present-day *senzalas* partly explains why those outside—those who live on the asphalt—tend to ignore the repression and killing that goes on so close to them. The other side of the coin is the mentality of those who live in the *casa grande.* One might fairly compare many residents of the rich Zona Sul to the occupants of the *casa grande.* Developing the image further, the state, in carrying out its policy of armed invasion to repress drug traffickers, can be compared to the *capitão de mato* (slave hunter) sent into the forest to recapture fugitive slaves. In the case of the favela, the target has changed. The police enter a favela, now redefined as a "subnormal agglomeration," to arrest drug traffickers and seize their drugs and weapons.[6] They prefer to view the residents as accomplices, much as the *capitão de mato* might have viewed all slaves as likely runaways. The similarity to the State Military Police and BOPE, who carry out orders to repress and keep order in the favelas, contain them within their boundaries, and make sure that they do not cause disorder in the city's wealthier areas, is apparent.

These terrible images recalling the repression of Brazil's enormous slave population are revived by the repression that has come with the controversial security policy of confrontation. According to Governor Sérgio Cabral, the stress caused by such confrontation is something that everyone in Rio shares This is misleading, however: Anyone can see that the stress is felt much more in favelas under siege than on the asphalt or in Zona Sul neighborhoods such as Copacabana and Leblon. In an interview with the newsmagazine *Veja* in 2007, Secretary Beltrame stated that Rio had reached a point at which sacrifices were required, and that although the proposition was difficult to accept, lives would have to be "decimated" to end the bandidos' firepower. However, the sacrifices are made in the favelas. Beltrame also said at a public security forum in 2008 that infants in favelas emerge from the womb already criminals due to the environment around them, in which bandidos brandish automatic weapons as routinely as other people handle cell phones.[7] Further, in an interview in 2007, Cabral referred to the bestseller *Freakonomics* to echo the argument that legalized abortion in the United States had been a blessing because it allowed poor mothers to terminate unwanted pregnancies and thereby reduce the pool of likely criminals.[8] To cut crime, he said, poor women in the favelas needed the same access to abortion that middle-class and upper-class women had. Marcelo Crivella, a bishop in the influential Igreja Universal do Reino de Deus (Universal Church of the Kingdom of God), took this idea a step further when he ran for mayor of Rio in 2008, proposing that the age of voluntary sterilization for women and men be reduced from twenty-five to eighteen. Sterilization would avert pregnancies entirely. Crivella even sought the endorsement of Cardinal Emeritus Eugênio Sales of Rio de Janeiro for his campaign. Although such views were contested, only a few prominent institutions and individuals stood with the people of the favelas against them, principally human rights advocates, some NGOs, and a handful of public security researchers who had condemned acts of police violence and the policy of confrontation. Favela residents continued to protest acts of violence that led to the deaths of innocent neighbors in their communities, especially children and adolescents, but they felt largely alone in an unequal struggle to prove that they were not criminals.[9]

In 2009, Cabral and Beltrame introduced Police Pacification Units (UPPs), designed to occupy favelas to expel or repress drug gangs. They were an answer to a long-standing demand to "reconquer" territory lost by the state to traffickers. UPPs, which were composed of newly recruited and trained Military Police and commanded by carefully selected officers, were occupying or were in the process of occupying nine favelas at the end 2009, and Beltrame projected that 300,000 favela residents might be living under UPP occupation forces by the end of 2010. However, as of this writing in early 2010, several questions remained to be answered. Would the Rio state government continue to create and sustain UPPs? Would the UPPs become the actor of choice in policing Rio's favelas so that residents might look forward to fewer police invasions and less shooting in the name of confronting bandidos? Finally, would specially trained UPP Military Police prove able to resist the temptation to engage in crime themselves, as had happened too often to other police groups, and thereby win the confidence of residents?

Favelas Follow the Money

The favelas appear and grow where economic opportunities present themselves. The continued growth of income in the middle-class and upper-class neighborhoods of the Zona Sul has brought even more rapid growth in the favela populations because so much work has become available in the service sector. It is common enough to hear that the residents in Zona Sul favelas such as as Rocinha, Chapéu Mangueira, and Cantagalo work as domestic servants in neighboring middle- and upper-class areas. Of course, hillside favelas give residents spectacular views of the beaches, which are also open to them, and of the hotels and condominium developments down below. But this overlooks the need of favela residents to live near whatever work they can get. Public transportation is expensive and often infrequent for low-income people, which drives them to look for housing as close to their workplaces as possible.

Therefore, growth in the favelas is not mainly a result of leniency or irresponsibility of past governments in allowing irregular occupation of urban soil, as many politicians have stated. There are sound economic reasons behind the continued growth of the Rio's favelas. Living outside the Zona Sul might mean traveling two hours or more to get to and from work in Copacabana, Leblon, or Barra de Tijuca. Further, in Rio, riders pay each time they change from a subway to a bus or from one bus to another, often having to pay three fares to get to work and another three fares to return home. It is not uncommon for workers in Rio de Janeiro to sleep in the streets during the workweek, because their wages allow them to go home only on weekends. In 2008, Hélio Luz, former chief of the Civil Police, described the Federation of Passenger Transportation Companies as a sort of parallel state or mafia that imposes its will on governments and prevents programs from being put in place to provide affordable transportation for low-income workers who ride multiple buses.[10] Eight thousand buses descend into the streets of Rio de Janeiro on a normal working day and become a major cause of traffic congestion. These buses, running in packs and often half-empty, jam the streets of the Zona Sul but may run infrequently in certain distant suburbs, which has led the militias to start operating illegal van fleets as an alternative. Past governments tried to deal with this problem by enacting a law that required employers to pay for transportation vouchers. However, in practice this kept workers who lived farther away and who had to take several different kinds of transportation from being hired, because the employer does not want to pay the multiple fares. The institution of one ticket with the multiple-transfer rights and other forms of fare relief would be a great help to workers, but the private bus companies have consistently vetoed such alternatives. Their power over the politicians and the state seems overwhelming.

The Rio de Janeiro favelas therefore are fixed in place, and the pressure to grow will continue, despite a countervailing discourse in favor of building walls to stop them from spreading and even some talk of a new round of removals. Meanwhile, urbanization goes on in the favelas, often with the state as a protagonist. The federal government's Program for the Acceleration of Growth (PAC), begun in 2007, has designed public works projects for the favelas in the areas of housing, sanitation, health, education, social services, roads, sports and leisure, and reforestation. In the Alemão complex, a cable-car line with several stations is being built, with a capacity to carry 30,000 people a day. This shows that, despite the recent history of conflict between police and drug traffickers, it is possible to proceed with urban development to the benefit of everyone. Confrontation, it would seem, is often a security policy of choice rather than of necessity.

PAC has been on the drawing board since 2007 but was behind schedule in 2008 and 2009, with much less money being spent than originally intended. Despite the delays, nobody expects the government to abandon the PAC projects. For the government, having something to show by the 2010 elections was an obvious goal, a key to doing well in the elections.

Growing Significance of Favelas

The residents of the favelas are acquiring greater demographic weight and social significance. Expectations are that living conditions will continue to improve. As stated earlier, many favelas have long since moved beyond shantytowns to become solidly established, recognized communities. The state has been taking more and more responsibility for developing infrastructure within the communities, including, since 2009, the construction of walls to prevent further expansion up the hills. This is being done in the name of preserving the remains of rainforest and of strengthening public security by controlling the access and egress of drug gangs.

Race and color also are no longer quite the disadvantage they once were. Much has changed since the government took its first census of Rio de Janeiro's favelas in 1948, which stated: "The fact that blacks and browns are most prevalent in the favelas is not surprising. Hereditarily backward, lacking ambition and badly adjusted to modern social demands, they furnish the greatest contingents for the lower classes of the population."[11] Publishing such an undisguisedly racist statement today would subject both the author and the publisher to criminal prosecution. Brazil has been putting policies in place to overcome its history of discrimination and inequality based on race. Black and brown Brazilians have made important strides relative to whites under democratic government since 1988, and especially since 2001. A study by the Institute of Applied Economic Research (IPEA) in 2008 found that gaps in income and education between blacks and browns, on the one hand, and whites, on the other, had lessened significantly since 2001.[12] The steady real rise in the minimum wage and government initiatives such as the *bolsa família* (family grant program) have significantly increased the income of

poor Brazilians, most of whom are black or brown. The gap in primary education had closed since opportunity at this level was universalized in the 1990s.
The official position now is that all Brazilians are able to read and write by
sixteen perhaps a generous assessment. Black and brown Brazilians were
largely unseen in universities in 1988. Although they still attend university in
significantly smaller numbers than whites, quotas that reserve admission for
blacks and for students from public schools are starting to redress this. The
quota for public-school students was needed because prosperous middle-
class and upper-class families can send their children to private schools that
provide far better preparation for the university entrance exams. Although
quotas have been controversial, with opponents arguing that they have
brought to the foreground a divisive discussion of race in place of the old discourse of racial democracy and the blessings of miscegenation, the government and the universities have persisted in implementing them, with support
from the public. And more black and brown Brazilians are showing up in
places they were not previously seen, such as on the Supreme Court.

In consequence, Brazil's black and brown population is growing more
rapidly than the white population. This is partly due to a higher birthrate, but
it is also occurring because more Brazilians are self-identifying as black or
brown. This marks a reversal of historic importance, a correction for past
practice when people showed a preference to identify as white because of the
discrimination and poverty that were the legacies of slavery. It was estimated
that sometime during 2008 blacks and browns became the majority. Gone
were the days when a document published with the imprimatur of the Ministry of Foreign Affairs could claim that the Brazilian population was white
and that the number of blacks or mixed-race people was minute.[13]

Prosperity without Peace

Government programs to combat race-based exclusion and to reduce poverty
along with the growth in income and size of the favela population work
together to make the political system more attentive to community needs.
Since 2007, this has been demonstrated most obviously in public works
urbanization projects such as the federal government's PAC. However, public
security policy has changed very little. State authorities in Rio de Janeiro
who make security policy insist they must have the option to confront armed
drug gangs in favelas with force. Favelas might be sharing the prosperity of a
growing Brazilian economy, but the police will still come in shooting. In
1991, Governor Leonel Brizola asserted that nowhere in the world were so
many people killed as in the state he was then governing for a second time.

The victims, he said, were "in the majority black and poor."[14] A study of homicides in the state of Rio de Janeiro conducted in 2008 by the Center for the Study of Public Safety and Citizenship (CESeC) at Candido Mendes University, based on figures provided by the Civil Police, showed that from 1991 to 2007, there were never fewer than 5,741 (1998) or more than 8,438 (1994) homicides in a given year. These counts did not include people killed in so-called acts of resisting the police and people who disappeared. If one adds these numbers to the official homicide count, the annual figure is higher than 10,000. The homicide rate for Rio state during this period was as high as 63 (1994) per 100,000 and as low as 38 (2007) per 100,000, but even the lower rate was significantly higher than for Brazil as a whole in 2007 (25.7 per 100,000).[15] A United Nations report on summary and extrajudicial executions in Brazil released in 2008 noted that Brazil had one of the highest homicide rates in the world. "Murders by gangs, inmates, police, death squads, and hired killers regularly make headlines in Brazil and around the world," the report commented, and of the Brazilian states, Rio had one of the worst records.[16] Overwhelmingly, the weapons used to kill were firearms. The victims were principally young men age fifteen to thirty. In some years since 1990, the homicide rates for men in that age range have reached 200, and even 300, per 100,000, rates comparable to those in the war zones of Yugoslavia during the 1990s and in Iraq since the U.S. invasion in 2003. Nor has antidiscrimination policy been extended to security policy. Black and brown men have two to three times the probability of dying as white men in the same age range.[17] They reside in poor communities, especially in the Northern and Western Zones of the city of Rio de Janeiro and in the Baixada Fluminense.

Clearly, homicide has both an ethnography and a geography. One day in 2008, we had a brief conversation with a man we had never met while riding an elevator in a large office building in the center of Rio de Janeiro. He suddenly told to us that his eighteen-year-old son lived in one of the *comunidades carentes* (poor communities) and was just starting university. He also said that 60 percent of the men in his son's cohort were dead. He concluded by saying the authorities in Brasília should address this serious problem instead of spending their time stealing public money. The elevator reached the ground floor, the door opened, the conversation ended, and the concerned father walked away.

The interviews that follow contain testimony by people who lived through the police actions in the Alemão complex in 2007 or who otherwise live in the shadow of police and drug gang conflict. They tell of the terror and disruption of community life they have experienced. However, two interviews

are hopeful, bearing witness to the tenacity and resolve of people. The inter-
viewees describe obstacles to overcome and the difficulty of living in some
favelas at the present moment, but they also talk about the advantages and
satisfactions of community life. The interviews provide snapshots of institutions in favelas and elsewhere that are working to guide, employ, train, and
educate community residents. Two interviews with community leaders give
perspective on the growth of crime and violence over time and the state's
failure to link up with favelas as a permanent presence and partner in a successful public security program. Finally, a priest from a parish in a Zona Sul
favela describes community outreach to the state following a moment of violent crisis, and the state's responses, which eventually led to the occupation
of the favela by a UPP in 2009 as the state struggled to put in place a new
security policy in selected communities.

Chapter 3

Communities under Fire

Four Teachers: A Discussion with Maria Helena Moreira Alves and José Valentin Palacios, May 20, 2008

We visited a school in an area of great conflict. This interview was conducted with several teachers on the condition that we would not identify them. They feared retaliation by state educational authorities, the police, other government authorities, members of the local militia, and even drug dealers active in the region. We wish to make clear that this school is not within the Alemão complex; it is in an entirely different community. Because of our commitment to the safety of those who provided testimony, and their families, however, we have made it a point to disguise the locality and all other evidence that would allow those state agents responsible for the violence to identify the teachers or the specific school.

Despite the fear, we could see evidence of the dedication that both the teachers and parents had to their elementary-school-age children. All of the children were dressed in uniforms, some of which, although worn, had been handwoven, as well as cleaned and ironed with care. The girls wore ribbons and barrettes in their hair to look their best. Both girls and boys had well-shined shoes that had been repaired so that one could barely see holes in the soles. The community was poor, and many of the children wore hand-me-down uniforms from their older brothers or sisters.

We noticed that the school served an excellent lunch and commented on this to the principal. She smiled proudly and told us that the food and the physical appearance of students and teachers was a fundamental part of the children's education and that this was especially important given the extreme violence with which they lived every day. "It helps raise their self-esteem," she said. "It also keeps the parents close to the school and believing in a better future through education for their children."

We were asked not to take pictures, except of bulletholes in the walls and of the seventy-six rifle bullets that had been taken from the walls and kept as evidence of the war. Even a photograph we had taken of a young girl whose long hair was braided with a pink ribbon was deleted at her mother's request. Though the picture showed only the girl's back, the mother was afraid she might be identified by the ribbon and hairdo.

Teacher A: Each year that passes increases the challenges. I have ties of great affection for this school, because I was raised here, as were my brothers and sisters, and we still have a rented apartment here. It's a public school and depends on the state, and it was always very important. We have many students who continued their studies and later went to the university and are professional people today—people with technical skills, people who have managed to advance in life. Even now, we have many students who are enrolled in higher education: students who took entrance exams for technical schools and passed and others who passed the university entrance exam. What is happening now, this year, has really made our work difficult. It is becoming more difficult every day.

Question: Then the difficulties are really greater this year (2008)?
Teacher B: Violence has been here for some time. It began in 1989. In 1990, '91, '94 we had difficult moments due to a crazy bandido element that couldn't live in harmony even with others in their own faction, and we had gunfights. But that was nothing compared with what we are living through now.

Question: By "now," you mean since 2007?
Teacher B: Yes, since last year. Before, we had episodes of gunfire, but it was sporadic. In '94, '95, and '96, we hardly took it seriously because it was everywhere in Rio de Janeiro. Since last year, the school has really been on the firing line. It has been targeted directly. We have bullet marks on all the walls, and I can show them to you. From May until July 2007, we moved to an Integrated Public School Center (CIEP) because we could not remain

here. My condition for returning to the school was to demand that the school be surrounded by bulletproof walls to give a little more security to the children. They built new walls, walls of concrete, to resist rifle bullets. Because the school had a lot of open space, bullets would ricochet from one area to another, and we didn't have a minimum of security, even during classes. A team came from the mayor's office and put a wall around the school. It gave us a little more security, but the episodes [of gunfire] continued.

Question: Was it day and night?

Teacher A: Any time. There wasn't a regular time. You don't know when it might happen. Who keeps us informed are residents who are responsible for the children. They arrive and say, "Professor, it seems that something is going to happen today." They maintain contact with the traffickers and stay on the lookout to save the school. I maintain contact with the community, with the parents, because they are the ones who bring information to me and are never without information.

Even when school was out, we had meetings with Colonel Ubiratan.[1] I liked him very much, but in truth he was not able to do much. I went to him with the hope that someone might do something for us, but he said, "You have to continue under these conditions, because it's a situation of confrontation. The Military Police are confronting the bandidos directly." He even came here to look at the work that had been done to see if we could return to the school. But the struggle between the police and the bandidos continued. Last year, we spent three months out of the school because the commander of the Sixteenth Military Police battalion, which is closest to us, said, "Don't return, because we are not able to provide security for you." The battalion commander himself came and asked where the school was located, because our school is in the middle of everything. Up above, you have a drug sales point; in front of the school, you have another; and on the other side, you can see that they also have one. He wanted to know where each drug sales point was located and where, exactly, the school was. He saw that the problem was a big one and that the bullets came from all sides. And now what happens? The police arrive already firing from inside the Big Skull. First, they enter firing from the street in front of the school. After, they enter through the school's main gate to get inside the patio with the Big Skull, and from inside the patio they fire in different directions at the bandits. This couldn't continue. When the bandidos are alone, they don't fire on the school, but when the constituted power arrives for a confrontation, using the school as a shield, after that there is a gunfight, and the school is in the middle of it. The constituted power does this. They are not interested in

knowing if there are children or aren't children, if they are in class, or if the
teachers or the mothers are in the middle of a gunfight. I spoke with them
wanting to know what they were thinking. Because the bandidos are up
there, they—the power of the state—enter the school and start to shoot.
This really is unacceptable. We can't work anymore.

Question: When you spoke with the police, what did they say?

Teacher V: Commandant Ubiratan always said that it was not convenient for us to go back to work at the school, that we had to have a little
patience. He would say, "Does a mother want to live in a peaceful community, or does she want to live in a community dominated by the traffickers,
the bandidos?" Colonel Ubiratan was saying it was better to lose some
schooldays than to live in a community where the bandidos were dominating
all the social space. You had to have a confrontation to remove the bandidos
from the area.

Question: This is interesting, because they are not managing to do this.

Teacher C: Now that I've arrived at the meeting, I want to say that the
authorities think they have to act with guns and weapons of war. This isn't ever
going to solve anything. It's militaristic thinking. The only form of state action
here in the community is to make a war. There is this idea, as the governor
says, that the Alemão complex is a den of bandidos, the "enemy of the State."
This seems to me a highly exclusionist, even fascist, vision that the poor are all
enemies and should be considered bandidos. It's not important if it's a school,
if you have a thousand children inside, because all are criminals. You can see
that we receive purely militaristic treatment, without any respect for us.

Question: You have said that the state doesn't exist in poor communities, that the only state presence is repression.

Teacher C: The only state presence here is the police. We don't have a
health clinic; we don't have a place for local administration, not even to
receive documents. We don't have anything. Even trash collection stopped
because the sanitation workers were collecting in the middle of crossfire and
did not want to face the danger. They had to make an agreement with the
Residents' Association, and it's the residents who collect the trash and leave
it on the street, far away, so that the government directs it to be collected.
The community organizes itself for everything, everyone together, even to
collect trash. The Military Police cut off the supply of water and electricity,
and it was the residents who connected them again and maintain the supply.

Question: Then besides the school, you don't have the presence of the state?

Several teachers: We only have the school and guns. We don't even have the telephone. People only use cell phones, because the land line needs maintenance, and this doesn't exist. Everything here is like that, and the community ends up solving everything together. Even here at the school, we depend on the parents who organize themselves in groups to bring the children safely to school. When you have a gunfight, and the Big Skull comes into the school, we call the parents, and they organize themselves to take the children away in groups. They come running to get the children who are in the school when the gunfight stops for while.

Question: Also the water and electricity?

Teachers: Last year they blew up the transformers, and we were without water and electricity for days. There was a gunfight for three days in a row. The whole time there was shooting. Then the residents worked together to maintain the systems themselves because neither CEDAE [state company for water and sewerage], nor the electric company, nor COMLURB [municipal urban cleaning company] wants to come here. Neither do we have mail service anymore. The residents have to take the letters either to the Central Post Office in downtown Rio, or to the post office in Olaria, where mail is sorted, and the residents organize themselves to go and get the mail for the community.

Question: All together, how many students are in all of these schools?

Teacher B: Here in our school, we have a thousand students. We only provide elementary education from the first year to middle school, from six to twelve years of age, more or less. Middle school instruction is provided in a nearby school. Middle school instruction is proceeding normally, and they are learning how to cope with the difficulties of gunfire. For them it's easier to operate normally, because they are located where there is less violence. It's only when you have conflict that the students can't go to school, because no one is out on the streets in a moment of conflict. But overall, the middle school is operating. It's a big school, very old, and important in the community.

Question: Are you now able to operate normally?

Teacher B: We are operating one day at a time. The maxim of the school is, "Just for today, let's survive!"

Question: Why?

Teachers: Because there is no longer a set time for shooting. One day, it starts at eight in the morning, when the children are on their way to school. Another day, it starts during recess, when they're on the patio, and the Big Skull enters shooting.

Question: Why do the authorities do this?

Teachers: Because they don't have a policy. They don't have anything except confrontation. It's the policy of war itself. You don't have an established time to make war—or concern for the children.

Teacher B: One time I said to the police commander, "Look, I understand your problem. because as a resident, I know that it's difficult for the police to enter the community. There are many exits on all sides, and the bandidos use them." The commander said to me, "Professor, it's more difficult for us to occupy X than Y. In Y, there are few exits, but here it's like a fan. In X there are various exits, and I need many men, and I don't have the numbers for this." For this reason, he doesn't attack at night or on Sunday. The commander told me, "On Sunday, there are many people on the street, people drinking beer, walking around, and I would have to put many lives at risk." The commander asked what I would suggest. I said, "It's not my role. I'm a teacher. I'm not a security agent. I don't understand security, but it seems to me that you might give a warning so we can prepare ourselves and remove the children from school and not leave them in the middle of a gunfight." It's very difficult for us to protect a group of five hundred students in the middle of a gunfight. In May, a grenade exploded inside the school and smashed classrooms to smithereens. The Military Police were at the door of the school and firing toward the hill behind the school.

Question: Then the Military Police don't enter the school?

Teacher B: The Military Police were at the door of the school and firing toward the hill behind the school. Before, they didn't come into the school. Now they come onto the patio. They come up the ramp and set up on the patio to have a better position facing the hill. For this reason, I say that they are not worried that the children are inside the school. It's been very difficult. We couldn't teach in 2007 from the second day of May until the end of June. Later, we had two hours of class each day to give some instruction to the students. Now we're back at the school and trying to keep a normal schedule—normal, that is, within this situation of conflict when at times we can more or less work.

Question: And they keep saying that you must have this confrontation.

Teacher H: Their only policy is armed frontal attack. There is no policy of intelligence gathering, of investigative work. What they only really know is how to shoot. The state considers all of us bandidos. They don't make any distinction. And you have professional people of every type living here in the community but without the least security. People are hit by stray bullets and die and are viewed as bandidos. The other day, a barber was killed at work. They said he was a bandido. He wasn't a bandido. He had been a resident here for more than thirty years.

Teacher D: They invaded his house and killed him. They took control of his house. He came home and was greeted with bullets by the Military Police.

Teacher A: They do this. The students tell us that [the Military Police] enter their houses. They invade the houses of people, eat yogurt and cheese, even make the mothers cook for them.

Another teacher: On April 11, they invaded the house of a friend of mine. They ate everything he had in the refrigerator. They threw things on the floor, left the place a mess, broke many of his things. The guy wasn't at home. He was lucky, because if he had been, perhaps he wouldn't even be here to tell the story, because they kill people.

Question: During the past year, did the National Security Force also do this?

Teachers: No, not the NSF. It's only the State Military Police who do this.

Question: Where was the NSF during the encirclement of the Alemão complex?

Teacher H: They stayed at the edges, at the principal entry points and streets of the Alemão complex, on the periphery. They didn't come into the community. It's the Military Police who enter.

Question: Did you have help from human rights organizations, the Brazilian Bar Association?

Teacher D: No. Some years ago, there was a meeting here of the Association of Journalists when Tim Lopes was assassinated.[2] They wanted to have a demonstration, and representatives of various communities came. They organized a demonstration, but it didn't take place. The bandidos found out and pressured the Residents' Association, and [the association] didn't allow it.

Question: Then the bandidos give the orders and allow or don't allow something?

Teacher D: Yes, and they don't like demonstrations in the communities because they interfere with their business. Even the secretary of education hinders making contacts, hinders our speaking, for example, with churches. They want an image that all is normal, that everything is fine. The truth is that it's gotten much worse. The government of Sérgio Cabral has already killed more [people] in one year than were killed in the eight previous years of under the Garotinho governments.[3] There is a report in the *Jornal do Brasil* about this—about Getúlio Vargas Hospital where the Big Skull frequently takes people who are already dead. It's the hospital near here where wounded people and even the dead are taken.[4]

Teacher A: When I was a child, this school was already a community reference point. I was raised here, and I attended this school. But it was very different. The area was all occupied by favelas. My mother sent me to the favela to buy eggs because there were residents who raised chickens, sold eggs and other things, and had vegetable gardens. Then, we went alone to buy things in the favela. My mother said, "Buy lettuce; buy eggs at the house of so and so." We went into the homes of people we knew. There was much poverty but not the violence of today. The violence came little by little, and from 1990 to today it has grown much worse. Already in the 1980s, with the passing of the dictatorship, it was getting bad, and during the 1990s it got even worse. As for today, it's worse than ever. Since 2000, it's gotten much worse.

Question: Teacher E, you think the school ought to leave here, to close, correct?

Teacher E: Yes, because within the community we don't have the means to continue. Are we going to serve as cannon fodder for the police? I don't think we should play this part. This is not a role for education.

Question: All five schools should be closed?

Teacher E: All should be transferred to a more secure place, since the police have not been able to contain the bandidos. For example, the city government can rent a building, or construct a building, in the center of Rio and put the students and the teachers there, even if only provisionally, until the violence is contained here. But I do not believe the violence can be contained, because public power is present only in the form of the police. Public power is not present with other public services. We do not have basic sanitation; we do not have a health clinic; we don't have work; we don't have good transportation. How can the bandidos be defeated without these means? What good does it do to repress alone? Until today, no one has died inside the school, which is a miracle of God, because if you look around the school you can see all the bullet holes. Any of these bullets might have hit someone—a child, a teacher, an administrator. The community turns to the school, because the administration of the school is good and has the school in hand. It has a good relationship with the community. The two principals attended the school and afterward worked here as teachers. They know the children by name; know the life of people in the community; know the mothers, many of whom were also students at the school. They have a life dedicated to this community.

I think it's a lack of respect. Each time there is a gunfight, we remain here, abandoned, living through hours of terror. No one is concerned with our life, with our situation—no one. Not the city government or the secretary of education or Regional Coordinator of Education (CRE), which is directly responsible for the schools in a determined area, including ours. We have sent documents and the principal has spoken to the CRE various times about the situation we are living through. Nothing happens. And this is being repeated with greater and greater frequency. Before it was shooting only in the late afternoon, after five o'clock. Not anymore. It happened in the afternoon during class time, from noon to 5:00 P.M. We can have a week with two or three days of gunfire.

I'm going to provide you with a detail confidentially since I'm not going to be identified. When the children arrive at school at seven in the morning, they already know whether there is going to be a police operation. I remember one time they arrived a little after nine in the morning, and the police operation did not succeed. The secretary of security, the one we have now, the blond one, said that the community was to blame for the failure of the police because the bandidos were warned about when the police would arrive. This causes me to believe that the bandidos are warned by someone inside the police. There is nothing to cause me to believe otherwise. We all know it. I can't accuse anyone, because I haven't got the proof. It's logical that the bandidos know. They already begin to put up the barricades well before the police arrive. What I mean to say is this shows an even greater lack of respect for the school, because [the Military Police] know that the bandidos know and still are not capable of getting us out before shooting starts. Of course, they are going to attack the bandidos, but first remove the population. Take children off the street, the teachers and population away from danger. Suspend classes. Respect our lives. Say, "Look, the police are coming here today. We're going to have a confrontation. Close the school."

Before you arrive and start shooting everywhere, you first have to offer what the Constitution guarantees to every citizen. But, no—here we don't have anything. The public power is not present in the community. We are abandoned. Are you in a shootout? Die, die, you're finished. One more statistic about stray bullets. We already saw this happen in other schools—children being wounded. Did it lead to something? [The teachers show bullets they found on the school's patio. In one day, they found seventy-two bullets.]

Question: And PRONASCI, this new federal government program. Do you think it can work? There are many community projects.

Teacher E: They say that it is going to change something. Frankly, I don't know. What we see here every day is gunfire. PAC [the Program for the Acceleration of Growth] doesn't have anything for this community. There is something in the Alemão complex. It seems that they are going to build a cablecar line. They talk about schools, about sewer infrastructure, about a health clinic. But this is not for our community or for others that we know. Here we haven't heard about PAC, about anything.

Do you know what we also fear, besides dying? I am going to confess that I'm afraid to die, but I came here to work. We are teachers. We did not come here to confront the bandidos who are in our area. My fear is that one of the children may be wounded. In that situation, even if I survive, if a child is wounded by a bullet, my life is over. Imagine living like this: my student being wounded, dying here without me being able to help or do anything. I know that I'm not responsible for the death of the child, but we feel responsible for them. . . . I'm going to feel guilty for not having been able to protect him, understand? I know that I'm in no position to protect these children. Not I or the other teachers or the principals. Not anyone here. We don't know where the bullets come from. We don't know the time that [shooting is] going to begin. You are giving a class, and suddenly the shooting starts. At any minute, a bullet can hit one of these children. This is my greatest fear: to spend the rest of my life crying, feeling guilty, because of something I didn't do and for which I was not responsible. I'm not in a secure situation to work, and the children don't have a secure situation to learn. People only know how to complain about the results of public school education; they forget that the one who relies on the public schools here is the child who is poor. How can a child living daily with violence like this learn something? I'm still impressed to see that some are learning when the conditions are so bad.

They come to school stumbling over cadavers, jumping over barricades, seeing bandidos armed to the teeth. The same bandidos say to them, "Today there is going to be a gunfight. Use that street because you can't walk here."

Question: Are the children beginning to adapt themselves to this violence, as if it were a normal part of life?

Teachers: No! They are still shocked. And they react in the same way. During recess, we see them fighting; they attack each other at random. To the contrary, this violence is influencing their behavior away from what is normal. When they fight, they quickly want to hit someone in the face or they pretend they have a gun and say they are going to kill. They do this as if they might be firing at a fellow student. I've already seen this. And any small thing—someone gets bumped—and they raise their hand to strike. Dialogue, conversation has stopped.

Teacher A: I work with adolescents. They sometimes stay and talk with us. They can't sleep; they're afraid to come and go. They fear what will happen to their fathers when they come home from work, and the police are in the house. They are afraid of everything because of the ongoing conflict. It's real fear. They live in a state of panic. They have cell phones with them and will say, "Let me call my mother. My mother is leaving to go to work." Or "My father is going to arrive from work, and if he encounters the police, they can kill him." It's heart-wrenching to hear the testimony of the students.

Teacher E: Then you are not able to teach because shooting begins in the middle of a class, the students begin to scream, they begin to cry, and so do the teachers. All run and throw themselves down on the floor. They don't know where to hide. There is gunfire on all sides. We have to remain calm. We don't have the right to cry. Many times, after it happens, I hide in the bathroom and cry. But at the time of the shooting, I can't even do that, because I can't abandon the children, abandon the ship. If I did, I would become unstable. Afterward, I feel like a person whose body has been run over by a tractor. I react at the time. I show strength. I help. But after, I feel very bad. So much is demanded of us emotionally. What can I do? I can't do anything but wait, to see if we can leave, to get the last child home safely. Sometimes the parents are not able to come.

On Wednesday, there was a shootout here. A child was here more than three hours after the school closed. The mother could not come. Many times, the parents cannot come and get their children because it's not possible to leave the house. That would put a life at risk. And many times, they have other, younger children. They think that the child is in the school and the teachers are there, and they think that it is safer here. The worst thing is we know this isn't going to stop. We are afraid that a child is going to be hit by a bullet. This is terrible pressure. We use a saying of Alcoholic Anonymous: "I'm only going to work today. I'm only going to survive today." This is how we are living.

We cannot program anything at the school, because suddenly we have shooting. I prefer programs outside the school so the children can leave the community a little, so they can see other realities. Here, it's gunfire everyday, violence, the Big Skull. When it arrives, everyone is terrified. According to the students, they [the BOPE police inside the Big Skull speaking through loudspeakers] say terrible things regardless of who they're talking to. If it is a bandido or a community resident, it doesn't matter. They say, "I'm going to get you. I'm going to kill you. I'm going to take your soul." The children are terrified of the Big Skull as if it's an alien from another world. When they say, "Big Skull is here," it's the end of the world; they're panic-stricken. We have to help, to try to calm them and protect them. And do you know what happens? The bandido ends up getting more respect from the community than the police, because the police arrive, speak in this way, and treat residents in this manner, and the trafficker doesn't. If you don't cross him, he doesn't do anything against the community. For him, it's a good thing that the community might be on his side. The bandido is never going to shoot anyone in the community unless he has a problem with that person. If there is no problem, the resident can breathe easily. But the police enter full of aggression, saying terrible things to the residents. Then the community ends up being against the police.

Question: Then it's true that they come in with the Big Skull saying things? They have music, don't they?

Teachers [*speaking emphatically*]: It's all true. "Get out of the way! I'm coming to take your soul." Calling us "*vagabundos* [tramps or bums]" and the women "whores." All this is real. They're inside this armored vehicle saying these things. It's cowardice. We don't even see their faces. They can go on speaking, playing the music, saying what they want. And suddenly from within they're firing in every direction.

Is there a solution? You can ask entrepreneurs to put businesses in the community to employ the population. The government can offer tax exemptions to such businesses—saying, for instance, "For ten years you aren't going to pay any taxes, as long as you construct your enterprise or factory here and give jobs to the community." And principally, the public power has to be present. You have to have a local police station with many police who

know the community. You have to have a health clinic to take care of the
population, because otherwise they have to descend the hill to Getúlio Vargas Hospital, which might not take notice of them. There are so many
patients with illnesses that aren't complicated and don't require hospitaliza-
tion, but you have to go there anyway, because the community doesn't have
a health clinic. An enormous population such as this and the community
doesn't have a health clinic! Why don't they establish one up here? Why
haven't the schools got the necessary security? We remain here like a target
for the bandidos and the police. It's as if the public power might say,
"Teacher, it's this way." And we have to protect the students.

Teacher A: The other day, on Wednesday, the bandidos blocked access
to the hill. They parked a bus, closing one entry, and seized a garbage truck
and closed entry from below. The bus couldn't make its route; the van
couldn't get through; there wasn't any public transportation. The Big Skull
was circulating and firing, and the bandidos were shooting, Before it was
one Big Skull. Now there are three or four. It's chaos.

Fernando, a Teacher in the Baixada Fluminense: A Discussion with Maria Helena Moreira Alves and José Valentin Palacios, June 10, 2008

This discussion with Fernando, an elementary-school teacher, centered on
drawings his students made about their lives and the violence that surrounds
them. Fernando explained that he gathered several classes to discuss the frequent shootouts near the school and the many incursions of the Big Skull,
which came to shoot near or at the gate of the school. The Big Skull was
shooting at targets on the hill, where drug dealers were believed to be hiding.
Return fire then reached classrooms. Children had to hide in closets, behind
walls, in the bathrooms. Fernando told us that many children suffered from
shock; some had developed heart conditions; and their fear made teaching
difficult—at times, impossible. Therefore, he decided to use a common psychological technique—that of drawings—to get the students to express their
deepest anxieties and fears. He asked them to answer three questions: The
first was, "Do you think that what is going on here is normal?" The second
question was, "Do you believe that your school can help and have some influence to change things?" And the third was, "If you had a chance and were
capable of changing things, what would you do?"

Some of answers amazed him; others saddened him. Only one child
believed that the school could reach the authorities and be heard so that the

violence would stop. And even that child believed it would happen only if the director of the school could speak to the President Lula himself. Many children responded to the question about what they would do to change things by talking about peace and working for peace and by drawing white doves. The answer of one student, a ten-year-old boy, stood out: His only desire, he said, was to leave the place where he lived and move to the "other side," to the area of the rich people, with the high buildings and fine condominium apartments.

Parents, teachers, and psychologists discuss what is going to happen to a generation growing up in such violence. If they do survive beyond age twenty, will they be permanently harmed? How can those who work with them, love them, parent them expect to guide them out of the hell in which they are living and heal the deep trauma?

Question: Do the current mega-operations by the police since 2007 represent a change in public security policy by the current state government?

Fernando: Definitely. Since the siege of the Alemão complex, it is evident that there has been a very strong policy change. Large-scale police operations have become frequent.

Question: Are you saying that there wasn't as much police violence before as there is now?

Fernando: There was none that I know of. The main proof is that the school had to undergo physical repairs. New concrete walls had to be built as a result of the bullets that were fired directly at the school. Before that, the hallway windows facing the community were left open. It was a calm setting, one that allowed light to enter, with the hallway open on one side, and the classrooms on the other. But everything had to be closed, and air vents had to be created, which were also pierced by the gunshots. The open spaces—the recreation areas for students and for sports—also had to be closed. They cannot be used now because they are very vulnerable to shooting. During the mega-operation, the police entered the school, crossed the yard, and removed part of the roof so they could climb up and ambush a guy who was on a hill. They caught the guy by surprise. The next day, the drug traffickers demanded explanations from the school administration. "What's this?" they yelled at the principal. "You let the cops in? We don't go into the school. We respect the school. How is it you allowed the cops in?" The head of the traffickers demanded answers from the principal. And she said, "Look, how could I possibly stop the police from entering the school?" It was truly a difficult situation.

Question: I'd like to know how life is for the people in these communities. Do they remain hidden?

Fernando: No, they don't remain hidden. Once the shooting is over, everybody is out on the street, having a beer, shopping at the food market, going to work. They move about normally. People believe that they have to go on living normally. They have lived in the community longer than the period of police invasions and police conflict with drug traffickers. They're grandparents, parents, children. They have to go on living somehow. They hide when the shooting is going on; they organize in groups to pick up the children from school; and after the shooting ends, they go out again to do the normal things they need to do to live day by day.

Question: What do they do during the shooting?

Fernando: They hide wherever they can. I asked students, "What do you think the school can do?" I found their answers sad. When they have a problem that affects them all, like a flood, they all come to school. It's a public space that they believe belongs to the community. But with the police invasions and shootings, the children say that the school can't do anything. This means that they have lost the school, which is important to them. I ask myself: "How is it possible that people have developed this attitude?" They can't do anything. The state came in shooting, and there is nothing they can do. To me, it's very sad.

Question: What about community organization? How does the community react?

Fernando: People generally hide and have their way of organizing. For instance, they help out one another a lot. It's a community thing, especially when it comes to . . . escorting the children back and forth to school. They know beforehand when shooting is going to take place, so they organize to have a group of parents pick up the children of neighbors who may be working and hide them until the parents return home. Sometimes the parents cannot come home if the shooting continues until the day after an occupation by the police. Then the children stay with relatives, neighbors, and friends. The organization is truly impressive. It's a matter of survival. They arrive at the school from everywhere, spreading the news along the way: "Listen, the Big Skull is coming and making its rounds, though I don't know exactly where it is now." The neighbors know. The news travels quickly, and they show up at the school to pick up their children. In fact, it's the community that warns the teachers. Sometimes a student will tell me where there's going to be a shootout, and when I go over to talk with the principal, she already knows and is already organizing the children's departure. The neighbors are very well organized, and the principal won't release a child to just anyone. Everyone knows one another, and they have a plan in place for emergencies—when there's a conflict or a shootout with the police. Neighbors also organize to do food shopping for one another. During the police mega-operation, there was a period of time when some people could not shop for food. So those people who could get out shopped for their neighbors, and vice versa. People know that demonstrating won't achieve anything. They know they have no voice. So they organize in a silent way. But they know that the state is the guilty party.

Question: How do you relate to the mothers and fathers and to the community as a whole?

Fernando: The school is the heart of the community and much respected. It's interesting to see the enormous respect that people have for the school. It's the police who don't have respect and invade the school. They shoot at it from close range, any time of the day. Students must come to school well dressed, clean, with their hair properly combed and with neatly washed and ironed clothes. The principal says that this is important for the children's self-esteem, especially amid so much violence. The community supports her efforts and tries very hard to honor them. When we

Big Skull. *(Photograph by A. F. Rodrigues/Imagens do Povo.)*

Drawing by a child providing a panoramic view of a conflict between police (identified as "P") and bandidos (identified as "B") in a favela. A bandido is firing a large automatic weapon at a police helicopter.

have a theater presentation on weekends, the school fills up with parents. It's a very beautiful thing to see. Everybody is happy seeing their children in the production, so they laugh and clap. The theater is very important. Sometimes, students write pieces about their lives.

Our theater has really developed. One of the first plays the students put on was a new reading of Shakespeare's *Romeo and Juliet*. It was called *The Montagues and the Capulets, and Us* and was an adaptation of *Romeo and Juliet* to the favela, based on the fights between opposing drug-trafficking factions. It was beautifully done and gave the community much to talk about. Well-known authors and people involved with the professional theater world came. They did presentations for the students and helped them put on the play. The students did the play in the school's dining hall. They moved all of the tables aside to have enough space and set up a stage. They charged one *real* for admission, and the whole community turned out to support them. It was important to the students to earn money and see themselves as professionals. It was the beginning for the group to become strong and became the entry point into professional theater life for many students. The

Drawing by a child depicting war and peace.

theater group is always involved with the school and the community. That's
a beautiful thing to see. They embrace community, and the community
embraces them.

A Mother from the Alemão Complex:
A Discussion with Maria Helena Moreira Alves
and José Valentin Palacios, June 12, 2008

This interview with a mother from the Alemão complex was conducted under
a guarantee of anonymity. The mother participated only after mutual friends
discussed the purpose of the book with her and why it would be important

for people outside her community, and outside Brazil, to hear her testimony. She identified herself as an ordinary resident and described how she lived, with her husband and four children, through the Miltary Police and BOPE invasions of her community in 2007 and 2008.

Mother: I have lived here since I was a child. I have four children, and my husband has always worked. I also worked, but when the violence increased, I had to stop because I have to stay with my children. One is six, one is eight, one is nine, and one is an adolescent. We live here because we don't have the income to live in a better place. At least after many years of effort, the house is ours, and we live next door to my mother-in-law. My brother-in-law also lives nearby. Everyone here is a good friend, and all help one another. We all want to move because of the things that are happening, but where can we go? We don't have a place where we can go.

Maria Helena: When you were young, were there so many gunfights?

Mother: No, not gunfights. Drug problems and drug traffickers, this we had. But it was this way: The authorities didn't bother about it. They didn't bother to note that it existed. From time to time, a dead body was seen. Today, it's different. Somebody is killed, and the police themselves remove the body. Before, the police came, killed many people, and left the bodies. But we didn't have armed bandidos. We didn't have this confrontation that we have today. It was much less.

Maria Helena: Fewer drug traffickers or fewer police?

Mother: Fewer drug traffickers, and they respected the residents. Not today. There is no respect. He [the bandido] is there in front of everyone; he is walking around with guns, selling drugs in front of everyone. Before, we didn't have this. The police came, and it was this way. They knew who they had to kill. They arrived already knowing who the bandidos were. Today, we have no respect from either side—from the police or from the bandidos. To the police, everyone here is a bandido. There is no longer a distinction.

Maria Helena: Then you are on the firing line?

Mother: Correct. In the area where we live, we don't have a street, only alleys. There are houses on one side, then an opening in the middle of the alley, leaving space for only one person to walk. The first house on the corner is my mother-in-law's, and the other is mine. Then you continue climbing the hill, with many houses and many children. Up above, the bandidos shoot at the police. They [the bandidos] made a big hole, with a concrete block on one side and another concrete block on the other side. The bandidos take up a position in the hole, firing when the police climb the hill. I live in the target area.

Maria Helena: Does the Big Skull go up, and do they fire on it?
Mother: No, not the Big Skull. The street is too narrow. It's the police themselves who come on foot.

Maria Helena: What do you do when there is a gunfight?
Mother: We hide. We go to the back of the house and hide. It's more protected. We stay on the floor. We stay together in a corner on the floor behind the walls.

Maria Helena: And if you were on the street, what would you do?
Mother: God help me, I have never been caught on the street. But [that's] also because I no longer have a normal life. I used to go out, and I wasn't afraid. Now I am, and I only go out to take the children to school and to buy food. Sometimes my daughter says, "Mommy, let's go to the market." And I answer, "We'll do it Saturday." Because it's dangerous. Suddenly you have a gunfight in the market, and the Big Skull invades.

Maria Helena: If you can't go to the market, where do you shop?
Mother: The market that we talk about is a place where they sell clothes, shoes, these things. We always go on Saturdays because they have pretty little things, and it's cheaper. To go to the market to buy food, we only can go when it's all clear. We call and ask, "Is it safe?" Then we go and buy on the run. When the police invaded and the confrontation began, we were without food. I wasn't able to leave the house, especially at the worst time of the gunfight. There were four days of terror. My husband couldn't leave the house for three days; he was not able to go to work. And I was hidden in the back of the house with our four children, unable to leave.

Maria Helena: Without food and water?
Mother: Without water not because we don't have running water, but because in some places they shut off the water. And without food because we couldn't leave the house to get it.

Maria Helena: This was when?
Mother: It was in May of last year [2007] when the operation began. We stayed trapped there. We were prisoners in the back of the house on the floor

for more than four days. Later, in April 2008, it was also very violent, many people were killed. We were trapped in the middle of gunfire. My husband called people who lived down below and asked, "Is it all right for me to leave the house?" When it wasn't, he lost a day of work. When he did get out to work, he would phone before coming home and ask, "How is it there?" Every day, every hour, he called. At times before we knew he was coming he would call to tell us where the police were so we could get ready and find cover for the children. If he couldn't come home, he had to sleep at work or even on the street. Many workers here sleep the whole week on the streets in Rio.

Maria Helena: What did you do with four children, four days without food, and feeling so frightened? I'm a mother, and I can't imagine how you lived that way.

Mother: You eat what you have until it's gone. You try going to the neighbors' houses to get food, but at times you can't even do that. But the worst thing I experienced was a big gunfight when I was with my six-year-old son. My other son was at school, and when I managed to get there, he was acting like a cornered animal. He was under a table shaking. I began to cry because I was seeing my son there, a little animal shaking with fright. And my older children were upstairs crying, one hidden inside the teacher's closet. The teacher came to me and said, "Stay calm," because if I didn't give strength to my children, who would give it? And there was a helicopter firing overhead. I had to find strength, I don't know from where. I swallowed. I took a deep breath to be strong. And the little one, poor little thing, he didn't know what was happening. He didn't have any notion of what this was all about. He stayed where he was because the teacher ordered him to, and he was terrified by the gun shots and the helicopter.

Afterward, my nine-year-old had to stay at the hospital for observation. She had a sort of heart attack, a cardiac problem caused by fear. The doctor told me that, when this happens, I have to take her immediately to the hospital. My other daughter, the oldest, who attends a middle school, suffered the most. Her classroom was hit. There was so much firing that the bullets struck the classroom walls, and shrapnel wounded the children. A piece of a bullet struck her ear, and she also had to go the hospital. Now she has panic attacks.

It's enough to say that the Big Skull arrived at the school. It broke through the gates to the patio and through the school building's door and smashed its way into classrooms, with machine guns in the hands of the police. They destroyed classrooms where there were children; they destroyed the computers. The police jumped on the tables and made a hole in the ceiling to shoot from the roof of the school.

Maria Helena: Was this the Military Police or the NSF?

Mother: It was the BOPE. The BOPE did horrible things. Where I lived, they broke into houses. They knocked down doors and entered. If a man was inside, they killed him. I thank God that they never caught my husband in the house. They would have killed him. They don't even care to know who he is. They kill right away. With us, with women and children, they beat us, they curse at us, at times they rape and kill. They don't have any respect. They went into my neighbor's house and destroyed everything. They threw everything on the floor. They tore apart the sofa in her living room. Then there was a case of a friend of mine. She was wearing a black blouse, and they tore off her blouse and beat her. We're not allowed to wear black because black is their color—only theirs. They left her with only a bra. She kept quiet. If they come here, I'm going to wear a black blouse. I'm not going to keep quiet, because I think this is absurd. Now you have to wear clothes the color they want in your own home. They also eat everything that they find in the house. They even make you cook for them.

Maria Helena: You're joking!

Mother: I'm not joking. It's true. One time, my mother came to visit. She's from Minas Gerais. She doesn't know how Rio is. She went to open the door, and they entered. I told her, "Don't open the door. Stay quiet so they'll think no one is home. But if they enter and order you to cook for them, you cook. Don't confront them, because they even beat old women." They entered, they ate everything, they used the bathroom, they left everything dirty. They have gone into the houses of many people I know.

I have already told my mother-in-law that she will have to bulletproof the walls of her house. Bullets are fired on all sides of it. Her house isn't standing up to the gunfire. I told her to make a door from her house into ours so she can run to the rear of our house, as we do. The other day, a grenade fell—one grenade from the bandidos, and one tear-gas bomb from the police. Our good luck was that the door was closed. I was with my oldest daughter inside the house when I heard, "Listen, anything happens and we kick in this door." I was frightened to death that the police might break the door and enter my house. I closed everything as fast as I could, and we hid in the back. When I went to hide, the shooting began. There were many, many bullets. I heard a boom at the door. Something struck the wall, and I heard a hissing sound. I said, "A bomb fell." But it didn't explode. I didn't know what type of bomb. On the weekend, when my husband went to clean the yard, he found it. It was tear gas. The other one was a grenade. It didn't fall inside my room because of the roof. If fell under the stairs and went down to the laje.

Maria Helena: Then both sides threw bombs?

Mother: Yes. One time, the school principal was caught in crossfire at the school, and she asked me to come to get my daughter. I told her, "I can't leave the house." And she said, "Then wait a little while." After, she called again to say that the situation at the school was difficult. I had to say again, "I can't leave." It was a moment of desperation because of what was happening. There on my corner, the police were under cover on one side, and the bandidos were on the other. Whoever happened to appear was shot. To leave the house was to die.

Maria Helena: What do you do then to get your daughter from school?

Mother: When it's calm, we don't have a problem. We go without worry. But if somebody shoots, then how do we do it? If on one side of the community there is shooting, people there can't leave and can't get their children. But if on the other side there is no shooting, then people run and get their children and the children from the side where there is shooting. Sometimes my daughter stays with neighbors for several hours, until things get better on our side.

Maria Helena: Then the residents help one another in these emergencies. And what about when your daughter is in school and cannot return home?

Mother: At times, the shooting is on all sides, and she cannot return home. She has to remain under cover in the school. If she were to leave, she could die. Go out on the street, and you're shot. We get it from both sides—the police and the bandidos. At times, you go to get your child, and when you arrive at the school, a gunfight begins. Then you cannot leave the school. The school is full of mothers, teachers, and screaming children.

Maria Helena: In the school, do you take cover until the gunfight stops, until late at night?

Mother: At times, we dare a little. When you see that it has calmed down a little, you run. Running is a risk until you arrive home. I have the problem that three of my children study in one elementary school, and the oldest is in middle school. Then I have to run the risk of getting all four. You can see how difficult it is. They're in separate schools. Three study in the morning, and she studies in the afternoon. Then we spend the day very nervous each time we have to go out and get them at one school or the other. Is there going to be a gunfight? What am I going to do with my children? If I leave the little ones at home to get my oldest, I'm scared to death that there will be a shootout around my house, and they are there alone. So I take them with me, run the risk of a gunfight on the street, with three small children.

Maria Helena: I know mothers in Maré who made a large aluminum shield big enough for three or four people. They stayed between the shield and walls to protect themselves from shots when they went to get their children. Has anyone done this here?

Mother: It wouldn't work here. It's worse here than in Maré, because they shoot from rifles. They [the bullets] go through everything, even walls. They only don't go through cement, but even sometimes they do. What good would aluminum be? We thought about doing this because the mothers told us that in Maré they did this. But it's too thin. We have to pray that it will be calm when we're out on the streets with children. What's worse is that the gunshots here come from two sides. At times in the morning, at the hour to take children to school, you arrive and see pieces of the wall, of wood, of the pavement, shrapnel everywhere. Then you can't take the children to school. Everyone stays at home, taking cover on the floor at the back of the house until things calm down a little.

Maria Helena: You told me that when you were a child, you went to school alone. Then, this violence began a short while ago?

Mother: There was plenty of violence before—not when I was a child, but since then. The police now use the school as a shield. I think it is absurd that a power that is supposed to protect us forces its way into a school, breaking things and even stealing equipment. In truth, they curse as much as the bandidos, but the bandidos never go into the school. To the contrary, they have a rule that no one can interfere with the school. The school has a computer. The school has many things of value. I'm saying that the school was safe inside and that the bandidos never stole from the school. Now the police, the Military Police, come and do all this. The Big Skull positions itself at the door not only of this school but at many schools. They force open the main gate, and the Big Skull goes into the schoolyard, firing in all directions. The school's walls have the marks. In the school that my children attend, the Big Skull remained in front of the door. I was terrified because it was shooting from the door, and we already knew that at the other school, it had forced open the gate and gone into the schoolyard. We are terrified of the Big Skull. We called the secretary of education, but nothing was done.

Maria Helena: Is it a public school?

Mother: Yes, it is. The school belongs to the city government of Rio de Janeiro, but they never help with anything. We have called, we asked the secretary of education for help, but nothing was ever done. So we deliver ourselves into God's hands.

Maria Helena: Then you go out only when you have to and when you can? You go to the market and take a walk with the kids?

Mother: No, going out for a walk is a thing of the past. On Friday, my husband said that we should go down to the street because he wanted to take the children to a movie. But in the afternoon, he came running back to the house because the Big Skull had arrived and was shooting. There were many bullets. He barely managed to get up the hill in time to stay with me and the children. I don't know how he made it home. He had to run, because there was a lot of gunfire. It's a long, steep climb, and he came up running. We don't have the right to walk anymore, to come and go. We no longer have the right to anything, because at any moment, there is a gunfight, we have the Big Skull and confrontation. The worst thing is that the Military Police and the BOPE pressure the residents with guns drawn, threatening them if they don't say who is who, where they are hiding, where the drug traffickers have their points for dealing, where they have guns.

Maria Helena: They force people to inform at the gunpoint? This puts people in danger.

Mother: Of course. And they threaten to kill us if we don't tell them anything. And the others threaten to kill us if we tell.

Maria Helena: How absurd. They don't do their own intelligence work and want the people to do it for them.

Mother: They get hold of us and talk this way: "Stand against the wall. You know where it is. We know that you know. You don't want to talk. We're going to get it out of you."

Maria Helena: Have there been cases of torture?

Mother: Yes, we had a teacher who was very much in favor of the BOPE invasions, but she changed her mind when she heard a group of residents, many of whom were parents of her students, say that they had been beaten and tortured in the square for everyone to see, so that everyone would be frightened and tell everything they knew. But people were afraid because the bandidos also threatened. The bandidos threaten to use the microwave.

Maria Helena: And, of course, everyone is afraid.

Mother: The other day, as I was walking up to my home with my three small children, a group of police at a barricade came to speak to the children. One played with my youngest and spoke to him and to me. I was afraid. The bandidos do not allow us to speak to the police. I thought, "What will happen if the bandidos see me speaking with them? What will happen to my children. Who will protect us?" The police are the first to inform against the residents to the bandidos, because they work together. That's the problem: There is much conniving. When you speak with the police, you don't know who you're speaking to.

[For example,] when a dance is held, the police don't come. There is a confrontation in the morning, but it's to force the bandidos to give them money so that they can hold the dance. Everybody knows this. There is no dance if the police don't get the money. We can see how the thing works. They get their money and fire their guns to say that there was an action, then they leave with the Big Skull and everything saying, "Enjoy the evening."

Maria Helena: And the Residents' Association, what does it do?

Mother [*laughing*]: The Residents' Association? They're working with them. You understand—they can't do anything. We don't have elections anymore. Yes, some communities still hold elections and have Residents' Associations that represent the people. But others, like here, don't have elections any more. We have one person [who has been in charge for many years].

Maria Helena: And that person is under orders from the traffickers or the police or both?

Mother: It's a person from the community, and both give him orders, knowing that he will stay in his position and not cause any problems. He's there as long as they want, just to say that we have a Residents' Association.

Maria Helena: Doesn't the Residents' Association organize courses?

Mother: It does. The Residents' Association is now carrying out a project for the government. It's a very good project, but only for the purpose of getting the children's attention. [It offers] a swimming course, a judo course, and a course in capoeira. It has courses to reinforce school classes. But what the community wants, it doesn't have. It doesn't have professional training courses; it doesn't have courses that help young people find work or courses that might get young people out of drug dealing. That would help resolve the crime problem. The government has a vision that it's important to have recreation for children. But we don't have any telecourses or any preparation for work.

Maria Helena: Do you have a health clinic in the community?

Mother: Not in our community. It's outside. I thought with the coming of PAC, [the government] might put a health clinic or a technical school here in the community. But we don't have anything.

Maria Helena: What is PAC doing in Alemão? Only the cablecar line, or is it also going to have a health clinic?

Mother: I think this cablecar line is an absurdity. So do many people in the community. The poor person doesn't need a cablecar. We want a health clinic; we want better education; we want professional-development courses and other opportunities for our children. As fathers and mothers, we are afraid that our children will begin to think that the violence we live with every day is normal. I said to my two youngest children, "If you get into drug dealing, you don't stand a chance. The bandido kills you. The police kill you. Drugs themselves kill you. And you will also die if you go to jail." I'm very fearful. Many parents are also afraid that their children will find this normal. The children will come to think that the bandido is the good guy because he is the one who is in charge, who has nice clothes, who has the prettiest girls. Do you understand? So we hope that PAC will confront these things with more professional-development courses, schools, and social support for children so they will know other experiences. What good is spending so much money on a cablecar line if the children grow up and are never able to leave this? . . .

One day a reporter arrived to get some information about the community. I said to her, "Look over there, the Big Skull is coming through." She said, "Let's take a picture. I'd like to photograph you with the Big Skull." And I said, "No way! It would be insane. How are you going to take a picture alongside the Big Skull. And then what are the others going to think? That you're giving information to the police, and then they can kill me and my family." She took a picture of the Big Skull anyway. After she left, I worried about what was going to happen to me and who was going protect me. She gave my phone number to other reporters, and they kept calling me, wanting information about the police. I had to say, "Look, I'm not giving you any information."

I only gave [the first reporter] an interview about family planning. I won't speak about any other community matter, because it's highly dangerous. You're here in this situation with family and children to care for. Some reporters said to me, "But you have to speak. You have to take advantage of this opportunity." And I answered, "Everything has a limit." How are we going to speak, identifying ourselves? In my case, I only speak with my husband: "You can come, but call before to know how things are." Because at times when it gets later in the day, the gunfight stops, and at times it's all right to return home.

Maria Helena: Do you think that they stop on purpose to let people return home?

Mother: I think so. They stop because there are many residents who have to come up the hill after work.

Maria Helena: Do they have a set time?

Mother: There's no set time, and at times they stop so there is not so much confusion down below on the avenue, with many people waiting to be able to return home. But many times, residents wait a long time, calling their families on cell phones to ask about the situation near their houses. Also, there are moments when the police don't allow us to go up or come down. Many residents end up sleeping in the streets because they can't go up or come down. They sleep on the street, at times for many days in a row. You can see under the bridges how many people sleep on the ground, but with their work uniforms hanging up so they don't ruin them. They're residents who can't return home because of confrontation, and they're afraid to lose their jobs if they go up the hill and the next day can't come down.

Maria Helena: The mega-operation began with two forces—the Military Police and the NSF, right? How long did the NSF remain inside your community?

Mother: The NSF never entered the community. It stayed in the surrounding area. Inside, it was only the BOPE. The Military Police had a station up there that it no longer has. They occupied a house and raised the black flag of the BOPE on it. The family had to flee, abandoning everything. . . . The BOPE also ran the police out. They no longer have a station there because the BOPE removed the police from it.

Maria Helena: I don't understand" The BOPE expelled the police?
Mother: That's it. The BOPE evicted the police.

Maria Helena: Is there rivalry between the BOPE and the Military Police?
Mother: Of course. They [BOPE] say that because the Military Police are corrupt and they are not, the BOPE has to take control of the place.

Maria Helena: And now, how are things? Can you leave? Can you take your children to school undisturbed?
Mother: Now it's quiet. But it's a peace that we think brings more danger, because at any time, it can begin again, and everyone can be taken by surprise on the street. . . . They [the police] are acting out of sight. I have already lost count of how many have died where I live. Bodies have been left in front of my house many times. I had to jump [over the bodies] with the children because they were right in front of the door.

Maria Helena: Young people or adults?
Mother: Young people, all young people. The last one who died was fourteen years old.

Maria Helena: Are all of them black?
Mother: No, it's not a matter of color. They kill all of them. This one who died was in a gunfight with the police. He was an adolescent involved in drug trafficking. Some are only ten years old. But do you know why I fear this peace? One day I was in my house with my youngest boy. The front door was locked, but it wasn't closed. I was inside the house binding his school books. Suddenly, a gunfight began, and bullets came into my house. I ran to the back of the house and took my five-year-old niece, who was with me. I made everyone take cover in the back. Then I heard some shouts that someone had been killed. A police officer shouted, "Get him. We have to take him out of here," and they dragged someone to the Big Skull that was left down below, because it couldn't come up here. They dragged him in front of everyone. I went carefully to close the door of the front room and to lock the front door. When I got there, I saw him, the one they called "*matador* [killer]." He was an enormous man, enormous. He was already at my front door entering the house. I went limp, completely limp. He stopped, looked at me, looked around the house and left.

Drawing by a child depicting
matador (the killer).

Maria Helena: This one called "*matador*," is he from the BOPE?
   Mother: Yes, he is. He returned the other day and went to another
alley. He seized some residents and put them against the wall and said,
"This here is a hiding place. You know where they hide. Tell us!" The residents were panic-stricken. One said, "Mister, I don't know any hiding place
here." And [*matador*] struck him and said, "Yes, you do." Another police officer arrived and asked, "How many people live here?" My neighbor answered,
"I live here, my brother, my sister, my mother, my sister-in-law." The officer
said, "But what have you got hidden here?" "Nothing," my neighbor said. "It's
our storage space. There are only clothes and household things." Another
police officer came and said. "Let's leave and go to the other side." And *matador* said, "I played with him, just like I played with that one on the ground
that I killed."

   Maria Helena: Like a cat playing with and killing a mouse. Was the
dead boy also dragged inside the Big Skull?

Mother: Yes. When it says in the news that there were four deaths, it's never four. It's five or six. When we had that operation up above in the CIEP, when the principal asked that the school be closed, inside [the school] there were two bodies. The press was told that four were dead, but two more bodies in the CIEP and another two nearby were not counted. It is only four who confronted the police with bullets; the others disappear. And if they are taken alive, they don't leave alive. Now they rip open their bellies. They [the police] have a knife that they plunge into the belly and remove everything.

José Valentin: It's the same as Operation Condor.[5] Without the intestines, the body can sink; it doesn't return to the surface and disappears. The same thing was done in Chile. They grabbed a knife with a curved point and cut the belly all the way to the top. After, they threw the body into the ocean.

Maria Helena: They open the belly and remove the intestines? Is this what you are saying? That knife, is it like he says?

Mother: I can draw it for you. But this thing about throwing [the body] into the ocean, I don't know. I can't say. I only know that they disappear, and the family never finds [the person]. Yes, they play with us, like animals. They open the belly, take everything out, and then they leave, dragging the body. The knife has a curved point [*she makes the form with a gesture*], and they leave shouting, "Get out of the way, we are taking away one more." And they drag the body through the community.

Maria Helena: Can you draw the knife you're describing?

José Valentin [*looking at the drawing*]: This knife is called the *"corvo."* This kind of knife was used by the military in Argentina and Chile to disappear bodies; when the bodies were thrown in the ocean, they would not float.

Mother: Here, inside the community, we experience many things that people outside cannot even imagine. The BOPE does this, and no one knows. No one! The authorities don't pay attention and are not even present when we die in this way. If you pay attention, you see they use this knife; they have this knife there in their belts.

Maria Helena: Who uses it?

Mother: The BOPE, because when the BOPE comes, it comes to kill. The Military Police don't. When they come we have almost no deaths. They arrest people, they seize drugs, they exchange gunfire, and they leave. The BOPE comes to kill.

Maria Helena: You told us about a day when the BOPE picked up a group of people. Were all of them killed?

Mother: No, they were shown to the press. They were drug users and were arrested. [The BOPE] knew who they were arresting. They picked out one in the middle and killed him in front of everyone. The others they showed to the press.

Maria Helena: As drug traffickers?

Mother: Yes, as traffickers, but they weren't. They hung out on the corner using drugs. They were consumers—drug users and unarmed.

Maria Helena: Did you ever speak with anyone—human rights people, authorities, lawyers, or the press—about this?

Mother: No. No one came here to ask about our life. If there is a demonstration, reporters come. There was one where we said that we had no lights and water, that the police had an operation but that they stole. They broke into a Lan House, and stole the computers. . . . A reporter arrived to interview the residents. They [police officers] made her leave, cursed her, and, after that, cursed the women who wanted to speak, calling all of them "tramps" and "bandidos' women." Why? Because you cannot speak, least of all to the press. It's like this up there. We're afraid to talk about the police and about the bandidos, because there are always people watching to see if you're X-9.[6] The BOPE kills whoever tells on them, and the bandido kills the X-9 who talks to the police.

Maria Helena: You can't go to speak with Representative Raul Jungmann of the Congressional Commission on Public Security or Secretary for Human Rights Paulo Vannuchi? As a person, you can't go to speak with a competent authority about this?

Mother: No! If I talk, I'm dead. I'm talking with you because I know you will not identify me. And my family, what would happen to them? If I talk, my family will be killed.

Maria Helena: You would suffer reprisal?

Mother: Of course. Here, it's the law of silence.

Gracilene Rodrigues dos Santos:
A Discussion with Cristina Pedroza de Faria,
February 15, 2009

Eight-year-old Matheus Rodrigues Carvalho was killed on the morning of December 4, 2008, by a single bullet in the head as he was leaving his home in Baixa do Sapateiro, one of the favelas of Maré. His mother had given him a one *real* coin to buy bread for breakfast. He fell dead on the steps of his home, with the coin in his hand. His death was witnessed by his mother, Gracilene Rodrigues dos Santos, and three of his seven brothers and sisters. According to Gracilene, who is thirty-three, married, the mother of eight children, and a lifetime resident of the Maré favela complex, the street was calm and quiet at the moment the shot was fired. In desperation, she ran screaming into the street in time to see policemen running away.

Soon other police came who wanted to remove Matheus's body before the medical examiner and a Civil Police detective arrived but were prevented from doing so by neighbors and friends of the family, as well as by Yvonne Bezerra de Mello, director of the NGO Projeto Uerê, who worked in the favela, and State Deputy Alessandro Molon, who came shortly after the event. The community photographer Rosinaldo (Naldinho) Lourenço arrived and photographed Matheus and the scene at the medical examiner's request. Lourenço put the photographs on the Internet, where they were widely downloaded. At the same time, and a few kilometers away, President Luis Inácio Lula da Silva was inaugurating the Territories of Peace project in the Alemão complex, promising less violent police intervention. Matheus symbolizes the many children—many unknown and unaccounted—who have died in this irrational "war."

Question: What happened to Matheus?

Gracilene: Around 6:00 A.M., I put on the television to wake up the children. I woke everybody up and got them ready for their morning bath. Afterward, I sent them off to school. Matheus waved goodbye and said: "Bye, Mommy, here's a kiss. I love you," as he did every day. I said, "Goodbye. God bless you."

Around 7:30, he came back, knocked on the door, and told me that he was going to have only one class, and that it would be at 11:30. I asked him to come in and change into his house clothes. He told me that he had not yet had breakfast, and I said, "Take a *real* and buy some bread." When he opened the door, I heard a bang. I thought it was a firecracker because it was Christmastime. I went to look for Matheus. I saw him lying in the doorway, shot here [*Gracilene points to the lower part of her face*] and bleeding all over. I froze for a moment, then ran into the street screaming, "They killed my son!" and saw the police. They saw me come out, screaming, and ran away. In my despair, I called my mother, saw people with cameras, saw all of my neighbors. I kept asking myself: "Why did this have to happen? What's going on?" Matheus was lying on the ground, with a *real* in his hand, one little coin. He didn't have the chance to drop the coin. He died with his little angel's hand open, coin in the hand.

   Question: How did the police act?
   Gracilene: The police arrived. Later, more policemen came. My relatives came and were talking. All of the neighbors were there, and other police wanted to take the body. I said, "Don't let them take him until the medical examiner gets here." Everything was in an uproar. There was a lot of confusion, and I don't remember anything else after that. I became ill and went to the hospital. When I got back around 9:00 A.M., his body was still here, and so were the police. Everything happened very early in the morning. Matheus's school is just a short distance below. He only had time to return, to say that there wasn't class at that time. Before coming in, he chatted with a neighbor who is in the street every day and who told me that Matheus said he was coming home to have breakfast. At the time, there were no policemen in the street, no disturbances at all. Everything was quiet, with cars coming and going. Some people who live around here told me that they saw the police. A woman neighbor told me that the police had fired a shot from down below, near a bar at the corner.

   The shot came from a distance. It wasn't from around here. A neighbor got hold of the shell. I believe that she gave it to Yvonne, and she, in turn, gave it to the medical examiner and to the detective. That's what happened. It was despair here on the street—people running, screaming, crying. Before people got to my house, I put my hand over Matheus's little heart. I kept saying, "Wake up, Matheus! Wake up and speak to Mommy!" I couldn't feel his heartbeat or his breathing, nothing. I saw that he was dead. He died with his little angelic eyes open. All of his teeth fell out. He was eight years old.

   Question: Were they able to stop them from moving Matheus's body?
   Gracilene: Yvonne, people who worked with me, [and] Alessandro Molon didn't allow the body to be moved until the medical examiners

arrived. When they arrived, my uncle picked [Matheus] up because not even the medical examiners were able to move the body. They were in a state of shock themselves. My uncle picked up the body, placed it on a stretcher, and covered it.

Question: How many people came from the medical examiner's office? What did they actually do?

Gracilene: There was a young man and a young woman. The young woman couldn't even get near Matheus. It was my uncle who had to put on gloves to move the body, and Yvonne helped. Yvonne was very supportive. She did not allow the police to remove him. If we had not had someone there to stand up to them, the police would have taken Matheus's body away. My family is afraid of anything having to do with the police. I was already afraid of them. After having gone through all of this, I am really afraid. The important person here who helped was Yvonne. People from work also helped me out a lot. It was all so hard for me. The only consolation is that I wasn't alone during this time.

Question: Do you know any of the results of the medical examiners' report? What's happening with the case now?

Gracilene: I don't know. I know that they concluded the shot hit the door, ricocheted, and struck Matheus. But they wouldn't let me near him at the time. I didn't want to let them take him. When they were ready to take him, I started screaming, but they took him anyway. The case is now being handled by the Legal Project, a human rights group, which is taking care of everything. They still have to take my deposition. I'm waiting for the public prosecutor to send me a letter or schedule a time for me to go there.

I think that they're taking too much time, because it's been three months since [Matheus] died. I'm just waiting for them to act. Last month, people from the Legal Project came to speak with me. They brought a psychologist to see how we were doing. If I could, I would resolve this as quickly as possible, because I have a lot of worries. A few days ago, a news reporter came by, but I told him that I didn't want to do any more talking. All last month, it seemed that everyone wanted to meet with me. The police chief here from the New Holland District wanted me to meet with him, but I told him I wasn't going.[7] He even sent me a letter, but I said I wasn't going because I was expecting to give my deposition at the Public Prosecutor's Office. Since then, the calls have stopped.

Question: What do you think really happened in your son's case?

Gracilene: I don't know. I think the policeman must have thought Matheus was a bandido, but that's strange, because he's not big. He's just an eight-year-old child, small, very thin. I suppose that the policeman was upset by something he saw here, or he came to get money, or he was using drugs, because early morning is not the time to start shooting people. It's the time when adults are heading for work, and the kids are heading for school. This is a very busy street. People walk up and down the street all day long. I think the policemen were very mistaken. Even if Matheus had been a bandido, they should not have come in shooting. And what if it had been my little daughter, who usually opens the door? It could have been any member of my family. This is a church, not a house. My mother lets me live here with my family. I was paying rent at another place. My mother saw that it was very difficult for me to continue paying the rent and told me that I could move in here with my children and my husband when church services weren't being held. I have a piece of land up above and was building a house on it, but I had to stop building because I just don't have the money. I sleep here on the floor with all the kids, all of us together. But it's also very difficult for me to stay here. Matheus slept here on this side [*Gracilene points to the place*]. Early in the morning when I would wake him, he would get up quickly, wash up, put on his shorts. He was an active child, a smart child. His dream was to have a videogame, and I told him I would get him one. I managed to buy that television set and to buy the videogame, but . . . [*Gracilene cries*].

Question: Who lives here?

Gracilene: My husband, my fifteen-year-old son, my twelve-year-old daughter, a seven-year-old [son], another son who is five, another daughter who is three, the baby daughter who is two, and me. I have eight children. Only seven are left now. I have a daughter who was living with us when Matheus died, but she was too upset and went to live in another community. We have nine people living here. I work as a cleaning woman at the Maré Cultural Center. The people there have helped me. They welcomed me when I was unemployed and helped the father of my children. He works as a doorman, in construction, as a handyman but is unemployed. I'm the family member who is working.

Question: Are your children in school?

Gracilene: Only one is not in school because she stopped after eighth grade. Everybody else is in school. The baby is in day care.

Question: What is your daily life like here?

Gracilene: It's quiet around here. When there's a shooting, it's generally down there, away from us. It's difficult to have a shooting here, because it's a very busy street. Many children live here. However, a young man we know died inside a kiosk where he worked selling food. The police came in shooting. The young man waved a dishcloth over his head to let the policeman know that he was a worker, but the cop didn't want to know about it. He arrived shooting and killed him. He was even wearing his work uniform. Matheus and that young man have been the only two victims here.

Question: Would you say that it's complicated to live alongside the police around here?

Gracilene: Yes, it is. They arrive firing guns without bothering to see who [they're shooting at]. For this whole week, they've been coming straight here to my house. I even had to ask my husband to take me to work because I'm still afraid to walk on the street. Neighbors tell me it's not safe for me to live here because the policemen are bad, treacherous. Now that the police know I'll be going to the public prosecutor to give my deposition, I'm frightened. When they're around here, I won't leave the house, and I won't let the children go out, either. Every day during the morning, they are here.

Question: Did the policemen come around before what happened to Matheus?

Gracilene: No. They only came that day when they killed my son. Now they come every day. A woman neighbor tells me that the same policeman who killed my son is among those who come around. She said that it was a lieutenant who killed Matheus. Those police over there must know because of the medical examiners' report on the bullet, the gun, and the shot.

Question: What do you think needs to be done?

Gracilene: The police cannot enter the way that they do now, shooting in the favela. They should come in quietly and try to find out what's going on. Of course, if gunfire is exchanged, the police have the right to defend themselves. But they can't come in firing their guns without knowing who's in the street. It might be a worker, a woman, a young person, or a child. They can't come in shooting like they do now in a street full of people, especially in the morning, when people are leaving for work and children are leaving for school. Also, they go into people's homes just for nothing. I have a neighbor whose home is constantly searched to see if there are bandidos.

Just think about it: You're sleeping with your husband, your children, and
[the police] enter the house. My children are frightened. The six-year-old
keeps repeating it was the police who killed his brother. His seven-year-old
brother saw Matheus lying on the ground, and he fainted right then and
there. One of his brothers remembers dreaming about Matheus. I know
because he says his name. When I draw near, he wakes up and starts to cry.
He has nightmares like that.

Question: What would you like to see happen in the future? How
should Matheus's case be handled?

Gracilene: I don't want to see the police coming into the favela just for
any reason, without any information. They should only come in when they
have a very strong reason to do so. They should come with an order, some
written document—or, at least, alert the residents that they're coming. After
what happened to Matheus, I leave for work in the mornings afraid to send
the children to school, thinking that the same thing could happen to one of
them. Nowadays, nobody around here buys bread in the early morning. They
go out only after 11:00 A.M. I would like to see the policeman who shot my
son pay for what he did. He might be expelled, unable to exercise his profession anymore. How can he say that he did not see it was a child? My son
had no shirt on. He was only wearing a pair of shorts and was barefoot. I
found out that the policemen said my son was carrying a backpack and a
small radio. How is that possible? Where's the proof? My son came home
from school. The only thing he did was change clothes. He was going out
just to buy bread.

Question: Do you have any hope that the police will discover who was
responsible for his death?

Gracilene: Yes, I do. Man's justice can fail, but God's justice doesn't.
Jesus will make things uncomfortable for that man and will make him turn
himself in. He will have no peace of mind for what he did.[8]

Question: What would you tell the world, people outside Brazil, about
what happened to your son? What would you like them to know?

Gracilene: People who live in a favela can never say, "This will not
happen to me." I was seeing news reports on television about incidents of
death, and I was thinking that this never was going to happen here, to my
own family. People die everywhere, but it's more dangerous here. I feel much
more vulnerable. I lack the desire and the will to remain here. Do you want
to know what gives me the strength to live and to stay here? My son,

"They killed my son." *Left:* Two photographs taken at the scene of Matheus's death. *Upper right:* Protester with a "Don't Kill Our Children" sign. *Lower right:* Gracilene, a friend, and Matheus. *(Photographs by Rosinaldo Lourenço.)*

Matheus. He lives in my heart. Also, his brothers and sisters. I have days when I wake up and fight the impulse to cry, to remember, because if I cry, my children will also feel bad. That is what is giving me the strength to carry on, because sometimes I just want to vanish, to forget everything. I didn't have any stimulus to live, no energy for anything. There are days when I cannot even eat the tiniest piece of bread. To have strength to go on, I remember that my small children need me.

It's still very difficult for me. I never thought it was possible to lose a child in this way, from a bullet. You might think about losing a child because of illness, but they killed my son as if he were a *bandido.* It could be me, but not my son. He was an innocent child. He wanted to work, to study. He used to say that when he grew up, he was going to buy me a home. He wanted to be a soldier because he was influenced by all of those army ads on television, and he would say that he wanted to be just like that. If I have to travel outside Brazil to speak, I will do it, because a police officer killed a child, not a bandido. He had no right to come in and shoot as he did. If it's possible, I'm going to speak everywhere. Nobody is going to shut me up. I'm going to tell what happened. I'm going to tell the truth, whether they like it or not. I'll go anyplace in the world. I'm going to show how this country is: what the police are doing and how they treat the residents of the favelas.

The police don't respect us. They act as if we are drug dealers. The police and bandidos are becoming mixed together. The police are the same as the bandidos. In fact, the bandidos respect the residents more. You walk past one, and he says, "Good evening, auntie." The bandidos never disrespected me. Not so with the police. They arrive at a house and storm in. They don't ask for permission to enter, and they won't give you even a "good morning." They don't respect anybody's rights. They don't bring a legal warrant.

Chapter 4

Voices of Hope and Renewal

Jaqueline Felix: A Discussion with
Cristina Pedroza de Faria, August 2008

Jaqueline Felix is a young photographer and a graduate of the School of Popular Photographers, a project of Imagens do Povo of the NGO Observatório de Favelas in Rio de Janeiro. In this interview, she tells the story of her life growing up happily in the New Holland favela in the Maré complex and of her work in theater performance and as a photographer, which took her out of the favela to other areas of Brazil. She also tells the dramatic story of trying to get to a maternity hospital to give birth to her son during early-morning hours when the Big Skulls were patrolling the streets of New Holland, where she lives with her husband. The interview describes the growth of violence in New Holland during Jaqueline's lifetime.

Jaqueline: My grandmother and my grandfather were from northeastern Brazil. They met at a textile factory in Rio Tinto [in Paraíba State], where they both worked. They were married there and came here to Rio de Janeiro. When they arrived, they did not come to Maré. In fact, Maré did not exist. All of the houses were built on stilts because this was all water. But my grandfather gambled too much. He was addicted to gambling, to cards, that kind of stuff. My grandmother only discovered these faults after they were married. He began to lose a lot of money—the money my grandmother had brought with her from the Northeast.

My grandfather bought a wooden shack on top of stilts in the Rubens Vaz favela. My grandmother was pregnant with her first daughter, but she lost her. Then my grandmother became pregnant again. She gave birth at home, with only a midwife to help out. They did not have time to get to the hospital. A year later, my grandmother became pregnant with my mother and my aunt, who are twins. They still lived in Rubens Vaz, and my grandfather was able to buy a larger house in the favela next to that one. Today it is called Parque Maré. They still live there. My grandmother worked at home, and my grandfather worked at a slaughterhouse. My grandfather was a "boner"—he removed bones from the cattle.

When my mother was sixteen, she became pregnant with me. My father also lived here in Maré, and he was about to turn seventeen when I was born. My father worked at a pharmacy, and he had given her a contraceptive drug, but she didn't trust it and did not take it, and got pregnant. When I was born, they went to live in a house behind my grandmother's house, but they ended up separating. My mother had a very difficult delivery. She was in the intensive care unit for a month with an infection and almost died.

I had a happy childhood. We had the freedom to play in the streets, to run to the middle of the street, walk on the other side. I never saw anyone smoking [marijuana] or sniffing cocaine. Also, it was very rare that we saw someone with guns or weapons. I remember that, when I was about eight years old, there was a murder in front of my grandmother's house. But it was the murder of one of these guys who are marked to die because I believe he was doing a lot of wrong things, stealing from other people. The residents were warned that all the children should be locked in the house, that everyone should go inside. No one was to witness the crime that was going to happen. This affected me. Today, people die right in front of us. Today, there is no concern for the children, for anything.

I played with dolls until I was fourteen years old. We did not have this idea that one has to start dating so early. My time was taken up with play. My whole childhood was like that. Everybody was in the street. We went to the street to celebrate our dolls' birthdays. My mother baked a cake and my aunt decorated it for the party for the dolls. We also had a party when we baptized our dolls. When it was my birthday, we did the same thing. I even teased my mom that my dream was to send an invitation to all my friends, only that there was no need to do that, because everyone already knew my birthdate. When my birthday came, all of my little friends were already there at my door, because they knew there would be a party. There was no need to send an invitation.

We did not have money to go to places. We did go to the botanical gardens,

the zoo, that kind of thing, but these were school outings. My friends were
all neighbors. When I was four years old, my mother met my stepfather,
Edson. They have been married for twenty years. When I was older, I joined
CEASM [Center for Studies and Solidarity Actions of Maré]. It was one of
the few organizations that mobilized the community. CEASM was very good
because it managed to reach everyone in the Maré complex. It was great
because they had a soiree on Saturdays. At one of the Saturday parties, I
met Geo, who belonged to the CTO [Center for the Theater of the
Oppressed]. He said that CEASM was developing a working arrangement
with his CTO and that they were going to form a theater group. I went to
the first meeting, but no one else came. More than ten people came to the
second meeting. It was a very good experience, because it was from my work
with the CTO that I began to see myself differently, to see my family differently, and to see the place where I lived differently.

The good thing about the CTO was that we worked with people's actual
daily lives. People told their stories, stories that they had lived. Then we
worked on themes. Sometimes they were about drugs or domestic violence. I
began to broaden my consciousness. I came out of a very small community
to get to know the city of Rio de Janeiro. From that point on, I became
aware that I belonged to the city, that I was part of the city, and I began to
see how much prejudice existed. Before, I did not notice the prejudice
because I only had contact with residents of the favela. I never felt that I
was inferior to anyone. And I always felt like a normal person. I had my toys.
I had my Estrela dolls. Every month, when there was marketing for a new
Estrela doll, I got one.[1] I had a nice house and potable water from the fau-
cets. In the bathroom, water came out of a small shower, which I also used
to wash my dolls.

When I began to meet people who did not live in the favela, I could feel
the prejudice. When I told them where I lived, they said, "Oh, my God! It's
dangerous there, right? Can you go out on the street?" They still think that
we live in wooden shacks built on stilts. This is when I began to defend my
ideas, because I already had ideas, and I began to tell them that this is a
place like any other place. I had a health clinic. I had a supermarket nearby.
I had water and electricity; I did not live with lanterns, as they thought. My
ideal is to defend the place where I live and to make people see that, today,
the favela is a part of the city. Since I became a mother, I have become even
more clear about this.

I began to go regularly to the CTO and to take parts in plays all over
the city—at hospitals, in prisons, at universities and schools, even in
other states. I had that wish to become independent. I wanted to "own my

own nose," as we say. I traveled a lot. I began to grow. I wanted to work. I worked in a clothing shop here, and later went to work with some friends of my mother and stepfather in the PT [Workers' Party]. I went with them to party meetings. I saw my mother and stepfather struggling for a better world, with less social inequality. In the meantime, my mother was accepted at a university. This was ten years after she had finished primary school. My mother had been a slave of work. She worked from Sunday to Saturday, without a single day off. She finished the university preparation course that CEASM offered, and then she left work to study. She was accepted at the Catholic Pontifical University in Rio with a 100 percent scholarship. But it was too far away for her. She had to wake up much too early, and after she finished the first semester at the Catholic Pontifical University, she transferred to the Federal University of Rio de Janeiro. At that time, my stepfather told me about the Observatório de Favelas, which was still a project of CEASM in Maré. The Observatório de Fave-las grew and later became an NGO. I went to the Observatório de Favelas and began to work with photography. I studied photography in the morn-ing and worked in the afternoon at the NGO. While I was finishing my final project of photographic documentation, I began to go out with Silvio, who is now my husband.

When I met Silvio, I was working at a clothing store next door to his house. He always went by, and I would say, "Hi, is everything OK?" One day, I stopped on Main Street. It began to rain. He was there on the street, getting ready to go fishing. I began to talk to him a little more. One day, I asked him out on a date, and after that, we were always together. I told him that I did not want to just fool around. I wanted something serious thing or nothing. "Do you want to be my boyfriend?" I asked. If you do, you must go to my house and talk to my mother. In my family, one had to ask permission to date and had to be inside the house, never alone. I was then nineteen, but I still had to have permission. He'went. I told my sisters that I had met someone, and they gave me a lot of support.

Now, let's go back to the subject of the photography project. Since Silvio fished a lot, he told me about a small colony of fishermen in the Parque União favela. I started to photograph the fishermen, and I liked it a lot. I left school and went directly to the colony to work on my project. Even after I graduated from the school, I continued to go there to photograph. We also photographed the Pan American Games [in 2007], and I did a lot of work for the Brazilian Society of Pediatrics and for magazines in São Paulo and Rio de Janeiro. I began to photograph not only the favelas, but also other places—paid professional jobs. This was very important, because I could see that I was able to do what I liked, to continue to document what I wanted, and could earn money doing it. In May 2007, I traveled with the project "Revealing the Different Brazils" and got to know southeastern and southern Brazil.

People from all over the country were selected to tell a piece of their story or someone else's story. They would come to Rio de Janeiro and study audiovisual production, then go back to their cities to make documentaries of the story that they had written to participate in the project. I took photographs of exhibitions of these films in towns with up to 20,000 residents. Enormous movie screens would be put up and people would come—people who had never seen a movie. The towns were small, with only one church in the main square that was the meeting point for everyone in town. People could themselves be participants; they could tell their own stories. This also had a lot to do with the project Images of the People, where we work to show the other, to give a voice to the other. We don't just go there to take photographs. We go there to listen.

I started to see myself reflected in these people because their stories were the stories of my grandparents who came from the northeast to try a better life here, people who also lived in wooden stilt shacks, people who every day also lacked food. I began to see my own family in these stories, and I started to be more sensitive to the place where I live. That is when I started to realize how good it is to give a voice to someone, how good it is to stop and listen. I arrived to take a photo of someone, and the rest of the time I stopped, just listening, chatting with these people who wanted to tell me their stories, who opened the doors of their homes for me to come in.

Question: This was in the interior of Brazil?

Jaqueline: Yes, in the interior in the south and southeast. I stayed one month there. But in the middle of the trip, I saw that my period didn't come. I was in Florianópolis and thought, "My God! It can't be." So I called Silvio. At the time we were only dating. We did not even live together. I told him, "Look, there is someone who is arriving, because I think that I am pregnant!" I did a pharmacy test and found out that I was, indeed, pregnant. I did an ultrasound because I wanted to know right away and found that the little heart was already beating. My life changed completely from one hour to the next. I had to stop the work I was doing. I returned to the work at the school. And I got financial support from UNESCO [the United Nations Educational, Scientific, and Cultural Organization]. I worked only Mondays,

Wednesdays, and Fridays in the morning, so I could fix the house where I still live today and I could buy the things I needed for my son.

Question: Did you and Silvio begin to live together?

Jaqueline: Yes, we went to live together. My vagrant life ended, that life of parties, of trips. Telling my family was difficult. The only one who knew about this was Silvio. When I arrived, I wore the largest blouse I owned so no one would notice. Then my grandmother said, "You came back chubby. You came back fuller." The next day, when I went to tell them that I had had an ultrasound, she said, "I already knew. When you went off on your trip, I already knew." But my mother did not expect this. My mother wanted me to go to the university. My mother wanted me to work more with photography and devote myself more to that. She did not want me to become a housewife at twenty-two. She felt a little hurt. My family was a little hurt. But then João Paulo was born, and it was all joy.

I stopped working when he was born and spent four months only taking care of the home and of him. Then I began to work again through Images of the People. It was difficult, because I am always thinking about the son that I've left at home. My breasts become very full and hurt and start leaking. Thank God, my mother is helping me; after the baby was born, she took care of him. I never needed to put him in a day-care center. I did not need to leave him with someone I did not know well. I don't think about having other children. I think only of this one son. I want to give him a very good education. I am very concerned, my husband and I are, about paying for health insurance for him, because I was worried about going to a public hospital. One arrives at the hospital and maybe will not even be seen, and there will be no beds available. So today we live around the needs of this son, and I make sure to pay for a health insurance plan.

Question: Did you have any assistance during your pregnancy and birth?

Jaqueline: My prenatal care was here in a local health clinic in Maré. But so many girls are pregnant, and one month went by and there was no doctor, then another week and there was no nurse. I thought, "Why don't they hire more doctors?" There is only one doctor. He is a gynecologist and obstetrician. He cares for those who are pregnant and for those who are not pregnant.

Question: So how many clinics are there here?

Jaqueline: There are clinics in Parque União, Rubens Vaz, New Holland, Parque Maré, Baixa do Sapateiro, and Vila do Joáo. Each of these communities has a health clinic, but there are too many patients. My pregnancy was very easy. I did not feel sick. It was a very pleasurable pregnancy. He was not a planned child, but he was a much loved child. I had the support of my family. I had the support of my husband. He followed everything closely and was very involved.

Then I had my baby. I began to feel bad around midnight on a Saturday, and I was almost forty-two weeks pregnant. The baby was way overdue. I began to feel ill, and then I felt a small pain. I said, "I will wait until it gets stronger so I don't go to the doctor for nothing, as I have done so many other times." At 1:00 A.M., the contractions came strong, unbearable, and I woke Silvio up. I said, "Silvio, I can't stand it anymore. I think the baby is going to be born." The problem was that night there were three Big Skulls here in New Holland and much shooting, people running, screaming. I said, "Oh, my God! How am I going to get out of the house to go to the doctor?" We were all very afraid of the Big Skull. It is a strong psychological terror we all feel.

Silvio called my mother, but she could not come from my grandmother's house, because there was even more shooting where she lived, and a Big Skull was there too. Then I said, "Mom, don't come." I did not want my mother to leave the house. I was with Silvio, and he could take me. I had to wait until 3:30 A.M. and was feeling so much pain. I couldn't leave the house because of the Big Skull. But the pains were stronger and stronger. They were becoming unbearable. Then I said, "Silvio, we're in God's hands. Let whatever He wishes happen. Let's go, because I cannot stand it anymore." So we left the house. There was no one in the street. It was already later than 3:30 in the morning when we managed to walk almost to Avenida Brasil. Then in the middle of Teixeira Street came the Big Skull. I said "I can't stand walking any longer." But we had to walk all the way to Avenida Brasil. There was no transportation. I said to Silvio "Let's go to the middle of the street because in the Big Skull they will see there is a pregnant woman walking just like a duck at 3:30 in the morning. They will see that I am going to the maternity ward. They won't have the courage to shoot us." And so, with the *boca de fumo* behind me, and Big Skull in front of me, I said, "My God! They saw the boys [drug dealers] here! There is going to be a big shootout, and we're right in the middle!" I was trying to walk fast with that big belly. We walked in this manner, right in the middle of the street between them, and with so much fear also. Then we walked very slowly past the drug dealers. Then we managed to get past the Big Skull. There were no taxis. No taxis at three in the morning! I had to walk across the overpass above the highway, and still no taxi. I walked to a gas station. When we arrived, there was a taxi. And when we were in front of a restaurant, the tire of the taxi had a blow out. But the taxi driver was able to stop another taxi in the middle of Avenida Brasil. This one took me to the maternity hospital in Praça XV which is near the boats that go to Niteroi. There I was immediately interned because I was not dilating and my son was really going over his time. It was an induced labor.

They try [to deliver by] natural childbirth until the last moment. They only do a caesarian section when they realize that there is no way the baby can come out by himself, so you just keep suffering. When I arrived at the hospital, I had to be given four bags of water in the vein so I would begin to dilate. At 8:00 A.M., I found out that my mother could come and be with me in the prenatal room. I asked a nurse to lend me her cellular phone and asked my mother to come. My mother arrived. I had been brought to the hospital at 4:00 A.M.; by now, it was 9:00 A.M., and my son was not yet born. Silvio couldn't stay with me, because the prenatal hospital doesn't allow men. It was a very painful birth process. I thought I wouldn't survive. There were times when I could not breathe. The doctor told me, "Look, if you do not begin to really help your son, he is not going to be born. He is suffering a lot, and so are you." . . . After that, when I felt a contraction, I began to push my belly down. My mother helped, holding my back so I could sit. An hour later, my water broke, and I applied even greater force, with my mother there, next to me the whole time. My mother was a fundamental part of the birth of my child. If my mother had not been at my side, I do not know if I would have managed, because it was so very difficult.

But to my daily routine today. I take my baby to my grandmother's house every day. I began to return to my more active life at work. I went to the Observatório. We had an exposition at a twenty-four-hour public health clinic here in Maré. That day was the first time that I ran from the Big Skull with my son in my arms. I got caught in the middle of a shootout, and I had my baby. I managed to get inside the minibus of a friend of mine who was also showing his photographs—his name was Michel—and we managed to arrive at the show. On the way back home, it was the same: There was a super-tense atmosphere in the favela. I couldn't go to the supermarket to buy anything for dinner, because at any moment the war could explode. At any moment, the shooting can begin, and we don't know where to run.

Today, I am afraid to raise my son where I live because he will not be able to have a childhood with freedom like the one I had. My son will not be able to fly a kite, play soccer in the middle of the street, with his mother tranquil and at peace, the way my mother and my grandmother felt. They could be at home, taking care of the house and preparing dinner, and not worry about the children playing in the street because they knew I was going to be all right and nothing would happen to me. On the other side of my grandmother's house is a playground, but not a single lamp works there, because once, during a brutal war between drug gangs, the police shot out all the lamps in the street and playground so the bandidos could not see where they were. It is terribly dark at night because nobody fixed the lights. I usually go to the playground around 4:30 or 5:00 P.M. to catch some sun, but twice I had to run because there was a shootout between bandido gangs.

I live with all of this violence, sometimes right inside our house. If the police tell us to open the door and want to come in and turn the house inside out, they believe they have the right to do this, without any warrant. If a bandido is running away from the police and wants to come into my house, I must open the door for him, as well. We do not have a say in this.

Question: With this happening, do you believe there is a solution?

Jaqueline: We cannot fight violence with more violence. I am trying to find other ways, other paths to improve my own life and that of my people. I am trying to combat violence by showing people that here, inside the favela, not everything is ugly; that is not all we have. There is so much more, don't you think? This "much more" is what we show in our photos. This "much more" is what is said in our defense when we speak on television, to a newspaper. I believe that this is the type of thing that can contribute to a real change. And when my son gets to be my age, if he has a bit of my desire for change and can continue to follow the path that I started now, maybe we can make things a little better. Today I live and work around this hope.

Francisco Valdean: A Discussion with Cristina Pedroza de Faria, September 2008

Francisco Valdean migrated to the Maré complex from Ceará, a state in northeastern Brazil, when he was fifteen. In this interview, he describes the difficult conditions sharecroppers face in trying to make a living in the northeast and the lure of distant cities such as Rio de Janeiro. Francisco's story is one of self-discovery and personal growth amid difficult conditions where the threat of violence hangs over daily life. His narrative reminds us that almost everyone who lives in the favelas of Rio de Janeiro knows one or more persons who have died a violent death or disappeared.

Francisco: I am twenty-seven years old and live in Baixa do Sapateiro, one of the sixteen communities of the Maré complex. I came from northeastern Brazil to Rio, and when I arrived in Maré, I lived in the community known as Morro do Timbau. Afterward, I came to Baixa do Sapateiro where I still live. I work for Images of the People, a databank of images of the NGO Observatório das Favelas. I also study social sciences at the State University of Rio de Janeiro (UERJ). Because I work and study, my days are very full.

I was born in a place called Cachoeira Grande, a small town in the interior of Ceará State, near the city of Poranga and bordering Piauí State. Today, the town has about 1,500 residents. The most important economic activity is agriculture. The place survives on the retirement income of the older people who inject money into the town's economy. My parents are from there. My father was born in the Piauí State, and my mother is from Ceará, but since the two places are so close, they become confused, and you don't know what is Piauí and what is Ceará.

I am a son of my father's second family. He was widowed and then married my mother. With his first wife, he had nine children, and with my mother, he has two—my brother, Isaac, and me. My father is seventy-four, and my mother is a little over forty. When my mother married my father, he already had a son who was the same age as she was, so I did not have too much contact with my half-brothers. I spent my childhood in Cachoeira Grande, and that is how I began to understand why young people left there. They go to the big cities because there is little work opportunity there. There people say something like this: "Look, when I'm eighteen, I'll get all of my documents and leave." And this is what happens. Today, everyone who is my age has left. If you return, there is almost no one of your own generation. The older generation has somehow managed to stay, but most leave. If they don't manage to get anything in the big cities, then they return.

My father was a small farmer, the activity of most people there. People work with a system of land rental: You rent the land from the farm owner, and he gets part of what you grow. The farmer works year-round, and at the end, part of what is produced goes to the landowner. It's a big problem when you don't have ownership of the land. Cachoeira Grande grew around a church called Maria das Cidades Nordestinas, and the lots where people built their houses are owned by the [Catholic] church. The church allows the people to live on the land and farm. But a time comes when people can no longer grow because they have reached the land of the big landowner, and the only possibility is to buy land from the big landowner, which is too expensive. My father continued to work under this type of rental so his family could survive.

When I was small, I noticed that, when we had little food to eat, we could buy a kilo of black beans for a certain price. When it was harvest time, the people who were buying from the farmers organized to lower the price. But the ones who work in the rental system had problems because they had to give a part [of what they grew] to the farm owner, and what was left wasn't worth selling, because they ended up having to sell cheap. People even preferred to keep the black beans in stock so they could sell them in times of scarcity. The young person who lived there saw all that, and believed that he had no choice except to leave. They said, "I am not going to stay in this place and go through life the way my father has to live." The best option was to leave the town and go to Rio de Janeiro, to Brasília, or to São Paulo.

When I was eight years old, my mother separated from my father. She went to Rio de Janeiro. In Cachoeira, my mother worked on the land. In the winter, there is great uncertainty. There are years when it rains, and other years when it does not rain at all. Sometimes you have two years without any rain. They are extremely difficult years. There are years when things get a little better because the government intervenes. It sets up work projects, and my mother worked on one of them. That is when she managed to buy a little house, because she worked with my father. The money that he earned was for our food, and what my mother earned was used to buy the house. She worked many years to buy the house. These projects are set up during times of emergency so people will not die of hunger. For example, once or twice I witnessed the construction of a dam and another time, the building of a bridge.

My mother went to live in Rio de Janeiro when I was eight years old. My mother had a problem in the uterus and needed surgery. She went to Rio de Janeiro for treatment. But she separated from my father and ended up staying in Maré because some of her family lived here. I thought "When I am eighteen, I will also leave." And it was not just me. Everyone thought the same way. I remember that when someone came back—I mean, a young person—we stopped everything just to listen to the stories of how Rio de Janeiro was. I remember that they said that Rio was a city full of glamor, a very chic city. It was much better to go there than to go to Brasília or to São Paulo. But there were difficult situations that we heard of. For example, one of the young men who was from Cachoeira went to live in Brasília and died there. He was killed. This was a very negative fact for us, the idea that someone could die in this manner. This showed that it was dangerous. There was another fact. A young man from Cachoeira disappeared, and it seems that no one has ever found out what happened to him. He simply disappeared. These facts weighed in our thinking.

When I was fifteen, my mother returned. She returned to get my brother and me. She stayed only one day and wanted to take us with her. It was an extremely difficult decision because it was my father who had taken care of us all that time. And then my mother arrived out of nowhere and wants to take us away. So I said to my brother, "We like our mother, and we also like our father. How can we just leave like that?" In the heat of the emotions, we decided to leave with our mother.

My father was devastated. This was wrong. My brother and I then decided that only one of us should go, and the other should stay with our father so he would not be alone. We decided that between us. Not wanting to say anything in front of my mother, we went to a river that was near my grandmother's house, and there, at the river, we decided what to do. I would go, and my brother would stay.

I came to Rio de Janeiro with my mother. I went directly to Maré. My mother did not have a house. She was living with a partner here, and already had a child with this guy. My mother lived in a small room. There was a bed, a refrigerator, a small bathroom, very small. When we arrived we went to live in this room. It was so small you couldn't move in it. One of the things that I missed most from Ceará is that we were very free. I remember that I spent all my time running around the street, going through the living room, leaving through the kitchen. There was so much room. Here, one of the strangest things for me was to live in just one room with only one door. I thought, "My God! How am I going to get used to living here?" There was only the door to enter, and the room was very small. But soon after we arrived, she got a larger house, with a bedroom, living room, and kitchen.

We took one week to arrive here. I think that three or four days after my arrival, I began to work. The work was very hard. I worked in a bakery even on Sunday. I only had a day off in the middle of the week. But in the middle of the week, all you can do is sleep. There is nothing else to do.

Question: And how was your life after that? Did you begin to study right away?

Francisco: I was fifteen years old and had only finished third grade in Ceará. It was already a long time since I had left school. I arrived here and went to work right away to help my mother. That made it difficult to study. I remember that I worked late into the night, so I only had the morning to study. At seventeen, I was in the following situation: "Everyone in the third grade is a child, and I'm not going to school with children." But not going to school was bothering me. Then I learned from a friend that there was a special distance-learning *telecurso* to complete your education, right here on the hill. I went there with my friend and talked to the teacher, Nalva. But the course was given in the afternoon, and at that time I had to work in the bakery. I tried to talk with the bakery owner about changing my work hours to the morning so I could study in the afternoon. But it was no good. The only option he gave me is if I wanted to study I had to quit my job. So I kept working a few more months. Then I regretted my decision not to study. I decided to study even if I had to quit my job. I talked to Nalva, but I had already missed three months of classes, and the whole period was nine months. "Look," she said, "I'm not sure that you will be able to follow the classes." But I managed to catch on to everything without much problem and to finish primary school.

I went to work in New Holland in a thrift shop that belonged to Nalva. Then I left work because we had a drug war here, and in 1997 it started to get worse. A war between drug gangs made it very difficult for us to walk around. It was extremely tense, and there was no way we could come and go freely, so I stopped working. I could not study, either, and for a time I was forced to do nothing. Then I managed to find work outside of here. I began to know other areas of Rio de Janeiro. I was able to work and to circulate in Rio de Janeiro and even got to know the city well. I understood that I needed to study more, but I had no way to do this. I worked at a newsstand. I worked as an office boy. I worked as a street vendor. My last job was at a company that made air conditioners.

Then one day, I was walking on Acre Street. A girl was advertising a course in computers, putting them together, and doing maintenance. It was cheap because it was being offered by a trade union, only 15 *reais*. "I'm going to do this," I thought. I finished the computer hardware course and the maintenance course. The second phase of the course taught how to make software. It cost another 15 *reais*. I did that, as well. The course was in downtown Rio. I liked learning about computers, especially when I got into this logical part of programs and software.

Question: Did you already have some knowledge of computers?

Francisco: No, but when I was taking the second phase of the course, I became fascinated and thought, "I'm going to take a course so I can get deeply into this." Then I took a really bad course. I bought a package of eighteen programs, and it cost me more than 2,000 *reais*. I had to pay in installments of 90 *reais* per month. I learned only basic stuff, such as Windows, Word, Excel, the Internet, and so on. In the middle of the course, I began to have difficulties because I had finished only the eighth grade and did not

really know how to write well and therefore could not type well. So I
thought, "I need to finish this course and get back to studying." I finished
the computer course and decided to complete high school.

In the high school course, I had many difficulties. I was very shy. Even
though I could express myself in the classroom, I didn't participate in many
things. I had to make many personal decisions and thought, "From now on,
I'm going to stop fooling around. I'm going to sit right in front and participate in everything that I can." I became a class representative and started to
participate. During the first year, I had contact with third-year students who
had been trying to create a student association. Since I was a representative
of my class, I got into a closer working relationship with them. We made a
set of rules for the association, and we mobilized people.

Question: Why did you want to create the student association?

Francisco: It was important because, to this day, the school does not
have student representation. I saw that there was not enough mobilization.
Only four or five students were working to get things done. And other things
interested us—food, for example. We studied at night, came from work, and
were very hungry. We wanted to have a kitchen and dining area in the
school for people who worked.

Question: So you managed to finish your studies?

Francisco: Yes, I did finish my studies, and then I was making plans to
get into the university. My family supported my decision, even though they
didn't really know what a university was. I did CEASM's preparatory university examination course. I decided to take social sciences because it is what
I most identify myself with, and because it is a political course. This has a
lot to do with the favela communities and with the city of Rio de Janeiro. In
Maré, there are university students, and the idea is that you ought not to
leave the community when you enter the university. There has to be some
giving back.

I decided to do social sciences because I had been concerned about popular causes ever since my time in Ceará. There, the problems are labor
questions. In the elections there, the parties and the candidates make a lot
of promises, but they don't do anything they promise. I passed the entrance
exam for the Catholic Pontifical University and for the State University of
Rio de Janeiro. I received a full scholarship for the Catholic Pontifical University. This was another decision I had to make. I didn't know where I
wanted to go. Catholic Pontifical is very good, but it is not a public university. Some friends who were going to Catholic Pontifical said, "You must be

crazy not choosing Catholic Pontifical and going to State University." But
that was my decision, and I am doing the course in social sciences at State
University.

Question: What does the community where you live signify for you?

Francisco: The change was abrupt when I came here [from
Cachoeira]. Maré has more than 100,000 people. When I left Cachoeira, it
had 600 people. I remember that I managed to adapt, despite the violence.
There was something that happened right after I arrived when I began to
work in the bakery that struck me hard. I saw a group of young armed men
with guns. I had never seen this. One day, I ran into a guy who asked for a
cigarette. I had to give it to him because he was a bandido. He was violent. I
didn't even look directly at him. Another memory. Almost a year after I
arrived here, I saw a young guy dead in a ditch. It was a very strong scene. I
thought, "I want to get out of here." Where I was born, people also died, but
when there was a death, it was a person over sixty. You died because you
were old. Young people didn't die there. Seeing a young person dead shocked
me. But at the same time that this was shocking, I was trying to understand
the violence that came from drug trafficking.

Today, my understanding is better. The fact that a young person dies is a
most serious problem. I have no doubt that people here are worried about
the fact that a young person dies. However, how they try to resolve this problem does more harm because it produces more death. Any place where a
young man may die—and not just a young man, but anyone in a situation of
death forced on a person, a death that is not natural—is strange. I never saw
this when I was a child. I remember when I arrived here, I knew some people who died. Some died because they did drug trafficking. This is a problem, but it's not the problem of the young man. He didn't die because he was
a shameless son of a bitch. He didn't die for this reason. He died because
there is a bigger game going on behind this that led to his death. In my opinion, what is believed will resolve this has not generated practical results
because young people continue to die.

Question: What are the solutions?

Francisco: They are coming from state institutions. These institutions
think it is easier to eliminate that young man. They reason, "He is the problem. He has to be eliminated," and they get busy eliminating. The bigger
things that are behind this are not eliminated. I came from the northeast. I
managed to study, pass the university entrance exam, but if you look around,
you can see this doesn't happen often. What you need to do is solve the

problem of the young guy who keeps migrating here. I'm not saying that you should close the city. There are problems to solve—rooves over our heads, agrarian reform, getting an education, having access. Here in Maré, in the communities, [the young man] gets segregated; he doesn't circulate in the city. If you leave Cachoeira and arrive here in Maré, the problem is a big one. In Cachoeira, it's less serious because the young guy doesn't die young, but the life there makes him come here. He arrives here and dies. I don't think that you should have to pass through a big system like this one, where some get through while others don't and therefore die young. It's not right.

Chapter 5

Voices of Community Leaders

Carlinhos Costa of Rocinha: A Discussion with Maria Helena Moreira Alves, Philip Evanson, and José Valentin Palacios, July 28, 2008

Carlinhos Costa is a community leader who was born and raised in Rocinha, in the Zona Sul. It is the largest favela in Rio de Janeiro and one of the largest in Latin America. He describes how Rocinha has changed and provides perspective on the rise of gangsterism in Rio de Janeiro during his lifetime.

Question: Tell us about your life in Rocinha.
Carlinhos: I was born in Rocinha. I was born of one mother and raised by another. At the time I was born, my biological mother had tuberculosis. She distributed her children to friends and to neighbors to raise. In my case, she gave me to a young woman who [was] my godmother. She became my adopted mother. My mother was cured and later returned to Rocinha. But given that certain values were even stronger at that time than now, she didn't have the courage to take back her children. She couldn't say, "Look, I'm well again. Give me my children." So I continued living with my adopted mother; my sister continued living with her godmother, who was one of my mother's first employers in Ipanema, and that was our life. Every Sunday, we had the ritual of visiting my mother.

My mother returned to Rocinha and fell crazily in love with different guys and had a child with each one—four children in all. My oldest sister died, and I have two younger sisters. But my father never took any interest in me, and I don't feel any affection for him. My adoptive mother was very methodical. I had to go to mass every Sunday and afterward visit my biological mother. We had this thing of respect for older people. We had to ask for blessings from the older generation. One time, I was with my adoptive mother on Rua dos Boiadeiros and an older man came, surrounded by women, and she said to me, "That one is your father." I had never seen him before. I was nine years old, and she said, "Go over there and ask your father to bless you." So I asked for a blessing, and he gave two little taps on my head and said, "No, no, no, you don't need to ask for my blessing. Don't bother me." I only remember that I felt deeply ashamed, but this established our relationship. Today, after all these years, he is proud of me and tells everyone that he is my father. Now we have a good relationship, and his children like me and are very close to me as an older brother.

I remember that his last wife—because he had several—once called me and said, "I want to ask a favor. My son looks up to you and he wants to ask whether you will allow him to call you his brother." I was pleased and said, "Of course. It's the right thing to do." From then on, I spent time with the boy and his sisters. So that's how my story begins. Two mothers and two fathers. One father with several wives, and many half-brothers and half-sisters, and I became friends with all of them. The father who raised me was an illiterate gardener who spent his entire life taking care of flowers and plants. He gave me all my values, all that I know about life. Really, I feel tremendous love and gratitude toward him. He gave me everything that I have in life: moral values, ethics, affection, attention, and so much of value.

Question: When you were a child in Rocinha, did it have bandidos, militia, and violence?

Carlinhos: No, nothing like this. Think about a city far in the interior, the neighbors, everybody knowing one another, everybody helping one another, everybody looking after each other's children when the parents were away or working. It was calm and very much a collective situation. The houses had little yards, an open field, that enormous space where you might play soccer, you could run, take a bath in a waterfall.

Question: Rocinha had a waterfall?

Carlinhos: Rocinha still has a waterfall. It used to have a lot more of them. We didn't have electricity. We didn't have piped water, but we had wells of pure water. Even today, there are places in Rocinha where people drink well water. They refuse to drink piped water; [they will drink] only pure well water, water that comes from the woods. People still go out to get it in bottles or with a big tin can on their head, as in former times, so they can drink pure well water. Generally, older people are used to doing this. It was a world to dream about.

I only saw what cocaine was in the army, in 1982, in Urca at the Command School of the Army General Staff, where officers are educated. It happened when a sergeant said, "You live in Rocinha? Bring me some stuff from there." I said, "What stuff? I don't know what it is." I really didn't know. He opened a little packet and said that it was that stuff there: cocaine. I had never seen it in my life. I had never seen marijuana or cocaine, because we didn't have organized crime. We had what were called *"vagabundos,"* someone who didn't like to work. We had a vagrancy law. When the police encountered someone on the street without his workbook [*carteira de trabalho*], he was arrested for being a vagrant and went to the police station. If the guy was arrested three times as a vagrant, he went to jail. I lived around *vagabundos*, but I never saw drugs, because the rule was that if someone had drugs or a gun, he kept it very much hidden. We couldn't imagine someone using drugs in front of someone. We were still all tied to good values and customs. For example, you didn't smoke in front of your father or mother, in front of adults. Or in front of children. This also was not approved behavior. We were raised in this way. What we saw mostly were pipes. We saw many adults, men, smoking pipes. Even cigarettes took a long time to be seen in public.

Question: How did this change? What caused so much change?

Carlinhos: I can't think when. I remember that in 1982, we were still living under the dictatorship, and I was doing military service in the barracks. I remember my first act of civic rebellion: On November 15, I went to vote wearing a "Lisâneas Macial for Congressman" T-shirt under my uniform. I had never voted for anyone. I didn't even know what the PT [Workers' Party] was, but there was a reason I had that T-shirt. The slogan for governor was, "Brizola in the Head"—at the time, cocaine was called "Brizola." The slogan was a joke, but it helped push Brizola's campaign, and he won the gubernatorial election in 1982.[1] But what I most remember was this strong thing about Lisâneas of the PT, that thing of grassroots effort. I didn't know anything about politics. I was wearing my army uniform, and several soldiers had election registration cards, because we were able to vote as soldiers. I remember that on the eve of the election, an officer collected all the registration cards. He didn't allow any soldier to vote.

By 1986, Rocinha was a highly politicized favela. All of the political movements were there, and the left and the right were very clear. A struggle was beginning already between the PT and the PDT [Democratic Labor Party]. The PDT, "Brizolismo," Brizola in power co-opted various community leaders, not only of the PDT. It was an enormous co-opting of community leaders within the public service sector. It began with people who were working in day-care centers and in the old community preschools. The communities began to suffer from the influence of party activists who were there to suffocate an independent movement of power. They didn't want movements making demands. They said, "But it's our government. Let's go there and converse with the governor. Let's speak with the [state] secretaries." Here you begin to exchange demands for favors.

Question: But there was no violence?

Carlinhos: Ever since I can remember, and until 1990, 1992, the police officer was part of the life of Rocinha. He made rounds. The people said, "Here comes a cop." You have to run, the police are making a blitz, frisking people, arresting people who had to be arrested. He walked through the community.

Question: But he wasn't walking around firing a gun.

Carlinhos: No, the police officer made his rounds, walked up and down, played hide-and-seek with the bandidos of the time. They shouted, "Look, here come the police," and the bandidos were running, with the police behind them and with their guns in their holsters. The bandidos were running, and the police were behind them, but without firing a shot. It was forbidden for the bandido ever to make an attempt on the police. It was a question of honor. You ran when you saw a cop. You didn't mess with the police. That was the order of things. Respect the police. When people were fighting at home, they went to the station to call the police. . . . The police officer went, conversed, arrested. He counseled. It was really community policing.

Question: After Brizola's first government from 1983 to 1986, was it then that there was greater violence in the community?

Carlinhos: The drug traffickers then became strong and established themselves on Second Street. No one could go up there without their approval. The police no longer went up there.

Question: They couldn't, or they didn't want to?

Carlinhos: They couldn't. They could no longer break through the barrier. The firepower of the bandidos was already great. And the police [only had] their old 32[-caliber] revolvers and, afterward, a submachine gun called an "INA" that the bandidos joked stood for "Isso Não Atira [This Doesn't Fire]." But it was one year later [in 1988] that the police avenged their honor and invaded Rocinha and killed all the drug-trafficking leaders. They killed all the local drug traffickers and where the traffickers had their command post, the police made a station that still exists today. They also killed the first child who was part of drug trafficking. He was known as "Little Brazilian" and was twelve years old, which shocked Rio de Janeiro. He was the first child we know who was part of the high command of drug trafficking in Rio de Janeiro. This was in 1988. The second was Carla of Dona Marta. She was also a child, but she was armed and commanded a drug-trafficking post.

What I mean to say is at that moment, we broke with being innocent, with the community moment. Now, except where we have GPAEs [Special Area Police Groups], police do not make rounds in the favela. The police don't even come into the favela, except during big operations. This means that if the hill is quiet, the bandidos do what they want to do when they want in any alley, on any street, on any narrow path, on any level paved area. They kill as many as they want. They do what they want to do, and no one can do anything. Now when the bandido wants to do something, he goes and pays the police, and everything is OK.

Question: Everywhere?

Carlinhos: Everywhere. But the favela police station is still a symbol. People like to have it there. Therefore, the drug traffickers allow them to stay. They [the police] don't do anything any more. They don't stop fights between married couples and between neighbors, as in former times. They don't do anything except help people who are sick or injured. You can say today that they do medical triage work. That's the role of the police today.

Question: And the militias: How did they begin?

Carlinhos: I don't know exactly how they began in an academic sense. But in certain places, there were migrants from the northeast, for example, who arrived with many people. They were afraid of the family being absorbed into the violence of Rio, of the son becoming a marijuana addict. They began to make a protection network among themselves, one helping and protecting the other, and this grew and became very strong. This strength turned into power, and the strength and power began to represent a political role—was able to deliver votes—and this began to interest the authorities. This model began to be sold to the authorities as an alternative to the drug traffickers, because it was strong enough to get the drug traffickers out of the favela and to control young people in places where the police couldn't work.

This began to get people's attention. On one side, it got the attention of the police, who began to want to sell protection in the periphery. That is how another model of protection got started: armed protection in return for money. I'll risk saying that this model began in 1994, during Brizola's second administration. These groups got started to protect themselves. Later, they began to protect an area, and then they began to sell security. Eventually, the possibility arose to get into other businesses, and they began to take power and organize over regions. The media started to promote this model as a financial boon that allowed money to be made; it "sold" the militia model as an alternative to drug trafficking. Diverse interest groups began to take over, especially in certain regions, such as the Zona Oeste of Rio de Janeiro.

Question: And so we have the League of Justice [militia group].

Carlinhos: [The League of Justice] came with another vision, that of financial and political domination over certain regions. When you go and look at the League of Justice, you have the police, politician, municipal councilmen, state deputies, and death squads. You have it all there. They sold security in order to protect the favela areas, but with political and police power. They charge prices that vary from 15 to 30 *reais* per house, and the way they begin to do it is not threatening. On the contrary, it's providing protection. They knock on a door and say, "Look we caught that *vagabundo* over there trying to beat your son, and we're protecting him. And the people say, "Yes, thank you." Then they say, "You can go to work without worrying, and we'll watch your house. No one is going to bother your wife and children, nor steal anything here because we're watching." They come by from time to time to ask, "Any problem here? If you have any, just tell us and we'll take care of it." And people ask how much is it, and they say, "If you want to give something, it's fine, but we're not charging anything." So they proceed by winning over people little by little, and with giving this support comes much political power, with many people elected and getting into all the spheres of public power. But it's to the contrary of demanding payment. They don't do this. They make people understand how they are important, and after they pass around a little list, asking for something, but it's only voluntary.

You also have militia throughout Zona Sul. The man who walks the street with a bullet proof vest, blowing a whistle from time to time, he receives money from the condominium presidents. Almost all the streets in

Zona Sul have people who receive something for making rounds. People end up paying more than the 15 or 30 *reais* in the favelas. Nobody believes any more in the [Military Police], and even fear the [Military Police]. They prefer to contract this "security" that isn't even licensed, and is from the militias, and many times the off-duty police. For example, my son who lives in Jacarepagua pays. But he doesn't pay by the month. What he does is to give presents and some money at Christmas, on Children's Day, Easter, during Carnival. But if it's necessary, he pays. He already saw examples in which the militia asked to go into the yards of houses, even with police cars, in pursuit of bandidos, and they were firing their guns.

Question: And when do the militias become violent?

Carlinhos: It depends. You have places where there has never been a case of violence against the residents by the militia. In others places, yes, they confront the drug traffickers and take the place of the boss of the hill and use violence to dominate the residents. Violence by militias is [found] only in places where militias substitute the drug traffickers and the bandidos. Still, there are places where militias take the place of the bandidos and drug traffickers but do not use violence against the residents. On the contrary, they don't allow bandidos to walk around armed. No residents are being held up; you don't have rape, because whoever does this disappears. The residents there think this excellent. They say, "What a great thing. I never smell marijuana here now. I never see a guy with cocaine. We don't have people walking around openly with guns." You ask, "Do you have a militia?" And they say, "Yes, but the militia doesn't bother us. It protects us."

Then there are the militias that take charge of selling bottled gas, cable television installation, and even drug trafficking, but outside the favela. Inside the favela, they protect the residents. It's similar to what the drug traffickers used to do. The residents feel protected; there are no more hold-ups; they can leave their windows open and their daughters can walk the streets safely, because nobody dares to bother them. "For this, I'll pay any price," the residents say, and they vote for the militias because of their real political and even judicial power. The militia represents the return of one's space as a resident, the return of public space. Before, residents had to ask permission to go out. Now they can leave, go to the public square, sit in a little bar, go to the market. They don't have the risk of a gunfight. If the police enter the community, they feel safe. They know that the police and the militia work together because they are in the same scheme and have the same benefits.

Question: Given what you are saying, do you support the militias?

Carlinhos: It's not that. I'm telling you what a resident thinks. Imagine, a while ago the bandidos walked around armed to the teeth, threatening the resident's family, killing his son, abusing his wife, at times raping his daughter. When the police arrived, they came in firing in all directions, and there were gunfights all the time. The resident couldn't leave anymore, couldn't sit in the public square, play soccer. He was also afraid of the police because of the gunfights. The militia came and took control of everything—confronted the bandidos and expelled them from the favela. It banned holdups and abuse of women and stopped people from walking around with guns. The police came now as a friend of the militia, which has also taken control of the sale of drugs, gas, and cable TV. What's important is that he [the resident] can go out into a public space without fear of gunfights. He doesn't see the consumption of drugs at his door anymore, without the power to do anything. He sees the police coming and going without any harm to himself. The resident is obliged to say, "I prefer the militia." In this way, the militias really exercise influence and control everything. They give the resident tranquillity in return for his vote and for influence in the areas of public power.

Question: It's the logic of self-protection.

Carlinhos: In some areas, the militias want to impose themselves by force, as in the case of Jerominho. The guy comes with a gun to the resident's door and says that Jerominho has to support the militia. The resident has to vote for their candidates. You see how it works. In the beginning, the militias go slowly, softly, carefully. They're winning over people. After, they don't want to lose anything. They begin to use violence to keep control. They turn into the bandidos; they become cruel: "Give me your vote, or I'm going to kill you. Give me your election registration card. I'm going to make a list of everyone who lives here and where they vote, and it's on you if my name is not voted in all those places where people who live here vote." It makes sense that he is not going to know which individual didn't vote for him, but he is going to know how many votes he has gotten, and it has to be so many or everyone will suffer reprisal.

Question: I heard charges of serious militia violence years ago—in 1992 and 1993.

Carlinhos: That's something else. It's what they called the "mining police."

Question: The "mining police" are different from the militias of today?

Carlinhos: The mining cop works like this: He says, "I know that you're a bandido. I'm going to leave you alone. But when I find out that you have plenty, I'm coming and will 'mine' you. I'm going to take it from you. That's how you're going to be able to continue." That's the mining police; he's there to "mine." The death squad belongs to those groups that don't tolerate anything. The mining cop tolerates crime because he profits from it by taking a cut. He says, "I always will tolerate you when you give me my cut and don't disturb the residents." The death squads are different. They kill the guy; they kill the guy's woman; they kill any person who may be close to the guy or that may be involved in his scheme. They finish off everyone. They're exterminators. They disappear the bodies; they do what they want. And they are almost all former police officers—or, properly stated, police who act when they are off duty. One can say that all criminal space that continues to exist in Rio de Janeiro has the support of state power behind it. Either directly or indirectly, it has the protection of state power. If it didn't, it could not continue to exercise its power. It has police power, it has political power, it has judicial power behind it.

Question: Do you think there was a change with Governor Sérgio Cabral?

Carlinhos: There was. And you have to be very much on the inside to perceive the changes. He went after criminals with much more violence than before, sometimes making the wrong decisions. I think the apex for Cabral was what happened at Alemão—unpardonable and unacceptable, but now some things are finished in the region. It can't be denied the so-called war of [drug] factions diminished with startling speed. The last war between factions we had this year was here in Babilônia and Chapéu Mangueira. Police operations have also been constant in the most diverse areas. Many people have died, and it can't be forgiven when innocent people die. We still have stray bullets and acts of resistance, which are deaths [that result] not [from] confrontation with the police but [are] intentional. But you have to admit that the "young men" are less eager.

Question: By "young men," do you mean the drug traffickers?

Carlinhos: Yes, at least in one place or another. A big difference now is that people aren't being arrested. Many have been killed.

Question: Then it's death-squad policy?

Carlinhos: I don't know. Contrary to what the press says, I think that [the police] are going into the hills to fulfill a mission. They don't find life easy. Society perhaps doesn't perceive it this way, but the death of the police officer is a victory for crime. Also, the death of someone innocent is a victory for crime. The innocent person doesn't have to die. Neither do the police. Neither does the drug trafficker. In the confrontation between good and evil, evil has to die. If in the confrontation someone has to die, then it has to be evil itself.

Question: You spoke about a demonstration in Rocinha to stop the police from doing certain things. Can you tell us about this?

Carlinhos: In July 2004, at the height of the war in Rocinha, the leader of the drug traffickers had been killed, and his lieutenant took command. There, in the middle of the woods, the whole bandido gang was cornered by 1,200 police in Rocinha. Then what became notorious is that, to provoke the population—and, according to some authorities, so they would inform against the bandidos—the police committed many outrages. There was a lot of aggression and violence against women, old people, and children. Young people were shot and wounded. The police fabricated information saying that they had found drugs on young people. They arrested people improperly. They forced their way into houses, breaking down doors. One night, the chief of the drug traffickers sent for me and the other two presidents of the Residents' Association. He said, "I know you're on television, in the newspapers, are with all the social movements talking about this, but it's not helping very much. The community is being victimized by the police, and if you don't stand up to this, I'm going to. Either you make a big demonstration, call the newspapers, call everyone and denounce and bring forward the victims of the police, or we're going to confront them. They call us bandidos. We are bandidos, and to kill or to die isn't a problem for us. We only want to avoid this confrontation in order not to make problems for the population. We only want to avoid the violence that we never committed anyway." We met among ourselves, the association presidents, and said, "They're right." We decided to act. Only we sought out the authorities, including the commander of the Twenty-third Police Battalion, and said, "Listen, we're going to organize a demonstration against police violence that was ordered by the drug traffickers, asked for by the drug traffickers, but it's going only to be residents, the population. We demand that that the [Military Police] commander bring together all of his secret police to see that there are no bandidos, no guns, no drugs—that it is not a movement to help the drug traffickers." Understand, we demanded that the commander put his men together to accompany us and to film and photograph the events to show that [the demonstrators] are only residents, to show that it was an organized movement of Rocinha. We put more than 800 people on the streets. We organized an enormous demonstration with cars, motorcycles, and so on. The order was given by the drug traffickers: The organization was ours. We counted on logistical aid from the community itself, from the merchants. And the authorities became concerned after they saw our capacity for mobilization. At no time did we demand that they remove the police from the favela. We wanted to stop the arbitrary behavior and the outrages, but we weren't giving up the right to the presence of the police.

Question: And did they stop?

Carlinhos: Bad police behavior diminished a lot. Did it stop? No. It's not ever going to stop. There will always be bad police who take advantage of a situation. But we can say this: the police as an institution stopped [acting badly]. The institution exercised more control. Those who continue [acting badly] are fearful because they no longer have the support of the high command.

Question: Was the Big Skull ever used in Rocinha?

Carlinhos: No. Rocinha is Zona Sul. Rocinha is São Conrado, Ipanema, Gavea. Secretary Beltrame himself has said that a bullet in the favela of Corea in Zona Norte is one thing; it is another in Copacabana. Rocinha is located in the heart of the best area.

Question: But the Big Skull entered Mangueira, and it was a disaster.

Carlinhos: Yes, they entered Mangueira, and it was a disaster. But look at it this way. The resident of the favela is not always against the Big Skull. The resident is against bad use of the Big Skull. Some organizations started a movement to ban the Big Skull and wanted favela residents to take up this idea. But favela residents understand and suffer when they see a police office dying in an alley, on a small path, in front of their homes. It reminds the community of a hostile feeling against the state.

Question: But the Big Skull drives in screaming threats, firing guns, saying that it is going to kill, that it is going to suck the soul out of the residents.

Carlinhos: But the vehicle doesn't speak. The armored car doesn't speak. What the population is against is the bad use of this armored car. It is very important that we say this, because I remember a meeting I attended with officers of the BOPE and a member of the group seeking to ban the Big Skull from the favela. A member [of the latter group] who was quite active and very much our friend said to the commander that he demanded in the name of the favelas that all of the Big Skulls be withdrawn from police operations. The mother of a young man who had lost a son in a BOPE operation said, "I want to say that this is not true. We only want the police to use well and with respect for the community this equipment that is meant to protect the lives of police officers." What she was saying was that favela residents live with this violence, with the drug traffickers, not because they want to, but because the drug traffickers they know are less bad than the police officers who don't know them—who act aggressively against them and kill their sons. What the resident was saying is that if the police arrive without acting aggressively, without residents' losing their lives, without their children losing their lives, without neighbors losing their lives—if the police enter an area in which crime exists against the will of the residents and give back to the residents the right to come and go safely—then the residents will support the police. The residents want decent, helpful police.

In the [police] occupation of Alemão that killed nineteen people, the residents were very upset, not once but twice: first, because the police killed those people; and second, because the police had mapped the bandidos' location but stopped 300 meters from where they were, killed a sizeable number of innocent people, and afterward left without arresting a single bandido.

Question: Why didn't the police reach them?

Carlinhos: How many rifles did the police sell [to the bandidos]? The deal with the bandidos was made at the expense of the residents, and many innocent people died. The residents were used—those who continued to live as much as those who died. They heard that the deal was being made, and those who didn't hear knew about it anyway, because the residents aren't stupid. The resident doesn't speak, doesn't see, and doesn't hear. Why can't he? Not because he doesn't want to. I always like to say: Do you want to know what the resident thinks? Listen to the resident. Don't call the leaders. Win his confidence and converse with the ordinary resident. Converse with the maid, the doorman, the sanitation worker on the street. Talk with the people and listen to what they say. Many times, they are unable to say whether they prefer the police or the drug trafficker.

Deley de Acari: A Discussion with
Cristina Pedroza de Faria, August 8, 2008

Deley de Acari is a well-known community leader in the Parque de Acari favela, which has been the scene of continual conflict between police and drug traffickers. Deley sees this situation as a slow but continual program of genocide directed against the communities. Also, he argues, while governments may change, public security policy for the communities does not. For Deley de Acari, a main community goal must be a program to reduce the number of homicides, which he and his supporters named the System for Reducing Injuries and Loss of Human Lives in the Acari Complex.

Deley de Acari: My name is Wanderley da Cunha; I am also known as Deley de Acari. I am fifty-three years old. I have been living in Acari since 1974 but have been in and out of the community since 1965 because of family ties. When I came here [to Acari], I was already an activist in the cultural and black movements, doing independent theater. I began to participate in the Neighborhood Association, and in 1979 I became vice-president of the Acari Park Neighborhood Association.

The Acari complex has eighteen favelas. In 1985, I began to work for a special public education program sponsored by the CIEP and put into effect by the Brizola government. In 1990, when the killing of children of the mothers of Acari took place, I was not living here. I spent five years living out of this area because my mother had died, and I had to take my sister and move away from here. Our family was left homeless and had to move out because of financial difficulties.

I came back in 1991. In 1993–1994, after the *chacina* at Vigário Geral, the most important and most violent police actions against citizens began in Acari. People began to pay attention to the complaints of some residents. Some people worked to denounce the violence through the Residents' Association. Eraldo was the president, and I was the vice-president of the association. The CEAP [Center for Expression and Art of Marginalized People] was around by then, and people would channel their complaints through the CEAP. We directed the relatives of victims and survivors to the CEAP. We established contacts, sometimes with police stations, and then went ahead to work for human rights.

Question: What were your achievements?
Deley de Acari: I didn't have any at that time. We would start processing a case, but after the anger and indignation passed, the family that had

submitted the case would fear retaliation by the police, go to the police station, and withdraw the complaint. When it was someone involved with some
criminal activity, the family would conclude, "He's a drug trafficker and
died. Let it go." There has never been a real change in public security policy.
It's remained the same even with the change of administrations because the
philosophy of government is one thing, the thinking of the battalion commander is another. The police themselves say to us, "The governor lasts four
years; the people in the batallion last twenty. We're the ones who know what
to do." A military policeman who can pinpoint a person's head from a Big
Skull 80 meters away is not a badly trained policeman. He may lack charac-
ter and humaneness, but technically our police are tops. They themselves
say that the BOPE is one of the best-trained police forces in the world, and
you believe that because you see the efficient results in the favelas where
those police act.

Question: What do you mean by a "reduction of losses"?
Deley de Acari: The traficante Berico came back to the favela from
1996 to 2001, and in 2002 Acari was occupied by the police. Berico spoke
with me during some community leadership meetings, and we said that we
needed help. We said, "You get into confrontations, shoot a policeman, and
the next day twenty police come and kill two bandidos and ten residents.
People want to know what you gain from that." Then we began the struggle
to convince "the boys" and this reduced the number of deaths.

One time, a prison guard came here, got out of his car to buy drugs, and
the guy who was selling drugs recognized him and told the others. They
came and nabbed the guard. Then another young guy who had been in
prison said that he was one of the few guards who had treated them well.
They let the guard go on his way. Four months later, they grabbed a Civil
Police officer who lives here and released him. Last week some of the boys
caught another police officer. They only took his gun and sent him away.
That's the result of these conversations. But the truth is that people don't
understand this. Down on the asphalt, people think that everything here is
linked to drug trafficking. What matters is reducing the losses.

The advantage that we have here is credibility. Most of the boys involved
in drug trafficking were my soccer students. When they were younger, they
never went hungry, because neighbors would pull together and help the family. It's a bond of trust that we have built over the years. We know that the
issue of reducing the losses is a fruit of our labor. Every day that people
wake up to see those boys alive is a day of joy. Here in Acari, the community
has joined the struggle against police violence. As far as I know, Acari is the

only community that has filed so many different cases. Granted, it's very little considering what we have here in terms of dead people. The fact is that
they are only six or seven cases, but they cover a lot, such as death threats,
which I have received, and another person who was shot in the arm. The
accused are now before the courts facing justice, and some are being tried.

Question: Has the number of deaths decreased?

Deley de Acari: The Public Security Institute has information about
that. Let's take the example of a community where there is a struggle for
control of drug trafficking. After a particular gang takes control, there is a
tendency for the number of deaths to decrease. Another example: When a
militia takes control, some deaths take place, but after that the militia is in
charge, and the number of new killings lessens. The state credits the fall of
deaths to its security policy, but from the moment that someone "takes control," the person in control wants to avoid deaths. No one will kill without
his approval. That's just the way it is. Still, what the politicians do is give
themselves credit for reducing the number of deaths, and they sometimes
get elected [because of that]. That's what people care about: reducing the
number of deaths.

As we see it, there is a clear public security policy of extermination, but
it's difficult to accuse the police of extermination as such, because they don't
kill many people at the same time—say, fifty people at once. The police kill
five people in one place, fifteen in another, twenty somewhere else, and so
on. So it's difficult to say, "Those cops are a group of genocidal exterminators." They also try to justify their actions in many ways, saying that these
are isolated incidents, not the result of a policy. In the case of the Alemão
complex, for instance, they'd say that it's a place of bad people and terrorists.
It has also been said that "the womb of a favela woman is a factory for making drug traffickers." They hold to what Beltrame says: that criminals learn
the culture of crime while in their mothers' wombs. It seems that they
believe that stopping the birth of more poor people will also stop the birth of
more criminals. You go either to prison or to the cemetery.

However, if you walk around the Acari favela, you will see almost a
hundred pregnant eighteen-year-old girls. What's going to happen to those
girls? You'll find an equal number of girls holding babies in their laps. We
have an interesting saying here: A twenty-five- or thirty-year-old woman
"gets pregnant," but a sixteen-year-old girl "catches pregnancy," just like one
catches a cold. I think we need to practice responsible sexuality, because in
a favela like Acari, if you have large numbers of pregnant girls, it's obvious
that boys and girls are having sexual relations without condoms, without any

precaution or means to avoid pregnancy. If you have a high rate of adolescent pregnancy, it is also possible to conclude that you will also have a high rate of AIDS and other sexually transmitted diseases. But getting back to what I was saying, I am convinced that health policy today—human reproduction policy—is a public security policy. Government personnel believe that family planning is a way to reduce crime in the medium term.

But there is also a very important issue that people don't yet understand. The women in the communities who will go out and join the struggle for justice because of the death of their relatives are a new contribution to the social movements. They are not revolutionaries; they are not the Mothers of the Plaza de Mayo. But they are beginning to politicize their speech and actions. None of those women chose to be activists. It was a personal tragedy that shook them up, and some of them, in the struggle to punish the police or the state for the deaths of their children, met other mothers, with whom they found solidarity. They also received support from some human rights organizations. That's what made them activists. Now they argue that the more the police are punished, the more impunity is reduced, that this, in turn, will have a broad effect. It doesn't help much to struggle for the punishment of one person. It's better to struggle for a change in the public security policy.

There is very ambiguous talk nowadays about the criminalization of poverty. Some academics are systematizing this, but nobody has yet defined what it means. So I am also saying that a process is under way, and not just in Brazil. It's a world process about the criminalization of poverty. It's like what Mike Davis says in his book *Planet of Slums*: about one-sixth of the planet's population lives in favelas. Within the perspective of neoliberalism, of the minimal state, what's left for the poor of the world is jail or the cemetery. They don't have jobs, schooling. They are what Davis calls "surplus humanity." The only thing to note here is that the "surplus humanity" is us, the favela dwellers. The politicians know what they want to do with the people, but we must determine what to do. We can't just walk around seeing fifteen-year-olds carrying guns and saying, "Everything is fine; [they are] 'surplus humanity' and are going to die anyway; they're headed for the cemetery." That boy is only fifteen. He has his entire life ahead of him. It's not right to believe, as Beltrame said, that the unborn fetus is already a drug trafficker or criminal. Many people don't like Davis's book because he doesn't propose a solution. It's clear that he did not write for the neoliberals; he wrote for us, the surplus portion of humanity.

Question: But there have been advances in terms of organizing popular movements.

Deley de Acari: Yes. Take, for example, the people who participate in the movement [for] the homeless who have occupied three or four areas in the center of the city, as well as in the Baixada Fluminense and Nova Iguaçu. Each movement has its own characteristics, but they all have a common thread. No matter how difficult or complicated the actual occupations are, people believe that they are responsible and must stand firm with people of different political tendencies.

Question: What about the arts? What role do they play here?

Deley de Acari: Here at the Cultural Social Center, we offer classes in music, capoeira, and Jiu-Jitsu. We also promote funk and hip hop shows. Funk itself has become as a social movement, a bridge between favelas controlled by rival drug factions. It's a broadly based movement, and people are in favor of it.

Postscript. This interview took place in August 2008. In November 2009, Deley de Acari announced the failure of the System for Reducing Injuries and Loss of Human Lives in the Acari complex. He and others had tried to persuade youths in drug gangs to leave their lives of crime, give up their weapons, and enter the legal economy. Jorge Rodrigues de Souza, nicknamed "Uerè," accepted the challenge—one of thirty such youths to do so, with another twenty interested in joining them. Ueré surrendered his submachine gun to a Civil Police officer, who immediately shot him at point-blank range and killed him. Deley partly blamed himself for Uerè's death. He and the other leaders, he said, "forgot" to get "agreement with the state government and the police high command to end the policy of confrontation, extermination of the poor, and ethnic cleansing." He wrote, "Our strategy for peace failed because it was romantic and unilateral." This tragic event is one more reminder of the absence of communication and chasm of mistrust that separate many favela communities and community leaders from state government and police leaders in Rio de Janeiro.

Frei Antônio: A Discussion with Philip Evanson, July and September 2008

Our Lady of the Rosary Catholic Church looks out on a street in middle-class Leme in Rio de Janeiro's Zona Sul. Steep hills rise behind the church and are occupied by the long established favela communities of Chapéu Mangueira and Babilônia. The church is led by Domincan priests and has a chapel in Chapéu Mangueira. Church and chapel offer religious services and educational programs to local residents. In May 2008, the calm of this peaceful area was broken by armed conflict between rival drug gangs. Police entered in force, a community school and day-care center were closed, and condominium residents reported that stray bullets penetrated their buildings' walls. The presence of the Duque de Caxias Army Base nearby apparently had no deterrent effect on the conflict between the drug factions. Frei Antônio, rector of Our Lady of the Rosary, describes the impact of these events on residents, church programs, and the community efforts led by the Residents' Association to reengage the state in the affairs of Chapéu Mangueira and Babilônia. Frei Antônio was interviewed twice, the first time on July 8, 2008 (six weeks after the violence began), and the second, on September 29, 2008. In 2009, a Police Pacification Unit occupied the two favelas.

Question: What is the situation today, six weeks after the violence started in late May?

Frei Antônio: I don't think things are getting better. People who talk with me, residents sixty and seventy years old, say they never have lived through such a situation and do not see a solution. Why? Because you see so much power in the hands of the bandidos. Also, there are people who say they are more afraid of the police than the bandidos. They cannot tell the police, "Look, this is happening, that is happening." There are people who say that the police are hostages of the bandidos.

Question: What is happening to the programs of the church?

Frei Antônio: We have a literacy program for adults here at the church that is for workers in condominiums and for other illiterate adults. It is held from 8:00 to 10:00 P.M. Right now we are not able to offer it, because a 9:30 P.M. curfew has been imposed by the drug traffickers that does not allow people to go up the hill. They do not come down, because they cannot return later to their houses. We also offer a computer course in the morning and afternoon for students who have completed the fifth grade. We had to stop giving it in the evening. In a world where everyone is becoming computer-literate, children are losing the chance to learn the first things about computers because they cannot go up and down the hill. They do not have the right to come and go. Even our children's catechism program is much reduced, because parents do not allow children to go out of the house, or they send their children away, take them out of the community, send them to other states to live with relatives because of the violence. Before, forty or sixty children attended mass. Today, we're lucky to have ten.

Question: It is now late September, and it seems that peace has returned to Leme.

Frei Antônio: They say that all the violence has stopped, and things have calmed down. We are again giving the evening course, with fewer people, but they are returning. The children are coming back to take the computer course and to receive catechism instruction. More children are coming because they have returned to their homes.

Question: How did this happen?

Frei Antônio: In truth, the state was called on to act. A series of meetings were held with the Residents' Association. The citizens were not able to come and go, not able to have normal lives, not able to go to work, to go out for a walk. It was through the Residents' Association that we brought the state to the neighborhood. We wanted to know the following: How is it that we live beside a military base and we do not have any security? The citizen does not want to know if it's an army, navy, or whatever kind of military base. He wants to know who has the power of the state. We were told, "The base does not have police power." The citizen does not care to know this. He wants to know that he can have security, that he does not even have it living beside a military base.

So the Residents' Association organized to demand action by the state. Secretary of Public Security Beltrame came with his staff. The commander of the Nineteenth Military Police battalion came, the commanding general of the Duque de Caxias base came, and the commander of the Sixth Military Police command post of Copacabana came. Through organization and complaints, we were able to get another precinct station in the area and cameras placed on Atlantic Avenue. This helps the resident have confidence in the state. We asked ourselves, where is the state? Why do we pay tax on everything? For everything we purchase, we pay something to the state. What does the state do with the money? The least the state can do is guarantee the right to come and go.

Question: What were working conditions for you during this crisis period, with bandidos in command of the hill and a police battalion down below and ready for action?

Frei Antônio: We have a chapel and we provide religious instruction in the community, not only in the parish church. One time we went up, and there was a checkpoint of armed men who said, "Go ahead, Father." But once we went up, we couldn't return. We stayed there the entire afternoon because, it was said, the bandidos were undergoing "a change of command" and there was a quarrel in the community. It was difficult for us to walk there with all the children, putting the children at risk. I already know a child in my parish who was wounded by a stray bullet. I've already had to collect money to send an adolescent to stay with relatives in another state because he had been wounded. Families in the communities tell me all the facts, keep me informed—when I should go up the hill and when I shouldn't—but I do not know anyone who died during the police occupation in this crisis. In brief, it was a very difficult situation, but we, as a church, and I as representative of the church, have to reinforce hope. We have to strive so that these people have the rights of citizens and so the state acts in a correct way. My message in homilies is always for political consciousness, to be aware of citizenship, that we have the right to demand the presence of the state and that the state has to act with respect. Many people in the community listen, and they call me to attend their meetings so that I can witness the situations in which they are living and so we can have programs to help young people.

Question: How would you describe the orientation of the archdiocese to priests and parishes in these difficult situations?

Frei Antônio: The archdiocese directs us to evangelize. But as Dominicans, we have a more political conception. I would say, more down-to-earth. We do not only stay with the idea "because you are going to have a better world later." We want a better world here and now. God gives us life so we can construct the Kingdom of God here and now and give greater value to life. The church has campaigned to place greater value on life. Before, the church had great authority. Today, it has less. Today, if some people need to beat a priest, they beat him. But he still has a voice and the means to take the voice of the people to be heard in other places. A priest has means to be an intermediary. Yes, he has a voice. And it's very important.

Question: You had a worker who was a victim of violence in the favela.

Frei Antônio: Yes, we had a worker who was helping to build houses, and someone suspected he had done something and said so. Based on this, he was beaten, and one of his fingers was cut off, amputated. We gathered his things and sent him back to the state he came from, because he could no longer stay in the community. He was given a warning. Poor guy: He hadn't done anything. It was a mistake. But it was impossible for him to remain in the community. He was terrified, as any person would be, and told me that he was not able to continue working, that he had a family.

Question: What is the situation with education in the community?

Frei Antônio: There is a university prepatory exam course, a community school, and a day-care center. I organized a library up in the community. The school is run by the Residents' Association. We had a public school, but the municipal government transferred everything to the Residents' Association; even the teachers are contracted by the Residents' Association. The government gives something to the Residents' Association to help pay the teachers, meaning that it exempts itself from all legal responsibility. It doesn't sign contracts with the teachers. The Residents' Association now has all of the legal, financial and even labor-law responsibility for the teachers and is not able to meet all the costs, because the municipal government only helps with some of them. The association had to close the school as a public school. But we continue to teach adults how to read and give the university preparatory course, which we call the "Little Course."

When people talk about the bandidos, [they're talking about] the minority of the minority. But they are armed and have power. If they were not armed, they would not have power. There are many good people both within the Residents' Association and in the community, people who want only to work, raise their families, live well. They are upstanding people who show great effort, people like the people who live down here on the asphalt. They only want to better themselves. In truth, many good things are being done. I now have a computer-equipped "smart" classroom for young people who are preparing themselves for their first job—meaning they are getting ready to improve their lives. Things are returning to normal. The bandidos are still there, but they do not interfere with us, and we have liberty to come and go and to continue our programs. We can provide more help. We have better policing. As I said, if the state is present, the citizen feels more secure.

Question: Is community policing a good option here?

Frei Antônio: We do not yet have community policing. It was begun but was not put in place. I don't know why. It would be a good idea, because we used to have a police officer everyone knew. He conversed with people, drank coffee with them, was always here. He was always blowing his whistle, walking here and there, attending to security. I think community policing would get community support. People treat the police well.

They treat well those who are up there with them—not those Military Police who go up the hill shooting, all that stuff. The police officer who stays there with them is different, and they treat him well. The police have to get the confidence of the community. They have to provide service and not act violently. Then the community will to support them. The people are good; they are kind; they are a people who treat others well. That was obvious when we had a flood; when the people were called on, they came. . . . If it's necessary to call the people to help the police, the people will come and help. If the police were good, they would not enter shooting like the Military Police do.

Part II

Voices of Public Security Officials

Chapter 6

Security for Whom?

Ensuring human rights and, at the same time, providing efficient policing has become one of the most difficult challenges Brazilian authorities face. Democracy was restored to Brazil in 1985 after twenty-one years of military dictatorship, with a coinciding increase in crime and violence in Rio de Janeiro. The emergence of a robust illegal economy in drug trafficking and an arms race between drug gangs and the police brought on the violence. Police were sent to attack drug gangs in the favelas, which unleashed a civil war in metropolitan Rio de Janeiro. This background and the low salaries of the police made possible new and unprecedented levels of police corruption. Raids by well-armed police on well-armed drug gangs brought great harm to innocent citizens, primarily in the favelas, a cost in human lives that is dramatically expressed in the soaring homicide rates since 1985, especially for men age fifteen to thirty. Real hatred exists in this war. Many police live incognito in the favelas in danger of discovery and execution by members of drug gangs.

Civilian leaders were slow to respond to these unfolding developments and to foresee long-term dangers. Politicians seemed reluctant or unable to deal with a police force composed largely of remnants of the repressive dictatorship. Furthermore, nobody envisioned that the end of military rule would leave any group of Brazilians more insecure in their persons and property. From 1964 to 1985, opponents of the dictatorship fought against tyranny and, apparently, defeated it. The stern, unloved, and now mostly forgotten

General-Presidents had constructed, and governed through, a national security state. National security state doctrine sought first and foremost to identify the "internal enemy," defined as anyone who opposed or otherwise
denigrated the government or armed forces. On this doctrine was built a
repressive apparatus that included a National Intelligence Service and a
political police, the much feared DOI-CODI.[1] The government drew some
distinctions between presumed enemies. Established professional politicians
in the opposition, even former presidents, might be *cassado,* or lose their
political rights, which meant they were barred from taking part overtly in
political activities. Intellectuals who wrote or spoke critically were silenced.
If they taught at public universities, they could be involuntarily retired.
Newspapers, television, radio, film, and theater were censored. Members of
the political or intellectual elite at odds with the dictatorship sometime chose
or were forced into exile. The military government regarded students and
workers as inherently antagonistic; it also quite rightly judged those groups to
be more dangerous to the regime than most professional politicians, whom
they disdained as corrupt or easily controlled. One of the first acts of the dictatorship in 1964 was to burn the National Student Union in Rio de Janeiro.
Strikes were outlawed, and the regime managed largely to prevent them until
1978. The dictatorship saved its harshest treatment for individuals or groups
who took up arms, and for their collaborators or perceived collaborators and
sympathizers. They could be arrested, tortured, and even killed in detention
centers.

     In the years since 1985, lists have been prepared and published of the
names of people who were deprived of political rights or arrested, kidnapped,
tortured, or killed by the dictatorship. The lists constitute an honor roll of
people who opposed or were victims of the military dictatorship. The individuals on the lists number in the hundreds, but the total is fewer than a thousand. However, they are relatively few in number when compared to the tens
of thousands of mostly unknown and unheralded individuals who have been
tortured, killed or disappeared victims of drug gangs and police in Rio de
Janeiro alone since 1985. Democratic Brazil since 1985 therefore has a much
poorer record in human rights than the preceding military dictatorship. This
seems paradoxical, since the Constitution of 1988 was hailed as a new char-
ter for citizenship, different from the 1967 and 1969 Constitutions of the
military government, which emphasized discretionary power and safeguards
for the state. Censorship may be a thing of the past; elections are held regularly; and certain social rights have been strengthened, but a geography of
public security shows that human rights have been largely absent in some
places. In areas with high homicide rates, nearly every family knows some-

one or has a family member who has been killed with a firearm, and the law of silence prevails.

Defining Homicides

Getting an accurate count of homicides in Rio de Janeiro has been a long-standing problem. The problem is tied to definitions, because an official definition of "homicide" has been contrived that excludes many individuals. That is, only victims of deliberate killings who die immediately are officially registered as homicides. Not counted are victims who suffer "deliberate injury to the body" and die later. This explains why police sometimes take bodies to hospitals and leave them, as if they were alive at the time of arrival. Also not counted are cases of "acts of resistance," in which victims are killed by police who supposedly are acting in self-defense. So-called acts of resistance are usually understood to be summary executions, since most of the victims are shot either in the back or in the head at close or point-blank range.[2] Because of inadequate firearms training, police marksmanship is poor, but they overcome this problem by killing at close range. Others not counted as homicides are discovered bodies or human skeletal remains. Finally, several thousand people disappear each year. Of course, not everyone who goes missing should be presumed dead or a homicide victim, but areas with high numbers of disappeared people also have high homicide rates, which gives cause to suspect the worst. The number of fatalities excluded from the official definition of "homicide" might well exceed the number of those officially counted in a given year.

There are also clandestine cemeteries in Rio de Janeiro. Who is buried in them? Are they victims of homicide? People know where these cemeteries are, but the state has made no serious effort to exhume and identify bodies or determine causes of death. Commanders of Military Police battalions feel pressure to keep body counts low in territories under their command, which is reason enough to remove bodies to clandestine cemeteries. There are also rumors that some bodies are disemboweled and cast into coastal ocean waters where they sink. For prosecutors when there is no body, there can be no crime.

Homicide cases are investigated, but in Rio de Janeiro fewer than 10 percent are solved. Compare this with a country such as Great Britain, where 90 percent are solved. When police officers are charged, fewer than 5 percent go to trial. Even a case serious enough to go to trial might not end in conviction. In July 2008, three-year-old João Roberto Soares was killed by police gunfire while he was in a car with his younger brother. The driver was their pregnant mother, Alessandra Soares, a lawyer, who had pulled off the road when she heard the police approach. Two police officers in pursuit of a stolen car mistakenly identified her pulled-over car as the stolen vehicle. According to the forensic report, they opened fire with intent to kill, and fifteen bullets struck the car. The victim was from a middle-class family, and the killing occurred in the middle-class Tijuca area of Rio. Several days of intense media coverage followed. The police admitted they had acted wrongly, were widely condemned, and the officers were put on trial. However, a jury absolved them on the grounds that they were only following orders. National Secretary for Public Security Ricardo Balesterei, commented: "If it were not a three-year-old white child, if it were not a murdered child—if it were, for example, three young, poor black men from some community—no one would have found what happened unusual. It would be registered as an 'act of resistance' or 'death in confrontation with the police,' and their mothers would spend the rest of their lives trying to prove that their sons were not bandidos but honest workers."[3]

Who Is to Blame for the Homicides?

Since the mid-1980s, blame for the high levels of deadly violence in Rio de Janeiro has been placed on the police and drug gangs. Both acquired and used automatic rifles and other heavy weapons, even weapons usually reserved for armies. In addition to conflicts with the police, the drug gangs attack one another to control territories. Drug gangs may impose curfews and decide who can come and go in a favela.

Drug gangs in Rio de Janeiro operate under different names, which have included the Comando Vermelho (Red Command), Amigos dos Amigos (Friends of Friends), and Terceiro Comando Puro (Pure Third Command). The history of these commands has acquired the status of mythology. They are said to have originated in prisons in the 1970s as inmates sought to protect themselves against officials, guards, and one another. Later, they maintained loosely affiliated ties outside of prison. They were supposedly encouraged and taught how to organize themselves by political prisoners of the military dictatorship who were incarcerated with common criminals.[4] The commands, once established, continued to organize in prisons. They were even able to mount operations that took place outside prisons, such as the one that shut down commerce in Rio de Janeiro in 2002.

Drug gangs' wars for control of territory have presented a major challenge to the police and authorities. Since 2007, Governor Sérgio Cabral has favored a policy of violent police confrontation with drug-trafficking gangs. This policy is partly driven by the hope to end conflict by expelling at least all but one gang from a favela and prevent new invasions by other gangs. It is easier for the police and the government, and safer for residents, to deal with one gang in control than with two or more in conflict. Thus, the drug traffickers seem to be able to cast a spell on public opinion and some officials; it is as though they set the agenda for public security. As Secretary Beltrame stated, "We have three well-defined factions of drug traffickers that hate each other and fight to control drug territories at any price and cause veritable wars. These were the people who introduced the automatic rifle here, introduced the 762 assault weapon, and now are introducing a group of explosives and 30 caliber machine guns and tracer bullets that are used in war."[5] In response, the police built up their own arsenal of lethal automatic rifles and invested in the heavily armored Big Skull vehicles that are used to invade favelas held captive by drug gangs.

The state police forces thus have been sent out to wage a war against drug gangs since the late 1980s but have ended up killing more people, including many innocent people, than drug traffickers. This explains why favela residents almost always say that, while they do not like drug traffickers, they like the police even less. However, in assessing blame for homicides, the police are following policies set by governors and carried out by their state secretaries of public security. In a sometimes acrimonious forum on public security in 2008 in which Secretary Beltrame participated, Julita Lembruger, onetime director of the Rio state penitentiary system and the state's first police ombudsperson, laid responsibility for the high level of violence at the feet of Governor Cabral, not the much maligned police or even the drug traffickers.[6]

Police Work: Theory and Practice

Understanding police work in Brazil should begin with a reading of the Constitution of 1988. Article 144 affirms that public security is the duty of the state and the responsibility of everyone, but it is exercised through a hierarchy of police forces headed by the Federal Police. At the bottom of the list are the Civil Police in fourth place followed by the Military Police and the Fire Brigades of the Military Police in fifth place. The Military Police, who are always uniformed, have the task of patrolling the streets to discourage and repress criminal action and to arrest people in the act of committing crimes. Arrested individuals are turned over to the Civil Police, who investigate crimes and prepare dossiers for prosecutors and judges.

Neither force is well regarded by the public. A widely circulating idea about the police is that they were created and deployed to control the lower classes so the middle and upper classes can enjoy their goods and privileges. In the favelas, where violent acts and threats can occur almost daily, residents' perception of police work is suggested in the words of a protest banner reproduced by the NGO Network of Movements and Communities against Violence that read, "The Rich Want Peace to Stay Rich. We Want Peace to Stay Alive."[7]

The ostensible enemies of the police are the drug dealers embedded in the favelas. Although relatively few in number, they represent a well-armed danger to residents and are willing and able to kill and tyrannize when effective public security forces are absent. Since many are willing to die themselves, they also pose a real threat to police, who are killed and wounded in significant numbers. Nevertheless, the police kill more, as homicide figures demonstrate. One recent report estimated that police kill forty-one civilians for each officer who dies. This is four times higher than the international average.[8] The police do not hesitate to shoot to kill in self-defense when they perceive danger. They even receive a certain level of public support when they eliminate criminals. When prosecutors and courts fail to try and incarcerate violent criminal suspects, public support for acts of extermination by the police is strengthened.

Police Grievances and Police Reform

The Rio de Janeiro Military Police are burdened by their recent history. In 2009, they celebrated two hundred years of existence, tracing their origin to a decree by the Prince Regent of Portugal (who later became King John VI) that created a royal guard in 1809. They were heroes of independence but became jailers for the military dictatorship when they were incorporated into the armed forces in 1969. As such, they became foot soldiers in the war against internal enemies of the regime. The Military Police were forced to become one more stern face of internal security, and though they remained on the streets, they were largely removed from traditional police duties. They were not the traditional "Cosme e Damião" or "Pedro e Paulo" police friends and mediators present to fulfill community policing needs. According to Ricardo Balestreri, the dictatorship in effect kidnapped the police for its own purposes and did away with any notion of neighborhood police forces. The main tasks of the police were to discourage and suppress opposition and to protect the regime rather than to safeguard the people. For many years after 1988, only sporadic efforts, at best, were made at police reform and to replace the national security state ideology of the military dictatorship with respect for the rule of law and the protection of citizens' rights. Instead, the older mentality and practices continued to the extent that the police were encouraged to view drug traffickers as a new incarnation of the "internal enemy."

The structure and inculcated values of the Military Police thus are more befitting an army than a civilian police force. Since they are soldiers, the Military Police are trained to kill. This undoubtedly has made it easier to employ the metaphor of war against drug traffickers, with its logic of weapons of war, such as the Big Skulls, and fighting in densely crowded urban areas. The large Military Police forces are organized into battalions; each battalion occupies a territory, with its own headquarters and barracks, and is made up of a hierarchy of officers and lower-ranking soldiers. Soldiers, or *praças*, are trained to obey their superiors and carry out their orders without question. Military Police are trained as soldiers to search for and to arrest or destroy enemies and seize their weapons.

Several serious problems have flowed from such militarization. The behavior of a battalion can change radically from one day to the next as battalion commanders change. Tensions are built into the relations between the better-paid, well-educated caste of high-ranking officers such as colonels, majors, captains, and lieutenants, and badly paid, lower-ranking *praças, or* enlisted soldiers, who patrol streets and make armed incursions into favelas. Unlike high-ranking officers, Military Police soldiers may have met only the minimal requirement of a ninth-grade education. At best, they can expect promotion to corporal or sergeant when they complete courses at the training center for Military Police soldiers.[9] In contrast, higher-ranking officers who took entry and promotion examinations for their positions did university-level courses. The career path for soldiers has not included entry into the higher ranks of planning and command. Little has been available to them by way of professional development. For various reasons, rank and file soldiers can feel oppressed and mistreated by superior officers. When the position of police *ouvidoria* (ombudsperson) was established in Rio in 1999 to hear complaints against the police, among those who complained the most were lower-ranking soldiers and officers with grievances against their superiors.[10]

Defenders of the Military Police model have argued that the hierarchical command structure and militarized organization is good because it allows the mass of poorly paid, badly trained soldiers to be controlled. This issue was addressed at the forum "A Policia Que Queremos (The Police We Want)," sponsored in 2006 by the NGO Viva Rio. It was attended by more than six hundred members of the Military Police, and stressed the need for promotion based on merit that is open to all ranks, thereby recognizing the grievances and aspirations of the *praças*. In 2009, the newly appointed Military

Police Commandant Colonel Mario Sérgio Duarte immediately praised the police on the street, contrasting them with a bureaucratized officer class that too often is insulated from patrol work. "Strictly speaking," he said, "the [Military Police] are the corporals and soldiers who are on the streets, the sergeants, the younger officers."[11] These words were at least a symbolic recognition of the soldiers' grievances.

Irrational behavior is built into Rio de Janeiro police work and institutional life. For example, unlike chiefs of drug gangs, commanding officers do not always have control over their soldiers, who often do as they wish when on patrol. In the formal code of police discipline, deviations in conduct such as serious violations of human rights might not be deemed as important as arriving late for duty, being improperly groomed, or not saluting a superior officer. Lesser breaches of discipline sometimes loom large in a soldier's record, and punishment may include arrest and confinement in a battalion barracks for up to thirty days. The Military Police are officially instructed not to use "excessive" force when approaching or arresting citizens, even in times of open armed conflict. But "excessive" is not carefully defined. In contrast, proper dress and grooming are defined precisely. Under such circumstances, it has been possible for an officer or soldier to have an unblemished record in matters of routine battalion discipline but to have committed human rights crimes while on duty, including homicides and summary executions, or to participate in schemes of corruption.[12]

Another example of irrationality is the wall that has been constructed between the Military Police and the Civil Police. Neither complete the full cycle of police work. The Military Police are on the streets, a presence to discourage crime and to confront it when necessary. The smaller Civil Police force investigates crimes. However, its record of investigation is poor. The Civil Police have a reputation not for solving crime, but for extracting confessions by applying torture in precinct jails, even though both the jails and torture are illegal. Like the Military Police, the Civil Police argue that they lack resources and, in the absence of resources, have been allowed to develop their own ways to operate.

The Military Police and Civil Police zealously strive to maintain distinct identities and to segregate themselves from each other.[13] This can lead to bizarre behavior. In 2008, for instance, a Military Police officer was killed in a Civil Police action. He was initially denied a Military Police burial with full honors because Military Police rules allow such burial only for officers who die on Military Police missions. Secretary Beltrame intervened and announced that he had selected the slain officer for the task. He praised the officer's courage and sacrifice and ordered that he be accorded burial with full honors. The Military Police relented, and a ceremony was improvised. But the Military Police still questioned the awarding of full benefits to the officer's family, which, following their rules, could be granted only in case of death while engaged in an official Military Police action.

Meanwhile, there are long-standing issues of low police salaries and corruption. Low pay is a festering grievance, a cause for complaints, demonstrations, and even strikes.[14] There is a common-sense understanding that low salaries are linked to the pervasiveness of corruption. Many police do not earn enough to buy a home, even in the poor communities from which many Military Police soldiers come. Most are forced to take second jobs, even while official rules prohibit off-duty work. Much of this outside work is in private security, which has grown into a large industry. Or a police officer might turn to crime by joining a militia or collaborating with drug traffickers. Commanding officers commonly permit the taking of a second job, which may even bring a certain advantage to senior officers by increasing their power over inferiors in the ranks for whom the worst punishment might be a change in work days and hours that schedule him or her out of an off-duty job.

The problem of low salaries and corrupt practices is reflected in the truculent behavior of some police in poor communities, such as when they forcibly enter homes without warrants, curse or threaten residents, demand food, and take possessions they they claim are stolen goods even when residents can show proof of purchase. Even more serious is the selling of weapons to drug traffickers, arresting them and then requiring that they buy their freedom, and extorting payments in exchange for the right to sell drugs as if they are leasing territory to an illicit business. People fear the police; they have little faith in them and are reluctant to report crimes such as theft because they believe such incidents are almost never investigated or solved. The exception is auto theft, which must be registered with the Civil Police in order to collect insurance compensation. Reporting a robbery in a home or office is commonly regarded as a useless exercise, even a risk, because a visit by the police to the home could set up a second robbery, this time by the police themselves. In the words of a middle-class Rio de Janeiro resident, "The last person I would call when I had a problem would be a police officer."[15]

Of course, the police themselves see that corruption is writ large in society, beginning with daily media reports of alleged involvement in kickbacks and other illicit schemes by members of a political class that also engages in blatant acts of nepotism. It seems clear that many middle-class and upper-class people and business groups prefer paying bribes to obeying laws. Brazil does not lack good laws against such abuses, but abiding by them can be inconvenient. Traditions of bribery and impunity are deeply engrained in Brazilian culture and judicial practices. For example, illegal slot machines operate unimpeded next to a Military Police battalion in Ipanema. Is it that all police in this battalion are corrupt, or is this illegal business of some interest to groups in a corrupt state?[16] Had the Brazilian elite found that a corrupt police reduced their liberty or threatened their property, they would have imposed the necessary reforms long ago.

While a long list of failings, weaknesses, and even crimes by police can be drawn up, it is still possible to see police from another perspective: as an ill-treated and even oppressed class. Many come from favelas and continue to live in them. However, living in a favela with the presence of drug gangs may force them to hide their identities lest the drug gangs or other bandidos mark them for assassination. The off-duty police officer is said to hide his identification in his shoe or dry his uniform after washing it at home by hanging it out of sight behind a refrigerator. Bandidos have been known to hunt off-duty police from house to house. The governors' favored policy of violent confrontation that sends police on armed missions into favelas, firing their guns and being shot at, can generate an unnatural reaction in which police learn to hate the communities from which they come.[17] Do police eat nourishing food or get enough to eat? Reports of police entering homes in favelas and demanding food are common and are repeated in interviews in this book.

Police work is clearly dangerous. In every year since 2000, more than a hundred Rio de Janeiro police have died violent deaths. The omnipresent danger helps to create a "shoot first and ask questions later" mentality. Even if instructed not to enter firing, the behavior and rationale for it may be otherwise as in the expression, "Better his mother's son dies, than my mother's son." Police corruption can be a threat for honest police. If the majority of police are corrupt and violent as some people think, the effect is to increase the sense of vulnerability of a minority who strive to do honest police work. This minority needs to do their work without alienating or raising suspicions of a corrupt majority, and thereby add to their dangers. Suicide also appears to be an occupational hazard of police work. The suicide rate for Rio de Janeiro police is six times greater than that for the rest of the population. Alcohol abuse is also a serious problem and recognized by the police themselves. Auto accidents, deaths in auto accidents and other violent deaths suffered by police are well above the rates for these in the general population.[18] At the same time, psychological services are largely unavailable, and health and dental care have been poor for low-ranking soldiers, as are recreation and leisure facilities.

Reformers within the police such as Hélio Luz, chief of the Civil Police from 1995 to 1998, have urged police to substitute a struggle for higher salaries for corrupt practices induced by low salaries. Luz supported his own police when they went on strike for higher salaries in 1998. Ten years later in early 2008, a police movement for better salaries received tacit approval of the Military Police commandant Colonel Ubiratan Ângelo, and culminated in a protest march in Ipanema directed toward the home of Governor Cabral. Cabral and Beltrame reacted by dismissing the commandant and ordering a general shakeup of the top command. The pressure for better salaries, the undoubted justice of salary demands, and various other overdue changes have opened the way for the federal government, which has money to make agreements with state and municipal governments through the new PRONASCI program to improve the situation of police that include salary supplements and to introduce innovations into public security policy.

Governors and Strategies

In Brazil, it is governors who command the police and have the power to set public security policies for their states, and to spearhead police reform. However, no Rio governor in the democratic period since 1988 has carried through a comprehensive plan for police reform, though there was at least a brief attempt in 1999–2000 to do just that. In his two terms as governor, from 1983 to 1986 and 1991 to 1994, Leonel Brizola tried to make police follow the law in the treatment of citizens. This was an effort to extend to favela residents something like the respect that has always been accorded middle-class and upper-class citizens. Brizola also built hundreds of public schools—the CIEPs, or the popularly named *brizolão*—most of which were in poor communities, and his governments strove to increase the availability of electricity and water in favelas.

Perhaps the good intentions of Brizola's security policy may be best understood by looking at certain key appointments. He selected Colonel Carlos Magno Nazareth Cerqueira to command the Military Police. In addition to being black, Cerqueira was an apostle of the community policing model, in which police become a permanent presence in a community and work closely with residents to build trust and reduce crime. Cerqueira's ideas represented an effort to redirect police work away from the national security state ideology of making war against an internal enemy. In 1999, Cerqueira was assassinated by a disgruntled or deranged police officer. However, his approach to policing had an extraordinary impact on a group of officers within the Military Police, who continue to honor his ideas and revere his memory. A second representative appointment was that of the sociologist Julita Lembruger to direct Rio de Janeiro's penitentiary system from 1991 to 1994. Lembruger has championed alternative penalties for those convicted of nonviolent crimes to prevent them from being incarcerated with violent criminals, to whom, she argues, they should not be compared. Alternative penalties to incarceration would also save money needed to invest in projects with greater social utility. These Brizola appointments represented efforts to link police and penitentiary reform to democratic institution building and to move away from practices of the national security state dictatorship. Lembruger's appointment also had the merit of putting a well-trained civilian professional in a prominent position in public security work. Public security programs appear to work best when both police professionals and civilian experts are present.

During Brizola's second term (1991–1994), the aging populist, seemed unable to get a grip on public security. Drug gangs flourished, as did the illicit flow of arms to them, and the homicide rate remained high. Two dramatic police *chacinas* took place. The *chacina* in Vigário Geral in 1993 left twenty-one people dead and was undertaken as revenge for the killing of two police officers by drug traffickers from whom the police were trying to extort money. In the same year, off-duty police killed nine children and adolescents who were living on the street around the Candelaria Cathedral in central Rio. The Candelaria *chacina* became an international incident and provoked a strong civil response in Rio. However, control exercised over the police has remained the weak link in the public security chain, and *chacinas* have continued. Perhaps the most infamous occurred in the Baixada Fluminense, near the city of Nova Iguaçu, in 2005 when ten Military Police officers went on a drive-by shooting rampage, killing twenty-nine people who were mostly outdoors in bars and restaurants. The police did this as part of a quarrel with a new battalion commander and as a show of strength.

Security policy in Rio de Janeiro has been described as swinging like a pendulum between the extremes of respecting human rights and violently repressing bandidos. A consequence of the latter is the loss of many innocent lives. Brizola's two successors, Governor Wellington Moreira Franco (1987–1990) and Governor Marcelo Alencar (1995–1998), reacted to his policies and opted for violent repression. Franco campaigned on the promise to end violence in a hundred days, but his government presided over a dramatic increase in homicides and death-squad activity. By 1990, the number of homicides and the homicide rate had reached unprecedented highs. In 1995, Governor Alencar named General Nilton Cerqueira, a veteran of the national security state dictatorship, as his secretary of state security. General Cerqueira is best remembered for introducing rewards for police who reduced crime. In effect, it was an invitation to police to reduce crime by exterminating bandidos. The rewards were salary bonuses and promotions.[19] The system was ended by Alencar's successor, but the bad example had been set. After a BOPE mission left nine dead in May 2008, Military Police Major Marcus Jardim praised the results, arguing that the Military Police should be seen as the best available social insecticide.

The pendulum appeared to swing back when Governor Anthony Garotinho took office in 1999. Garotinho, a radio talk show host, was the candidate of Brizola's political party and the heir to his populist political legacy. He ran on a platform of police reform and endorsed a plan designed by a group of police and civilian experts headed by the anthropologist Luiz Eduardo Soares. The plan was to introduce a reform program that combined public security with defense of human rights. Soares, a civilian, was appointed undersecretary for public security. Julita Lembruger was named the first Rio de Janeiro police ombudsperson. There was a short-lived effort to put a large-scale reform program in place in 1999 and 2000 based on ideas enunciated in the gubernatorial campaign. However, on encountering resistance mostly from the police, Governor Garotinho grew faint-hearted. Most likely, he lacked a sincere commitment to security reform in the first place. The fear of appearing weak or irresolute in combating violent crime could damage his reputation, as had happened to Brizola, whose party he now led. In any event, Soares was forced out of his position, Lembruger resigned, and the reform program was largely abandoned.[20]

However, an important effort in community policing started in 2000 in the Zona Sul favelas of Cantagalo and Pavão-Pavãozinho. Commanded by Captain Antônio Carlos Carballo Blanco, the community policing was successful in momentarily stopping violence. During the eight months before he took command, ten violent deaths had occurred. During the two years that followed, there was not a single violent death, nor was anyone wounded, and stray bullets did not pierce the air in these favelas. The great strength of GPAE community policing, in contrast to confrontation, is that although it does not end drug dealing, it has been shown to dramatically reduce gunfire, stray bullets, and death or wounds from gunfire in a community. It can also establish the police as a mediator and a welcome presence in a community.[21] Unfortunately, GPAE initiatives have been few. They seem either to have been pilot programs or an attempt to improve the bad image of the Military Police. Moreover, institutional support by the Military Police is often weak. The officer sent to command a GPAE unit might be strongly committed to community policing, but other police assigned to the unit might be there not because they were interested but because their superiors viewed them as a source of problems. Hardline Military Police officers engaged in the war with drug traffickers are not likely to think well of community policing, which may seem to them like social work.

In 2002, Garotinho resigned to run for president. His wife, Rosinha Garotinho, was elected to succeed him as governor. Her four years in office (2003–2006) were marked by continued high levels of violence and police corruption, which reached into the highest ranks. Two Civil Police chiefs and the chief of the state highway police were arrested and accused of various crimes. The 2006 gubernatorial election was won by Sérgio Cabral, who was supported by a coalition of left-of-center parties. Cabral campaigned in defense of human rights, better public security, and, in response to protests from favela communities and human rights groups who viewed them as a weapon of terror, he favored the removal of the Big Skulls from police arsenals.

Cabral was named after his father, an icon of journalism in Rio de Janeiro who in 1970 bravely joined a few like-minded journalists to found O *Pasquim,* a political humor magazine that opposed the military dictatorship. During ten memorable years, O *Pasquim* captured the imagination of critics of the dictatorship like no other publication. Its audacious satire and humor represent the spirit of *carioca* opposition to power at its most irreverent and irrepressible. The older Cabral may be even better known as a leading writer on popular music in Rio de Janeiro, especially music produced by samba composers. He is also a noted biographer of popular composers and a composer himself. His son entered journalism and politics, and after fifteen years in the State Assembly and election to the Federal Senate, was elected governor.

Governor-elect Cabral quickly began to reverse course. Two days after his election, he introduced José Mariano Beltrame as his choice for secretary of public security. Beltrame announced that the Big Skull would continue to be used in certain circumstances, and Cabral added that it would be irresponsible to scrap the armored vehicle because it had cost so much money. Beltrame was a vigorous, well-conditioned man of forty-nine and a twenty-six-year veteran of the Federal Police. He had spent the preceding two years directing a Federal Police program to improve intelligence work in mapping organized crime. His choice, which had been recommended by officials of the Lula administration, represented a tacit agreement between the new governor and the central government to work together on public security. It was made as President Lula and his public security group were planning to fund major new initiatives to be carried out in partnership with states and municipalities.

Whatever temperamental affinities may or may not exist between Cabral, who during his first year in office was criticized for spending a record amount of time on trips away from the state, and the workaholic Beltrame, who seems never to be absent, they marched in lockstep on public security policy. Also, both men were highly critical of the growth and development of the favelas. For Cabral, conditions in the favelas were bad because the favelas grew without planning or the presence of the state; their growth, he said, was due to years of government "leniency." Beltrame's views may be even more deeply felt. He is an outsider who hails from Rio Grande do Sul, the spiritual homeland of a positivist tradition in Brazil that exalts the authority of state. Favelas large and small are communities from which the state has been absent, where some people, to use his words, do not even know what the state is and where criminal groups may rule and impose a law of silence and obedience. Beltrame understood that this situation was deeply rooted in the history of Rio de Janeiro, a history he found full of irresponsibility and omissions. Not the least of the omissions had been to leave police forces in a parlous condition, demoralized and corrupt.

Both Cabral and Beltrame defended the policy of using the police to confront drug traffickers, enter favela strongholds to arrest them, and seize their weapons and drugs. However, there are not enough police to occupy territory everywhere after an incursion. When they fail to occupy, the enemy drug traffickers and other bandidos return. The policy therefore had a Sisyphean quality. In its defense, Beltrame has argued that confrontation at least prevents criminal groups from becoming even stronger. Critics have attacked the policy on both human rights and practical grounds. For them, it produces a high number of homicides and wounded individuals, many of whom are innocent. In 2007, the number of homicides for the Rio state exceeded those for much larger São Paulo for the first time, and criminal groups remained strong. Critics called confrontation a policy without *metas* (goals). For example, there is no stated goal to reduce the number of homicides by so many per month, which could be used when evaluating police tactics.

The Federal Government and Creation of the PRONASCI

By 2008, the Brazilian federal government had become deeply involved in public security. The United Nations Council of Human Rights had praised the results of government social programs but sharply criticized Brazil for its public security record, thereby questioning the progressive political paradigm, and even common sense, that saw a causal relationship between improving social indicators and falling crime and homicide rates. Also in 2008, the highly critical report by Special Rapporteur on Extrajudicial, Summary, and Arbitrary Executions Philip Alston was released, which reminded the international community that homicidal violence remained very high in parts of Brazil and that the human rights record remained bad.

In response, the national government, with much fanfare, launched the National Program for Public Security with Citizenship (PRONASCI). Justice Minister Tarso Genro came to Jacarepagua, a suburban area of Rio that had suffered from high violence, to unveil PRONASCI. Unlike the previous national public security program, of 2000, this one went far beyond symbolic statements.[22] PRONASCI was a package of ninety-four programs, later increased to ninety-seven, that came with significant financial backing. At least a billion *reais* (a half-billion dollars) was budgeted annually through 2012. The money would be funneled through states and municipalities that signed agreements with the national government. These agreements established the Cabinets for Integrated Administration of Public Security (GGIS). These were new administrative entities where representatives of municipal and state governments and the federal government worked together to select and start PRONASCI programs. The aims were to train better police professionals and to reduce crime and violence in so-called vulnerable areas. By 2009, several of the ninety-seven programs had been prioritized. The *bolsa formação* (education scholarship) offered low-salaried police officers a monthly stipend to enroll in certain courses. Distance learning proved the preferred method of instruction: Some 150,000 individuals enrolled in an online public security training course the first day it was offered. With pardonable pride, National Secretary for Public Security Ricardo Balestreri proclaimed it the largest such training program "on the planet." A second program offered low-interest credits to police to purchase a home. Yet another prioritized program was Mulheres de Paz (Women of Peace), which gave PRONASCI a presence in vulnerable communities by recognizing the leading role female residents have played in communities in trying to save lives and reduce violence. News stories had reported, and even shown, women in favelas confronting police who were trying to take away young men in an effort to save them from summary executions. Members of Women of Peace receive training in human rights and citizenship and are then asked to dedicate eight hours a week to identifying individuals age fifteen to twenty-nine who seem vulnerable to the lure of crime and direct them to social and job training programs. The women receive 190 *reais* per month for their efforts. However, as a police officer assigned to PRONASCI told us, it was important that they not become police informants or perceived as such for the program to succeed. Yet another PRONASCI initiative was the Project for the Protection of Youths in Vulnerable Territories (PROTEJO), which registered youths age sixteen to twenty-nine in training programs in tourism, for work as beauticians, and in community and recreational work. By mid-2009, the Women of Peace and the PROJEJO programs were present in at least eighteen Rio communities, sometimes in areas of continuing conflict and armed violence. PRONASCI-Rio organized a conference with representatives of both programs in attendance to draw up proposals to be sent to a National Conference on Public Security in Brasília.

PRONASCI therefore had become part of the public security framework for Rio de Janeiro. Governor Cabral claimed that the state led all others in the number of police receiving scholarships, though there were charges that some police were getting scholarship money without taking the course. PRONASCI money was also made available to construct gyms for police and municipal guards and to upgrade health services for police with treatment for post-traumatic stress and prevention of drug and alcohol abuse. Money was also provided to increase the number of beds in Military Police hospitals and to create a mobile dental clinic.

As welcome as they were, PRONASCI's contributions to the much needed expansion of health and recreation services and other benefits for police and community residents did not affect the setting of overall security policy, which remained in the governor's hands. At times, Justice Minister Tarso Genro and his public security team in Brasília were openly critical of the policy of confrontation. They were clearly committed to the alternative policy of reducing the use of lethal weapons and in favor of more community policing. Beltrame told us that in his view, PRONASCI was the salvation of the police, that he included community policing as part of the police training program, but he could not set up community policing units in places where the police had not yet established control.

Pacification: A New Phase in Public Security?

By the beginning of 2010, authorities in Rio de Janeiro and Brasília were facing growing pressure to reduce the number of homicides and to carry through police reform and strengthen human rights. The coming of the World Cup to Brazil in 2014 and of the Olympic Games to Rio de Janeiro in 2016 were adding to the urgency. These two international mega-sporting events were putting public security in Rio de Janeiro and Brazil under scrutiny as never before. Something new was needed in addition to the PRONASCI programs.

In Rio de Janeiro, this came in the form of the Police Pacification Units (UPPs), which first appeared in 2009.

Military Police UPPs were created to occupy selected favelas and expel drug gangs. For the authorities, the goals were to retake territory lost to drug-trafficking gangs and impose peace in targeted communities. Beyond this, it is not altogether clear what "pacification" means. In colonial history, the term "pacification" had been linked to control strategies and even the extermination of particular ethnic groups. More recently, "pacification" had been used to describe a strategy to control an enemy with strong community support, as was tried by the United States in the Strategic Hamlet Program during the Vietnam War. However, nobody can argue that people in the favelas strongly supported drug gangs and would resist their removal or suppression. Whether residents will support or resist the UPPs remains to be seen. Their attitudes are bound to be skeptical. Will Military Police who fill the ranks of UPPs and who are steeped in military discipline know how to respect the rights of residents? Will they be ordered to do so? Will UPPs become a version of desirable and trustworthy "community policing" close to the people and protecting them from crime? Military Police have not demonstrated these qualities during the long years of war against drug dealers. Will social programs such as those envisioned in PRONASCI follow once an area has been "pacified"? Will officers with a GPAE perspective emerge to command UPPs? Finally, will a UPP, once in a community, stay?

Media reports that have focused on UPPs in the Zona Sul favelas have largely been favorable. Children have returned to play in streets and other public spaces, and people are free to come and go. In the middle-class condominium apartments that face Dona Marta in Botafogo, bulletproof sheathing was being removed from windows, just as it was from the windows of the office of Mayor Eduardo Paes in the City Palace, which also faced the favela. In the Zona Sul favelas of Dona Marta, Chapéu Mangueira, and Babilônia, UPPs have been stationed in large new police stations overlooking the communities. In a gesture toward residents, tech centers have been constructed to make computers available to them.

However, Zona Sul has faced fewer challenges than other areas. Homicide rates had always been much lower than in the favelas in the Zona Oeste and Zona Norte, and it remains to be seen how far pacification can be extended and whether it will prove the best proximity policing program. That the middle class in Zona Sul feels a new sense of security seems clear. However, this is not entirely so for those who live in the occupied communities. There have been reports of police abuse and mistreatment of residents. In researching this book, we inquired about the level of support among community people in areas occupied by the UPPs. Many responded that "silence is not support but fear."

Public Security and Politics

UPPs and pacification have been publicized as one more step toward establishing democracy in the favelas by liberating them from the power of bandidos. However, can pacification or the completion of various PAC public works projects end or weaken a long-established informal structure of politics, a so-called parallel state that intimidates residents and allows chronic violent crime to be present? Enrique Desmond Arias has described this structure as one in which elected officials, resident leaders, businesspeople, police, militias, and drug traffickers collaborate for their own benefit even while they perpetuate crime and prevent formal state institutions from being established.[23]

The sinister side of this parallel state is the link with crime and refusal to tolerate threats to its power, including its political power, through elections. By 2008, militias had become a fearsome presence in certain areas of metropolitan Rio and were taking the coercion of voters to a new level in the elections of mayors and *vereadores* (City Council members). Voters were intimidated wherever militias or drug dealers were strong. One method was for militias to carry out a census of voters in different favelas. The names of residents were put in a book called a "*cadastro*," along with information such as the names of family members, addresses, and telephone numbers, as well voter ID card numbers. Once they have this information recorded, it becomes easy to intimidate people: All that is needed is to send representatives from house to house or even simply to "pass the word" that they expect to find so many votes in each particular section where a given number of people in the community vote. Failure to reach the number will be followed by retribution. Considering the violence perpetrated by militias, drug chieftains, and police with the complicity of local leaders and political parties, few dare to disobey.

As the 2008 campaign proceeded, certain candidates were barred from appearing in some favelas. Antônio Bonfim Lopes, or "Nem," the young drug lord of Rocinha, the largest of Rio de Janeiro's favelas, selected his own candidate for local city councilman, laid out the campaign in Rocinha himself, and barred competing candidates. Nem's wishes were duly recorded as decisions, or "Acts," of a meeting with community leaders over which he presided. They included his warning and exhortation, "I will not accept defeat."[24] Carlinhos Costa, a longtime Rocinha community leader and Workers' Party (PT) candidate for vereador, and City Councilwoman Andrea Gouvêa Vieira of the Brazilian Social Democratic Party (PSDB), who works with people in Rocinha, told us that they were not able to organize their campaigns in Rocinha or approach voting areas on election day. Nem and members of his gang walked freely in Rocinha. They carried weapons openly, including semi-automatic AR-15 rifles, in support of their candidate, who duly won and became a member of the Rio City Council. The election in Rocinha was never an issue of political-party competition but of control of territory by a local crime group. Nem's power was further consolidated by the wall built with government funds along the upper reaches of Rocinha. It ostensibly was intended to stop settlement of the favela from continuing to climb the hill and to save forest areas, but it also served to prevent an invasion by any competing criminal group.

It seems clear that security reform cannot be expected to emerge out of the politics of Rio de Janeiro. The civil rights of citizens who reside in favelas still find no support strong enough to prevail against the coercion and intimidation practiced by criminal groups such as drug gangs and militia acting with the complicity of local leaders. A structure of informal power has been in place too long. It may even be growing in strength. Too many powerful groups benefit—among them, political parties and individual candidates running for office, including the offices of mayor of Rio de Janeiro and governor of the state. Such a system is unlikely to be self-correcting. Authorities, experts in public security, and the police themselves may argue that better salaries, better training, and better equipment will improve the quality of police. The Brazilian Bar Association and human rights organizations can point out and protest the abnormally high number of violations suffered by poor citizens in favelas. Experts at universities and research institutes can identify and analyze the many challenges in designing public security policy and doing police work in Rio de Janeiro. Media coverage will expose violence and corruption and demand reform. However, the countervailing weight of parallel power long in place in favelas that has benefited political parties and elected local and state officials—and criminal groups—has proved too strong to break even in the midst of reports of violence, the killing of innocent people, and widespread violations of citizen rights.

Extending the civil rights guarantees of the Constitution of 1988 to citizens of favelas seems to require something new—either a powerful civil rights movement that recalls the social movements of the 1970s and 1980s in the era of military dictatorship or greater involvement by the federal government. Direct federal intervention is unlikely, given the division of power embedded in the Constitution.[25] The history of national governments in Brazil shows extreme reluctance to intervene in the affairs of states unless requested by governors who are likely to circumscribe an intervention in duration and scope. PRONASCI remains a promising federal instrument for broadly conceived security reform, with its bountiful offer of government funds, and with numerous programs that are suitable to favelas, with their traditions of self-help and solidarity. In 2009, the federal government sponsored its first National Conference on Public Security in Brasília in support of public security and human rights as part of a single program, a proposition long considered contradictory or unrealistic by some.[26] Finally, there is the possibility of international sanctions. If the country's human rights record does not improve, sanctions deriving from treaties signed by Brazil remain as a prod and a threat.

The interviews that follow provide views of public security professionals and of state and national authorities, including President Luis Inácio Lula da Silva, Justice Minister Tarso Genro, National Secretary for Human Rights Paulo Vannuchi, National Secretary for Public Security Ricardo Brisolla Balestreri, and Governor Sérgio Cabral. They demonstrate the complexities and challenges of designing public security policy in contemporary Brazil and in carrying through police reform. Brazilians like to say that they live in a complicated country. Nevertheless, they have clear ideas of justice and human rights and have enshrined them in good laws and the Constitution of 1988, which they need to enforce with greater conviction.

Chapter 7

Voices of Police Officers

José Mariano Beltrame, Secretary of Public Security for the State of Rio de Janeiro: A Discussion with Philip Evanson, August 2008

José Mariano Beltrame became secretary of public security in January 2007. He is a member of the Federal Police and was recommended to Governor Sérgio Cabral for the position by the Brazilian federal government. Beltrame, like Governor Cabral, has been a defender of the policy of confrontation, which in practice leads to confronting drug trafficker groups directly in densely crowded favelas. For critics, this means the police often come in shooting and kill and wound innocent people. While Beltrame does not deny the violence and mistakes of police, he has argued that these actions are necessary so that crime and violence do not become an even greater problem. He also argues that, over a long period, the state abandoned many of its responsibilities in Rio de Janeiro, including the responsibility to improve the quality of its police forces. The interview took place in August 2008, before the creation of Police Pacification Units (UPPs). Holding what is surely one of the most difficult positions in Brazilian public security work, Beltrame is widely viewed as an incorruptible professional. He has tried to set an agenda for crime control in Rio de Janeiro even as criminal groups have shown little fear of the state.

Question: Can you tell us something about your life: how you chose to become a police officer and how you came to Rio de Janeiro and took the position of secretary of public security?

Secretary Beltrame: I am from Santa Marta [in] Rio Grande do Sul. My family of Italian immigrants were people linked to farming. Later, with the coming of monopoly farming such as soybeans, introduced by Americans, the [immigrant] colonies came to an end, and the people went to the cities. Since the south of Brazil had a large immigration of people from various parts of the world—Polish, Italians, Japanese, Germans—this is reflected strongly in the culture of the places such as Santa Catarina, Paraná, and Rio Grande do Sul. I studied business administration at the Federal University of Rio Grande do Sul in Porto Alegre. I entered the Federal Police as an intelligence agent. I was always very much interested in intelligence work with respect to organized crime and drug trafficking and narcotics. In my career as a police officer, I worked in most of the Brazilian states in this area until I came to Rio de Janeiro and earned an MBA in strategic intelligence at the Higher War College.[1] I directed a large intelligence-gathering unit that the Federal Police established in Rio de Janeiro called "Mission Help Rio." This position led me to be named chief of intelligence for Rio de Janeiro, and later I headed Interpol in Rio. At the end of the 2006, I was invited to take this position which is twenty-four-hour-a-day work, as we are subject to be called at any hour.

Question: How should we think about public security in Rio de Janeiro?

Beltrame: I think there is a certain exaggeration in saying that Rio de Janeiro is one of the most violent cities in the world, because we have neighborhoods where the incidence of violent crimes is very low, such as Rodrigo de Freitas Lake and some areas of Ipanema, Leblon, and Barra de Tijuca. There, the indices of crime are very good, if this expression can be allowed. Beginning in 1980, Rio de Janeiro was abandoned. There was no additional investment in the police, and there was no type of concern about social conditions. Rio de Janeiro was invaded [by poor people] in a way that had no order. It was completely disordered. Rio de Janeiro has a topography and geography that allows this to be done. Why do 85 percent of the domestics of Barra da Tijuca live in Rocinha or in City of God? These people with low incomes install themselves in the central areas of the city.[2] These central areas are well located and, being areas of very difficult access, this allows the drug traffickers and organized crime to get established. It's a very good situation for the trafficker because access is difficult, and in general there are only two or three ways in and out. The trafficker has absolute control of the area, and the people who live there are under his command—or, rather, under the point of his rifle, and the law of silence is what reigns.

The drug trafficker, then, is in the center of the city. This normally does not occur elsewhere in the world. In other places, they are found on the periphery. Not in Rio de Janeiro. In Rio de Janeiro, drug gangs are in the center. The presence of violence is marked. To give an idea of this, the area of Barra de Tijuca has nineteen favelas on a half-dozen hills. The good citizen sits there watching one faction fight another. Here in Rio, we also have this difference. We have three well-defined factions of drug traffickers that hate each other and fight to control drug territories at any price, and they cause veritable wars. These were the people who introduced the automatic rifle here, introduced the 762 assault weapon, and are now introducing a group of explosives and 30-caliber machine guns and tracer bullets that are only used in war. The society watched all this helplessly. It is the inertia and ineptitude of the state that controlled nothing, including nothing socially, that brought us to where we are. Parallel to this in my thinking is that there was no investment in public security and in the police during this time [since 1980]. The Military Police and Civil Police did not keep up with the development and growth of organized crime. There was no leadership or an objective interest in the police developing themselves not only in the use of weapons but also in police work, in the qualifications of the police officer—in his preparation, matters of salary, and outfitting of the police.

Question: The federal government seems to have decided to invest money in the Federal Police in the past few years. What is being done in Rio de Janeiro?

Beltrame: The federal government invested money in the Federal Police, but it's difficult to compare the Federal Police with the state police forces. Today, the Federal Police has a contingent of 12,000 or 13,000 men. It's is a small force, and it's easy to invest in it. The competence of the Federal Police is only for federal crimes. The state police have all the rest. Here in Rio, we are mainly replacing equipment. Vehicles here have to swerve out of the way of a cigarette butt to avoid a blowout. We have put 1,335 new vehicles on the streets. The communications system is such that today we can speak with one another. Before we couldn't. The control center has two hundred cameras. When I started, there were sixty. In all this, with respect to equipment, we are giving a little more dignity to the police, because to the extent that the police officer wears a dirty uniform or rides around in a beat-up car, he absorbs this. We invested a little in improving this image. We have to deal with an Achilles tendon here, which is the question of salaries. The police earn very little. The states are all facing an economic crisis [left over] from the 1980s and 1990s. The states spend money badly; they do not invest well, and the Civil Police and Military Police are lagging in terms of salary. While we cannot correct this, we are going after other things. Rio Card provides transportation for the police, and we are investing in two hospitals for police and their families.[3]

We had to move up our project for a better-trained and qualified police as a result of the recent events and incidents that were publicized.[4] We were going to start this in October, but we are beginning now. All of the battalions are receiving training on how to approach and treat citizens. We are recycling all the battalions. There is training in the use of nonlethal weapons connected with the substitution of the assault rifle by the 40-caliber carbine, which is suitable for urban use. These are initial changes, but the big change is structure. We intend to initiate a major project to invest in camera technology for all of Rio de Janeiro. By 2010, we want to have a command-and-control center that divides Rio into twelve regional areas that will send all images there. And there is the project "All Police in the University," which is already under way in partnership with the Getúlio Vargas Foundation, where we intend to place Civil Police and Military Police in one training center.

This is our structural project for the long term. It is a big investment in technology and training of police. In the short term, it's recovering from the wreckage we found here with everything broken down and without any equipment worthy of use by the police. And we have to get police units up to strength. We are short twelve thousand or thirteen thousand men. We didn't have police entrance examinations; we didn't give importance to or admit new police recruits. We are very much undersized in the number of police per inhabitant.[5]

Question: PRONASCI is a new program for public security.

Beltrame: From my perspective, PRONASCI is a project that comes to the rescue. It is a vast program. It has within it more than ninety proposals that bring into alignment actions of all of the state secretaries. I know that Brazil still does not have a history of continual large social investments that have succeeded, but PRONASCI is the solution. It is a broadly conceived project—a project that attends to human dignity, that fosters development of human beings in all areas. It does not help to provide education if food is lacking. We have here a saying that "an empty sack doesn't stand." It does not help if today we invest in the Alemão complex by building large schools and children do not have food and a health clinic, are not able to get to school. In my understanding, we have to have combined actions of all of the state secretaries in the sense of making life worth living and developing actions in combination for the complete human being. If all the social dimensions were developed, public security surely would be in last place. Today, the situation is to the contrary: Because everything is in a state of disorder, everything falls into the lap of public security.

Question: What is being done to remove bad police officers?
Beltrame: This is a problem. I'll tell you about the obstacles. In Colombia, 15,000 police were removed, but Colombia did this at a time when the government had exceptional power. Who decided everything was the police commandant. It was, "I don't like you, and you're out, finished." In Brazil, we call this the "power of discretionary police authority," and it worked that way in Colombia. I remember when the Olympic Games were held in Sydney, they had some problems with police corruption. They established an ethics committee that had power to dismiss police who were not considered ethical. In Brazil, we cannot do this. We have the Constitution of the Republic, which guarantees among human rights the right of full defense. This right of full defense exists as much in administrative law as it does in a judicial process of criminal law. In a year and a half, I removed more than 350 police, but with their right of full defense guaranteed. There were 50 Civil Police officers and 300 Military Police, but respecting for all the right to a full defense. We had to prepare the charges, and this is very bureaucratic. To file all these charges, we have the internal investigation police.

When there is a deviation from correct conduct, I might want to expel the police officer. But then we have the obstacles that in truth are not obstacles, because it is necessary to have the right of defense. Even in the case of homicide, we do not have the right to expel a police officer without going through this process. This is the way it is in Brazil. Legal procedures take time. It's enough to remember the accident that caused the sinking of the *Bateau Mouche* in which so many people died at the end of the 1980s. The judgment on the case only was given at the end of last year [in 2007].[6]

It's the obligation of the state to guarantee human rights. I have to guarantee human rights. My problem is that, as I see human rights here in Rio de Janeiro, they come to us through a lens of forty years ago. I know the United Nations' view of human rights was that the state is the villain, that it does not allow people to speak and act freely. It's just that today, it is no longer the state that does not allow people to speak. The villains today are small groups of people who do not know the laws, do not know the state. We have codes of law. We have to obey the laws. These people, they do not know the laws; they do not know the state. They do not even know what the state is. There are people here who have engaged in crime for four generations. I don't know if you saw on television or in the newspapers how they say, "Here it's us. It is we who give the orders here." That is their cultural ethos, and this in effect brings conflict. But our obligation is to defend human rights. The police officer, when he goes up the hill, nobody orders him to kill anyone. But also, our police do not have to die. They have to defend themselves. They cannot let themselves be killed.

Question: What do you say about the fact that the bandidos know beforehand that the police are coming? Shouldn't you warn the residents about an impending operation so they can leave?

Beltrame: They know that the police are coming in an operation from the simple fact of seeing a police convoy on its way. The ideal would be to warn children and the larger population so that they can get away from the danger. But we have to act with the maximum secrecy or we will miss the opportunity. We are acting within careful guidelines in each of these actions to minimize the risk of killing innocent people.[7]

Question: Many people believe the police themselves supply weapons to the bandidos. Today one can trace police weapons and ammunition. Is there a program in Rio de Janeiro to stop the police from trafficking in arms?

Beltrame: The cycle of illegal transfer of weapons is not complicated [and is] a very old practice here in Rio de Janeiro, because formerly people kept guns at home The law that regulates the use of guns only dates from 1992. It is only since that date that control has existed over the stock of guns. Behind all of it is clandestine trade. In addition, we have arms trafficking from Bolivia and Paraguay. There are also illegal transfers from the armed forces. A fourth factor is that there are many illegally owned rifles. But there is also outsourcing on the part of criminals. It works this way: Some criminal group is going to undertake an action. It gets rifles from other areas—it rents the rifles or gets them on loan. This does not mean that the group does not have its own rifles, but when it undertakes an action, it always seems to have more rifles than it in fact owns. An example of this was last week when ten people died in Caxias. In that favela, you did not have ten or fifteen assault weapons, as there were on that day. Criminals from the Alemão complex were hidden there to take control of the area from a rival faction at night. When the police arrived, they found these people from the outside, and there were weapons from the outside.

Today, our police are tracing and controlling their own weapons. They know how many there are and if they are being illegally sold. What we need is control over our borders. That's the hitch, because we have 16,000 kilometers of land border and 7,000 kilometers of sea border. Because what we have in guns here inside [Rio state], we control. The underground market is very small, and the underground and criminal market is in old arms. We are even receiving ammunition stamped to be read with the naked eye. We can trace ammunition. Our problem is the underground market in weapons of the armed forces that are illegally sold that are already here, and the weapons that come from those two countries [Bolivia and Paraguay].

Question: What can be done about organized crime? For example, do you need special courts or new laws defining organized crime?
Beltrame: We need special courts for organized crime. We need specialized police to combat it. Here in Rio de Janeiro, we need a very large police force to have police presence on the streets. And we need to improve the quality of the armed forces, not so the armed forces will come to provide security in the states but so the armed forces can do their part on the borders—on land, in the air, and at sea. Today, the armed forces, following the example of the state police, use equipment that needs to be scrapped. To the extent that we give greater importance to the role of the armed forces on our borders, this is going to be reflected within [Brazil]. I have no doubt about this. But today we are in a phase in which we have to restore the police to full strength to start to combat crime.

Organized crime does not exist here in Rio de Janeiro. People have to know how to differentiate. Organized crime is silent crime. Organized crime is the illegal flight of foreign exchange, money laundering, tax evasion, money going abroad. It's white-collar crime practiced by big businessmen and by multinational companies that illegally transfer money out of Brazil. It is money that is transferred abroad that could be used here as investment in the police and social investment. The big drug-boss type does not exist here. You can have them, but they are few. You might arrest one or two in five years. Crime here is very fragmented. It is people killing one another to control a drug point for the sale of marijuana for 300 or 400 *reais*. We don't have organized crime here. The organized crime here is the militia. This is a tyrannical, bandido criminal organization. We are starting to get on top of this, and are going after these people, and that is what you are now seeing.

Question: What are your plans for community policing?
Beltrame: From my point of view, there is a simple answer. Community policing is the ideal program. It's police in the community, the police

nearby. But today we cannot put the police in a place where they are exposed, where the situation is inflamed. I cannot today send police out walking a beat, doing community policing in the Alemão complex. It's a fundamental requirement for community policing that it be in a region that has been—here I'm using an expression I don't like—pacified. Meaning, that you do not have any criminal presence—not militias or drug traffickers—because this is a situation where community policing has a basis. This basis is an exchange. The resident can go to the police officer and tell him something, orient him, and also the contrary. Today, I cannot put a police station in an area where the community does not feel secure, where there is fear, and if someone approaches a police officer, the drug dealer comes asking, "What were you doing there? What did you want there?"The last place we put a police station was Batan. We were able to do this because the community provided a guarantee. They came here with more than five hundred signatures. The police live there. They have one person who is an army officer. The community turned the Residents' Association over to them. Today, when any criminal cell tries to enter the community, the police battalion is warned, and it acts immediately. Where conditions are very violent, it does not work to put in community policing. We would expose the police to being killed without the community getting the police work that it deserves.

In the curriculum, the matrix of courses for police completing their training now includes community policing. Before it was not there. Today, all police leave their training program prepared to do community policing. The police officer has to be good in his police work. He has to feel good about himself. He has to wear a good uniform, be well fed and well rested and, without question, well paid. This improvement is going to be not only for police working in the community, but for all police. As to preparation for community policing, today every police officer who is being trained has it. The police officer I want is the officer on duty at his post and who, in the two days he has off, can remain at home taking it easy with his family on the first day and on the second can take a refresher course, even through the Internet, and then return to his battalion. It's just that given what he earns, he cannot do this. He has to find a second job.

The police institutions here in Rio have 50,000 men. It's not easy. Control is not easy, and the pressure is great. We also have our problems. If you compare [the Rio de Janeiro police] with the police of London or the United States, as well paid and as well fed as they are, yet there in London, a Brazilian was shot six times in the face by the police.[8] If this were to happen in Rio de Janeiro, heaven help us! The press would jump all over us.

Henrique Oliveira Vianna, PRONASCI Coordinator: A Discussion with Maria Helena Moreira Alves and Philip Evanson, July 2008

Officer Henrique Oliveira Vianna of the Civil Police was assigned to the National Program of Public Security with Citizenship (PRONASCI) as one of four coordinators in Rio de Janeiro. His responsibilities included working with state police and municipal guard units. One of PRONASCI's important administrative innovations was the establishment of the Cabinet for Integrated Municipal Management (GGIM), with representatives of the federal, state, and local government working together to select and develop PRONASCI projects. In addition, while working as a GGIM coordinator, Officer Oliveira Vianna was named undersecretary for human rights for the municipality of Niteroi in 2009, with responsibility to oversee construction of a Human Rights Clinic, an example of a federal government–municipal government partnership under PRONASCI.

Question: How do you view PRONASCI?

Officer Oliveira Vianna: PRONASCI is exactly this: It is security with citizenship, unlike the programs that were established in a very fragmented manner because they were either for security or citizenship. PRONASCI was created to implement the part of citizenship. It's easy to understand, but very difficult to do. PRONASCI also has something very important: significant investment by the federal government for the Civil Police, Military Police, the Fire Brigades of the Military Police, municipal guards, and prison guards with low salaries to take training programs in public security and human rights. Police officers receive a scholarship for twelve months and take a sixty-hour course. What PRONASCI does is improve the qualifications of someone who is already a police officer.

The heritage of the police in Brazil is the legacy of its authoritarian and, at times violent role, because it was always a force acting on behalf of the state. The real, true, and operative idea of the "citizen police officer" is far from the historic trajectory of the police in Brazil. The police were always an armed force of the state, disposed to attend to the interests, and even to the caprices, of our officials. Making the transition from an authoritarian police force to a citizen police force is a process that goes to the root of the problem and involves questions of education and training. Education only fulfills its part when behavior changes. It does not help much to have brilliant ideas, brilliant thinkers, if behavior doesn't change.

In changing behavior, I think PRONASCI can contribute, because it is going to make itself felt in the three spheres of government: the federal government, the state government, and the municipal government. It brings several things together. It is not restricted exclusively to security but brings together integrated social actions. It is a program that will serve the federation, but only in those states that sign an agreement. And [it will serve] the states that have an agreement, but not all municipalities—only those municipalities that [also] sign an agreement. And for the municipalities that have an agreement, [it will] not [serve] all areas—only the areas or neighborhoods that the GGIM chooses. It is important to keep these objectives in mind, because when the time comes to make an evaluation, we have to evaluate with reference to what was proposed. Brazil's problems cannot be resolved in two or four years. For those who know the problems, there has to be a group of special strategies.

Question: Will PRONASCI recruit police?

Oliveira Vianna: PRONASCI will not be involved in recruiting police. Not yet. But it will help to improve the police. As for the Military Police, a large number of their personnel are recruited in the communities, because the level of required education for entering the corporation is basic education [i.e., through the ninth grade]. This is the education that a large number of the police have. Becoming a police officer is a profession they can hope to have. This creates another problem: a person from the community overseeing or proceeding against another who is his equal, either in ethnicity or by social stratification; one person checking on and proceeding against someone equal to him. It is a way to control poor people and protect the free use of goods of those who are well off, of the wealthy. The "haves" controlling the "have-nots." The police end up being used to keep poor people separate from rich people so that the wealthy can use their patrimony safely. This is a distorted idea, but it's what we've lived with historically.

Question: How has PRONASCI been proceeding? Are there priorities?

Oliveira Vianna: In the first phase of PRONASCI, some actions were prioritized—for example, to make sure that the municipal guards understand that they deserved to receive the *bolsa formação*. Another priority is making financing available [to police] for a home. In another action, Brasília offered us a design for a building that would house the GGIM with a situation room to keep us informed and to follow crises, an auditorium to interact with the community, a camera system for monitoring. But not all municipalities received such a project, which does not signify that they lack physical space for the GGIM.

Question: How can public security reform with citizenship proceed in Rio de Janeiro, where there is so much violence?

Oliveira Vianna: At this time in Rio de Janeiro, where the police are received with bullets, with explosives, and where people often are killed by bandidos' bullets that are intended for the police, we have a very special situation, and we need to develop a strategy based on respect for human rights. The police on the front line, the police of the tactical group, must also have this vision. Evidently, when a police officer is on duty, he is going to employ all means necessary to defend himself. But he cannot have the elimination of the adversary as a principle of conduct, because it is going to lead him down the road to a summary execution, which is not correct in a democratic state based on the rule of law. We have to intensify actions of intelligence gathering and enhance the prestige of distance learning. The courses in this area are difficult, but we are proceeding. Also, we need to strengthen intelligence operations by having a defined and clear objective so that actions may be more surgical to avoid the problem of stray bullets. Where there is the cache of arms, where are they hidden? The police don't know. They undertake operations and invasions every day without having a clear objective, not knowing where people can be found, the location of stashed weapons, or the things they have to prevent. It might take five years to study an area well, but as a result, if the operation is well done, it has a greater chance of producing results while minimizing the bad effects on innocent populations and [of being] done in accord with the democratic rule of law.

There is some skepticism about PRONASCI on the part of police professionals. At first, they saw an opportunity to buy new equipment: a new bulletproof vest, vehicles, and so forth. But we have to hear what they say and to design community policing that will accord with reality. We are far from the pattern of community policing in other countries. For example, in the Japanese pattern, a precinct station can be located in the home of the police officer, and his wife will register incidents when he is out on the street. If we did this in Rio, his house would be machine-gunned. In Rio, we have the police officer who is in combat the whole time when he is not off duty.

The police of Rio de Janeiro have to be heard so we can develop a model of community policing that accords with the reality that the police are living—as, for example, when the commander says, "In my area this is not going to work." We can accept that it is not going to work today, but we need to have an objective toward which we should work. Otherwise, someone might decide that in his area community policing is not going to work and will continue buying bulletproof vests and heavy weapons and might think, "Let's continue with everything in the same way."

The police are tired of seeing a colleague die only for doing his job. When a police officer sees a colleague being shot, hit by a volley of automatic-rifle fire, he starts to think: "I do not want to be that colleague who died on yesterday's shift." He goes out to the street with the instinct to survive clearly evident. He prefers to fire first and ask questions after and then, later, to be able to respond in an administrative process because he is alive instead of dead on the last shift. It's a worrying situation. This is my opinion after twenty years of police work in Rio de Janeiro. This is a conscious or unconscious sentiment that dominates the mind of many police officers in Rio de Janeiro. It's not that the training course did not teach us how to approach situations. It's not the course of our dreams, but it taught us how to do our job. But when the police officer is out on the street, he sets the manual aside and has his finger on the trigger because he wants to live. For this reason, the policy of public security is going to have to be bold, because the man in the uniform needs help. Our society has been made a little sick with the culture of fear. Perhaps the program ought to foresee inclusion of psychological help for the police professional who faces the questions of life, death, violence, threats to family, and corruption every day. There is no reasonably good or even a medium-level program of psychological help for police.

The police have always and everywhere been the armed branch of the state. This has been true since the thirteenth century in England. But the transition from the policy of the police serving as the armed branch of the state to a citizen police has already begun in Rio de Janeiro. A good number of police already have absorbed this idea to a certain degree in their police training. But the reality is so hard and naked that this training in practice disappears on the street as if by magic, at the snap of the fingers. What interests me in a confrontation is my survival. Let his mother cry, not mine.

Question: The police professional, then, is an oppressed individual?

Oliveira Vianna: In fact, the totality of this situation in Rio de Janeiro makes the police officer an oppressed human being. He is badly paid; he generally comes from the deprived communities; and he has to be a psychologist, an anthropologist, a sociologist and to know well the activities of his profession in technical terms, and his salary and equipment are that of someone who is in a situation of an oppressed individual. For that reason, PRONASCI includes programs that help [police officers] acquire a home. The police professional urgently needs a program such as PRONASCI.

Question: Many charges have been leveled that elite BOPE units enter communities firing from the Big Skulls and playing rap music with lyrics such as, "I'm going to kill you; I'm going to steal your soul." Can you prohibit the playing of this music?

Oliveira Vianna: This music can be stopped. We can say that it's against the instructions of PRONASCI that [the BOPE] enter a poor community playing this music and threatening the population. But it's complicated for us in PRONASCI because we are the Ministry of Justice. We are the power of the federal government, and there are limits on federal power. In truth, only the governor and state secretary of public security can give these instructions to police units under the control of the state government. The Constitution of 1988 states this. The Brazilian judiciary determined that the state governments have competence and responsibility for public security, not the federal government or the municipality.

Question: Now that we have PRONASCI, which favors community policing, is the police view of violence changing?

Oliveira Vianna: If bullets could solve the problem of security in Rio de Janeiro, we would have already solved everything, because so many have been fired. It's not by firing guns that we will solve the problem of security in Rio. It is not acceptable that a police officer goes into a community shooting, making and promoting violence. There has to be methodical action to reduce conflict; the police cannot be the instrument to exacerbate conflict. It cannot be that way because people are living in hell. The child cannot go to school; the father goes to work, and you do not know if he is going to return; the family lives in fear that bullets will come through the walls of the house, depending on the material of the wall, and they are alive only by the grace of God. The police cannot make the conflict worse. Police thinking has to change. The police have to study human rights, the history of slavery and of runaway slaves in Brazil, the violence that is a legacy of slavery and of the slaveocrat aristocracy that used violence not only against the slaves and, later, against free blacks but also against poor whites. This is all connected. If the black is a snitch, he stays on good terms with his master. From this, we have a historical connection with the tremendous corruption of Brazilian society that persists and that consists not of the exchange of money but of the exchange of favors. It is a terribly corrupt connection that is much used as a bridge to political positions. Today in Rio de Janeiro, there is a very strong connection between public employment, politics, and organized crime.

Question: How do you choose a community where PRONASCI will intervene and be present?

Oliveira Vianna: Who chooses the community where PRONASCI enters is not the coordinator of the program or the Ministry of Justice. It is the GGIM, but with orientation by the ministry in the sense that it will be a community with much conflict and tarnished by a reputation for crime. What will be done varies. There are communities where it is recognized that the police have to enter first. Then it depends on how the police are received. You cannot think about programs such as Women of Peace as the first action. For example, there are communities where you have an estimated two hundred young men armed to defend the points where drugs are sold. They are armed not only with automatic rifles but also with different types of weapons to defend their drug-selling points. Either they allow the state to enter peacefully or, if they greet the police with bullets, then they can expect a strong reaction.

After this, you enter with the social program. Besides the Women of Peace, we have the creation of secure urban spaces with areas for sports, leisure, and culture. We have a study revealing that, in cities whose unemployment levels are high but where activities in the areas of leisure, culture, and sports are reasonably good, the incidence of crime is less. These new data show that, more important in terms of criminality and more important than unemployment are the levels of culture, leisure, and sports that a city has. Even with high unemployment, if the city is strong in these areas, it is able to solve many problems of young people. This is even true for cities that do not have high unemployment but have little culture, leisure, or sports, which still have higher levels of crime. This is very important because it shows that PRONASCI is on the right road. The idea is to enter with the social programs and not withdraw, not stop the program, and also guarantee that the security forces do not leave. The program is also social. It considers the cultural environment, such as having centers with access to computers, places to read, areas for sports. And the security forces have to be trained to act within the law, to use force only in self-defense and not to use violence as a model for routine, daily behavior.

Question: How does PRONASCI survive the changes in government that occur when new administrations are elected?

Oliveira Vianna: PRONASCI has to be a program of the state. It cannot be just a program of the Lula government or of Governor Sérgio Cabral. It has to be a policy of the state with its continuity guaranteed or it won't work. It's a policy directed toward public interests, collective interests. The policy can be modified in the sense of changing it according to the needs of the moment, but not by dismantling it.

Public Security Expert and Staff Researcher for the National Congress of Brazil: A Discussion, August 2008

As concerns with public security, human rights, and police behavior have grown in Brazil, so has the number of experts researching these subjects. The following interview with one expert focuses on the police of Rio de Janeiro. The interview describes a closed corporatist spirit within police forces and police resistance to criticism, even self-criticism, which many police believe will further damage their reputation. The interview points to connections between the police and organized crime and offers reasons for the lack of popular support for the police in favela communities. The expert spoke under the conditon of anonymity to protect his identity.

Question: The police have a bad image and resist reforms coming from the outside.

Expert: The police don't want to divulge anything that denigrates the police corporation. They are more concerned about keeping the internal corporate spirit intact than about improving the external image of the police. The commanders mistakenly think that punishing police lapses and divulging the punishments will worsen the image of the police. Since public opinion has a bad image of the police, the situation is exactly the contrary. If they would punish and admit to the errors of bad police officers, they would improve the image of good police officers and of the commanders.

I'll give you an example. A commission of the [National] Congress completed an investigation of about 1,500 firearms made in Brazil that were sold to the Military Police and ended up in the hands of bandidos. Congressman Raul Jungmann, who was charged with preparing the report of the Commission on Firearms of the National Congress, then made its contents known to the police as an example of collaboration between the government and the Military Police. The [commission] forced the arms makers to admit that they had sold the arms to the Military Police of Rio de Janeiro. These 1,500 weapons, among them fifty automatic rifles made for use in war, were sold to the Military Police of Rio and ended in the hands of the bandidos.

In the meeting, they expressed much thanks. The Military Police commandant was most grateful for the research. Then, the following day, an official statement was given to the press: "What they are saying is a libel. Why? Where is the proof that the weapons were diverted illicitly? Obviously, these rifles were stolen from our glorious police forces." In São Paulo, there was the same negative reaction. The Military Police thanked Deputy Jungmann when they received the study but afterward declared to the press that "the information was not correct," which is an absurdity. Why? Because the idea prevails that what is wrong cannot become public because the image is already too bad and something else would make it even worse. Two difficulties exist: first, corporatism; and second, the "don't wash your dirty laundry in public" idea. In fact, this attitude comes from the military regime, when any criticism was considered hostile to the institution, and contrary to the democratic principle in which an order to punish subordinates who do something wrong strengthens confidence in the institution. Our police forces were not democratized, and their norms and principles still keep much of the authoritarianism of the dictatorship.

The interesting thing is that, even though they did not publicly recognize the facts tracing the illicit transfer of weapons, the Military Police of Rio in practice got better at controlling its officers' weapons. Another important action was taken against the criminal transfer of ammunition. It is now possible to do this because the new Statute of Disarmament law requires the stamping and numbering of ammunition sold to the armed forces and police in Brazil. During the voting on this new law, there was an effort to require that all ammunition produced and sold in Brazil, even for civilians, be stamped, but that proposal was not approved. It was approved only for soldiers and police officers, which, however, was a great advance.

But the problem is that only ammunition sold to the police of the state of Rio de Janeiro is being stamped and numbered because of insistence by the police. The ammunition factories are not following the law, because they do not stamp ammunition sold to the military and to the other twenty-six Brazilian states. But at least in Rio, one can trace the ammunition used by bandidos and discover which police officer is selling ammunition to organized crime. That is a great advance. It is much easier to trace ammunition, first, because although bandidos run away with their weapons, the used shells stay on the ground and can be collected; and second, because a gun may be used for years, and the ammunition always needs to be replenished. The trade in munitions becomes more lucrative—hence, the resistance of many governments, including that of U.S. President George Bush, to accept stamping numbers on bullets.

As for gun control, although the Rio police publicly deny involvement with the drug dealers, internally they are acting to combat it. They are even testing a new method of control through the fingerprinting of police. When a police officer receives a gun and ammunition, he leaves a fingerprint register for the weapon and quantity of ammunition, which has to be returned at the end of the workday. This makes it impossible, for example, to take a gun in another person's name. This practice is still going through a test phase. For example, a police officer takes a certain weapon to perform his assigned tasks for the day. He leaves his fingerprint as a guarantee of the weapon and the type and quantity of ammunition that was provided. When his work shift ends, he has to return that weapon and all of the unused ammunition. In this way, there is control. If he receives thirty bullets and returns fifteen, he has to account for the difference. This, then, is very interesting. It is an instance of the only police force in Brazil that is exercising internal control over weapons and ammunition. This means that, internally, Secretary Beltrame is trying to impove control. Erroneously, this fact has not been divulged in an effort to keep the issue of the criminal transfer of weapons from being debated in public

The police in Rio de Janeiro have defended the policy of confrontation based on the argument that the bandidos in Rio are very well armed. The financial power of the drug trade permits the bandidos to buy many weapons and ammunition, including those made abroad. The police are not going to admit that an illicit transfer of weapons of war is being made from a corrupt police force to criminals, because that would mean that organized crime in Rio de Janeiro could be the best-armed group in Brazil. The argument of the police goes like this: Because organized crime is very well armed, it is necessary to defeat it militarily so that afterward the state can make itself present in the favelas with socioeconomic and educational programs. I even agree with this, but the error is to attack without warning, attempting to surprise drug gangs in the favelas which brings about conflicts that result in the deaths of many innocent people. The error is in the idea of exterminating the bandidos and not eradicating criminality.

The drug gangs protect themselves in the midst of a poor population, as the Vietcong [did in Vietnam]. If you attack without warning, you're going to have a massacre, as has happened. The population "protects" the bandidos either because it has greater fear of them and disdain for corrupt police, or because it is forced to collaborate with the terrorist power that the drug trade exercises over them, or because the people know that after an attack, the police will leave, and whoever collaborates with the police is going to be killed by the drug traffickers.

Question: But the policy of confrontation has led to the death and wounding of innocent people.

Expert: The governor is going to say, "It's inevitable. It's inevitable." I would look at the other side of the question. In São Paulo, police did not invade favelas by surprise. The police warned them, "We are going to invade and occupy the favela." What happened? The bandidos fled from the favela. So the difference is that the [Military Police] of São Paulo do not want a confrontation. They want to occupy land and remove the bandidos. They take charge of terrain and stay there. What is the problem of the policy of confrontation? The police enter; they confront; they kill many people, even innocent people; and afterward, they leave. The police are not able to remain in this hostile environment without the aid of the population and without being surrounded by bandidos. In São Paulo, they remain as a permanent force, protecting social investments in health, education, professional training, sports, and so on, providing police protection. Gradually, the assault police—which is what we have in Rio de Janeiro—are replaced by community policing, as is being done in São Paulo.

Question: Why isn't this happening in Rio de Janeiro?

Expert: The police high command is accustomed to saying that the police do not permanently occupy the favelas, as they do the rest of city, because they "do not have a sufficient number of officers, because there are 968 favelas in Rio [and] more than a million people living under the yoke of organized crime." This is a half-truth. In truth, one reason is that the police in Rio do not have the support of the favela population. It is a highly complicated matter for the police to remain in a favela. The favela resident knows only two types of police officers: those who are linked to organized crime and who extort, intimidate, and kill and whom the residents regard with fear, disdain, and hatred; and the "exterminator" police who come into the favela to kill bandidos and end up killing many innocent people. For these, they also have fear and hatred.

Good police officers who go into the favela to protect the population and arrest bandidos are lacking. In general, the police treat the poor people of the favelas so brutally that the population does not welcome the police as saviors. They receive them as enemies, as even worse than the drug dealers. The drug traffickers are from the community and are brutal only toward their rivals in selling drugs and toward residents who collaborate with the police or interfere with their business. With the population in general, they are not brutal, because they need support—or, at least, silence. The police come from outside. They bring death, destruction, extortion. They are the enemy when they should be the ally, the protector.

A large part of this police force is part of organized crime in Rio. Look at the composition of organized crime in Rio de Janeiro: the Third Command, the Red Command, the Friends of Friends, and sectors of the police. Normally, when the police are going to invade a certain favela, the local organized-crime commanders already know because their police accomplices have already informed them. What is happening in the Alemão complex? Alemão is the high command of organized crime. It is the most difficult place to be taken. Sixteen favelas constitute the Alemão complex. Concentrated there is the greatest fire power of organized crime. You can say that they [the police] began the war against the drug gangsters in the most difficult place. This is not a logical way to proceed. It is not Cartesian. You should begin in the easiest place and go forward occupying space and growing stronger little by little. Why did they begin there? To avenge the killing of two policemen—meaning it was not a strategy; it was not a security policy. It was simply a reaction. It was like this: "They killed two police, and this is not acceptable." It was an act of revenge so the police would not be discredited.

The police ended up having an attitude similar to that of the bandidos—a macho attitude of revenge, of saving their honor—and not a rational policy of standing up to crime. The justification of the police for the invasion was "You have to maintain the image. If we do not take our revenge, we are going to be discredited. The bandidos are going to feel all-powerful because they did this and nothing happened. And afterward, they are going to discredit our side. Thus, we have to react." Of course, there has to be a response, but a rational, intelligent one based on a strategy, not on being reactive only by invading. It was a mistaken policy. Why? First, they badly evaluated the power of organized crime and the lack of support for the police by the population. They went in, killed many more innocent people than they imagined, and did not smash organized crime. To want to avenge the death of a police officer is not a strategy. It is an emotional act—at best, a retaliation that only leads to the increase of violence and that does not isolate the bandidos, who continue to have popular support because innocent people are victims of shootouts. Second, the actions fell into a quagmire, became bogged down. The police entered and did not manage to stay. They did not remain inside because they were unable to occupy the favela and were obliged to remain on the outside, surrounding the favela. It is sad to recognize, but the drug

traffickers won this clash, because they are still there. Third, the government has PAC [Program for the Acceleration of Growth], which means public works construction. It is a program of the left. We always said that there
have to be social projects, infrastructure, basic sanitation, health, education,
and so forth. The PAC is being implemented in Alemão. The government of
the state of Rio said, "We took Alemão. We pacified Alemão. We guarantee
security, and now PAC is being developed there." What is the truth? They
invaded Alemão, they took control of Alemão briefly, but they were not able
to stop the drug trafficking there. The drug traffickers continue to dominate
Alemão, and the soldiers are there only encircling, surrounding. Eventually
they [the police] go up the hill, enter, and exchange gunfire, but they do not
remove the traffickers. It is said that the government negotiated with the
drug dealers. They won't admit this. Some say that they are trying to do
what was done in Medellín [Colombia], except that in Medellín, the drug
dealers really were removed, and afterward the government did social projects and infrastructure. The truth is the state government in Rio was not
able to do this and ended up negotiating with the traffickers to build and
realize the PAC projects.

It's the drug traffickers who are providing the necessary security for
PAC. This is the truth. Then what do you have in Alemão? The government
is making social investments in PAC projects: in health care, transportation
and a cablecar line, and education with the permission of, and under the
security provided by, the drug traffickers. What is the result going to be? Is
it going to improve people's lives? It will. Is it going to end drug tafficking?
No. In fact, the traffickers are going to come out of this much strengthened
because they are the ones who are making it possible for these things to
happen. They are giving total support and security for the PAC projects.
This means the total defeat of the policy of security. It may be that this
really will improve health care and education, but it is being done with the
stamp of approval and protection of the drug traffickers, and it is going to be
its great trump card in winning the support of the local population.

Why don't the police go in and stay? Because a good part of the police
are accomplices of the drug traffickers, and because the police do not manage to get the support of the favelados because the policy of exterminating
people and not respecting the rights of residents prevails. In Rio de Janeiro,
we had a Civil Police chief named Hélio Luz who used to say that 80 percent of the police of Rio de Janeiro are accomplices of crime, working for
organized crime. If this is true, it's like a war in which 80 percent of your
soldiers work for the enemy. You are defeated in advance. For that reason, I
think that without a cleansing of the police, we are going to get nowhere. A

great portion of the arms used by the drug traffickers was acquired through corrupt police, as the congressional committee investigating arms trafficking revealed.

Question: Wasn't it Hélio Luz who stopped kidnapping in Rio de Janeiro?

Expert: Yes, it was the only thing he managed to do. He put honest police officers to work on this matter. Finally, he was able to declare, "Now, in the Anti-kidnapping Police Unit, there is no more kidnapping." A large number of the kidnappings were being done by the very police of the Anti-kidnapping Unit. Or the police would discover a kidnapping, negotiate with the kidnappers, and divide the ransom. All of this was explained by the chief of the Civil Police himself of the period [1995–1998].

There is a report about arms taken from bandidos in Pernambuco. In it, one can sees that the arms apprehended by the Federal Police are excellent weapons, expensive weapons, the contrary of weapons apprehended by the Civil Police and Military Police, which are all old. Both the federal and state police seized arms from the same population of the same state, but the results were different. Why? Because the good arms that the state police seized were not delivered to the corporation. Either they remained with the police themselves, or they were sold back to the bandidos. It's similar to drugs. Bandidos are arrested, and the drugs they are transporting are seized; afterward, the bandido is sold his liberty, and his drugs. That is, the bandido has to buy back his own drugs to be set free. The same thing happens with guns.

The question of corruption thus is not a small one; it is something parallel to police work. It is basic. If corruption is not confronted in an efficient and total manner, it prevents police reform; it prevents having any policy of real, efficient public security. And there is another fact. Social policy in the favelas is advancing, and organized crime is stronger than ever, which is contrary to common sense, an enormous contradiction. It ought to be the opposite: to win the support of the population by bettering its conditions of life and by isolating and expelling the drug trafficker.

The federal government through PRONASCI is applying a lot of pressure on the state governors to reform the police and to implement a policy of preventive, investigative police work, not only repression. PRONASCI has plenty of money, and the government is making the democratization and modernization of the police a condition for receiving it. For example, the Ministry of Justice forced the police of Rio to exchange the AR-15 rifle and FAL assault weapon, which are weapons of war, for carbines that allow greater control over gunfire, reducing the number of innocent victims of stray bullets. They are also forcing all of the police forces of Brazil to exchange 9-mm pistols for 40-caliber pistols. The first pistol uses ammunition that perforates—that is, it can pass through victims and reach innocent people. The 40-caliber pistol uses ammunition that stops at impact—that is, the bullet stays in the victim, not causing harm to others. It is more appropriate for the police to use in urban areas.

Question: But the police are going to say that the bandidos of Rio de Janeiro have weapons of war.

Expert: It's true, and the guns are bought from the police themselves. The police are prisoners of a military, not a police, vision of fighting crime. If the bandidos have weapons of war, they feed a rising spiral of violence. It's as if a war were much easier. It would be a question of "surround and annihilate." But between the police and the bandidos is a population that is forced to support the latter. Either the police win over this population—start to respect it, to protect it—or they are not going to stay in the favela to do their police work. Either they have the support of the community, or they are going to be defeated.

The police do not warn a favela that they intend to invade because, on the one hand, there is a vision of exterminating the bandidos. On the other hand, if they really were to enter the Alemão complex, they might not be able to leave. The bandidos are so well armed, and because they have infiltrated the police force, they know beforehand everything that is going to happen. That is, they know the police better than the police know them. The drug traffickers have many men inside the police force. They know the firepower the police bring. They know the capacity the police have. So we have these palliative ideas, such as sending in the National Security Force. Not being men from here in Rio de Janeiro, it is believed, they are not linked to corruption. It's just that not being men from here, they also do not know anything about Rio. You need knowledge; there has to be investigative work, the winning over of local public opinion. A friend told me about a conversation he had with a corporal of the National Security Force from Rio Grande de Sul. He asked, "How was your experience in Rio since you were acting in Rio as part of the [NSF]?" He worked directly with the Rio police. He answered, "Look, we have corruption in the police in Rio Grande do Sul. We know this. Eventually, it is exposed. At times, it's taken care of in-house. But this is a minority. In Rio, the honest police are the minority."

The police have two enemies. The least important is the bandido that he confronts. For the honest police officer, the more dangerous of the enemies are other police involved with crime. The honest police officer goes out on patrol with four or five police who are not honest. The honest officer is always afraid of being killed by police linked to trafficking, because if they are going to do some illicit deal, they kill the good officer so he cannot incriminate them. Afterward, it is made to look as if the good officer was killed by bandidos. He is provided a burial full of glory, with honors and so forth. So you can imagine how it is to work with colleagues who are working for the enemy. They live in panic; they live in stress; they have serious psychological problems. Many take refuge in religion and create evangelical groups to help one another. Normally, what do they do? They speak directly to their colleagues: "Look, I'm not going to get involved in this, but you can count on me. I won't inform against anyone. Don't kill me." This is the testimony of a police officer. I've heard similar statements from others. Being a police officer in Rio de Janeiro is terrible. You go out on the street fearing you will be shot in the back by your colleague. You live in panic.

If you might be part of a minority, it's very difficult. In the Civil Police, there is a mechanism that is efficient in preventing people from informing or criticizing: A district police chief can transfer a subordinate without providing a reason. If you're a critic or don't enter into the scheme of corruption, and your family lives and works in Rio de Janeiro, the police chief can transfer you at his pleasure to a distant city on the frontier with Minas Gerais. He ends your life as you have known it. Your wife will lose her job, and your children will have to change schools, or you will remain separated from your family permanently. A police officer told me this. She said, "This mechanism alone is enough to give almost total power to the chief"—meaning that he can transfer anyone who is against him. It is a personal act. He does not have to explain himself to anyone. The structure, as we have it, gives enormous power to whoever is at the top, and if whoever is in charge is corrupt, you have to obey.

So it is said, "The police are corrupt because they earn little." This is not true. Who earns more through corruption are the high-ranking officers, who have good salaries. The higher you are in the hierarchy, the more you receive in schemes of corruption. The traffickers pay 60 percent to the colonel, and it's less and less until you reach the soldier, who receives little. The higher you are in the hierarchy, the more you earn. The film *Elite Squad* [2007] shows this type of corruption in the high ranks of the police.

What makes corruption possible is the lack of oversight. Internal oversight is not enough. You have to have external control, an ombudsman, people with autonomy and independence to investigate. The internal police investigators in Brazil are appointed by the secretary of public security—

that is, by the police authorities. How, then, can the police be investigated? In Rio, the police officer goes out on assignment, and the commander does not have the slightest control over what he is doing. This parking space here, for example, is only allowed because the person parking the car pays the police officer who is assigned to the area and who permits him to park his car. If the local police are not paid off, they will not allow taxi stops to operate. Then, the first myth, "The police are corrupt in Rio because they earn little," is not totally true. The good police officers earn little. The bad police officer earns a lot. A salary is one thing; the various forms of corruption in which the police are engaged is another. And no one has any control whatsoever over them. This permits them to do as they wish. There is graft of every kind beyond sharing the profits many times with the chiefs of drug trafficking. You can see that it is going to be very difficult to control all of this. External control is what is lacking. Without this, we are going to get nowhere. We need a real internal investigation unit.

We also have the issue of the preparation of police which is bad. The courses are poor and very brief. They do not even learn how to fire guns. They fire a half-dozen rounds because ammunition is expensive, and the commander does not want to spend the money. After six months, they are assigned to go out on the streets without even knowing how to shoot. They have to learn how to fire on the streets, and many times they end up killing innocent people by mistake. Also, there is the issue of the weapons they use, which are not adequate.

In a training course, I heard a civilian instructor ask, "Suddenly you find yourself on the subway. It's 6:00 P.M., and the platform is full of people. You encounter criminal number one, for whom you are searching. You identify him. He also sees you and pulls out a gun. What do you do?" Everyone answered, "We shoot him." On a subway platform at 6:00 P.M.! Why? First, because they were not taught that you cannot put the lives of innocent people at risk in combating bandidos. Second, with their poor training, they do not know how to shoot and end up making victims of third parties. Third, their mentality is very macho; it's the same as the bandidos': an eye for an eye. If you kill a police officer, I'm going to come after you and kill one of you and then kill three more. It's the same mentality. That is, the police have not managed to differentiate themselves from the bandidos. Police are recruited from the same strata in which this culture exists. They have the same values. They want to kill. It's similar to a child saying, "If you hit me once, I'm going to hit you twice." In this case, with weapons of war in hand, they kill. Various [police officers] have said to me, "We took some courses, but when we finished, our superior officers told us, 'Ah, you did this course.

This is only theory. Now it's time to get real. Now you're going to learn to be real police officers. The rest is only talk for the journalist.'"

We have to have good training courses that are practical, from real life and not disconnected from real life: how to arrest a bandido, how to question a prostitute or an older person. But the principle is oversight. In the United States and other countries, video cameras are spread over areas where there are police to monitor their activities. Here, we don't. The police can go out on the street and do what they want. At times, they even organize holdups in neighborhoods to which they are not assigned. It's necessary to have control. We have to have technology adequate for control. It exists but is not used properly. The structure of the police force does not help.

I think the police high command wants to change this but does not know how. [Secretary] Beltrame wants to improve the police, but he is not able to do this. The mentality of the military regime—the Rambo model— prevails among the troops. At bottom, they think that this business of community policing, to spend time conversing with the people, is something for women, that it's social work. They think the real police officer has to be trained to kill, which is the vision of units considered the best police units. On the other hand, we have the corrupt sectors who collaborate with the bandidos. When they reach a favela, the bandidos, warned by their police accomplices, leave behind some weapons and drugs so the police will not be discredited and can go to the press and say that they apprehended so many guns and so many pounds of drugs. In reality, the bandidos already know when the police are going to arrive and are prepared.

The police have sectors so closely tied to organized crime that they know exactly what to do. When they need to arrest a certain bandido to satisfy public opinion, they know where he is, and they go there and arrest him. Also, when the government needs to show that it is being efficient, it knows exactly where the drug dealers and drugs are. The government needs the corrupt police because they are the only ones who know where to find the drugs and traffickers. Intelligence work independent of organized crime in Brazil almost does not exist. The government uses police who are linked to organized crime, who receive a great deal in exchange and pass along information to the government. And the police arrest certain bandidos so that they and the government will not be totally discredited. When a crime occurs that horrifies public opinion and leads to much pressure, the government responds by appealing to the police who know where the bandidos are because, honest police cannot solve the crime. It is the dishonest police who can solve the case. When a drug-trafficking chief is identified publicly, when his name is published in the press, public opinion pressure grows, and the government orders his arrest. The police go and arrest him. They know exactly where he is and do not even have to fire a gun. This is why almost all of the drug chiefs that have been identified by the press are in jail. But for each one, there are ten substitutes, and the dishonest police immediately make agreements with them—and with the government—to allow the drug business to function in exchange for the arrest of bandidos who are in the public eye. Organized crime continues to be strong in this area. When it is necessary to arrest a bandido, he is turned over to the police. The police are then owed one. It's a negotiation and a diabolical logic. This is why Hélio Luz, former chief of the Civil Police, said ironically, "The best police in the world are those of Rio de Janeiro, because they have an intimate relation with crime: When it is convenient to arrest a bandido, they go and do it."

So as to not end on a note of pessimism, the government of Rio recently initiated two initiatives within the model defended by the minister of justice. Using young, recently trained police officers who have not yet been captured by organized crime, they promoted the occupation of two favelas: Dona Marta and City of God (the latter made famous in the film of the same name). But before entering, they warned people of the occupation, and the bandidos fled. There was an occupation, and the police simultaneously began various initiatives to benefit the local population within the model of the community policing. These are still isolated initiatives, but if they succeed and are not sabotaged, as happened with other local community-policing experiences, it could signal the beginning of the substitution of an archaic, violent, and authoritarian model with a democratic and modern model of policing.

Antônio Carlos Carballo Blanco, Military Police Officer, Rio de Janeiro: A Discussion with Philip Evanson, September 2008

Lieutenant Colonel Antônio Carlos Carballo Blanco joined the Military Police in 1984 and left for a time in 2008 following an unsuccessful protest by the police of Rio de Janeiro to improve their working conditions and salaries. He returned to active duty in 2009 and was named commander of the Second Battalion of Military Police in Botafogo in January 2010. Lieutenant Colonel Carballo has been a leading proponent of community policing, having commanded a community policing program in the Cantagalo and Pavão-Pavãozinho favelas in the Zona Sul in 2000–2002. He was given the Botafogo command at a time when this middle-class area was suffering from an epidemic of street crime. Carballo proposed to install more surveillance cameras, put more police on the streets working in pairs and with police dogs, and work with community institutions such as churches and schools. The interview was conducted in September 2008, when Lieutenant Colonel Carballo had temporarily left the Military Police.

Question: People might want to know more about community policing as represented by the GPAE [Police Group in Special Areas]. You commanded a GPAE unit in Cantagalo and Pavão-Pavãozinho.

Lieutenant Colonel Carballo: I spent two years in Cantagalo and Pavão-Pavãozinho [2000–2002]. In the case of the GPAE, the rules are very simple. The principal rule is what I call "moral authority"—in the sense that the police officer be a police officer and not equal to the bandido. This is the first rule. We have adopted other rules in the process of building relationships with the community. For example, there are two rules of police work: the preservation of life, and the right of people to come and go. For this to occur, though, people cannot be circulating in the community armed. Another rule is not to tolerate illicit police behavior. The police officer has to be there not only to be an example, but also to mediate conflicts, to try to resolve problems that arise, and so on. And the rule when a crime occurs is that the officer has to act within the law, arrest within the law, take the person to the precinct station, assume the risks. Yet another rule has to do with not involving children in criminal practices.

I was even "reprimanded" because as a police officer, I was acting as a sort of community leader. What did I do? I tried to raise the expectations and demands of the community. I was acting as a facilitator between the government and the community, and when there were conflicts, I acted as a type of mayor. The merchants were causing problems because they kept their businesses open until 2:00 A.M. I brought them together. I prepared a document, and I signed it as an agreement made by the community in relation to the functioning of that business activity. It was entirely informal. The city government was not present. I had to do something, a sort of state within the state. For this reason, I had a problem with the city government. This initiative was seen as a threat. Within the thinking of occupying space to make it a laboratory for anti-welfare, anti-clientalistic practices, the city government saw a threat. In this context, the city government tried to discredit the work, saying that GPAE was involved in crime.

Another thing, between January and September 2000, there were ten violent deaths. I took command in September, and during two years we did not have one case of violent death or a case of a stray bullet or of people who were wounded. We managed to bring some benefits for young people, such as courses in computer use, a [language] laboratory for English and Spanish, the Espaço Criança Esperança.[9] The city government viewed all this, became worried about the loss of a political dividend and decided on a strategy of trying to discredit us by saying there was still drug trafficking. Of course, drug trafficking continues—it is a permanent challenge—but there were no violent deaths.

The great merit of the GPAE is that, contrary to other police programs, it fulfills the Constitution. Article 144 of the federal Constitution says that security is the duty of the state and the responsibility of everyone. The GPAE does this. It doesn't put people at risk, which runs contrary to the public security policies that have succeeded one another and that do not fulfill the Constitution. [Those policies] maximize exposing people to the high-risk weapons used by both sides. The worst thing is that the police play an important part in situations of conflict with high-powered weapons that threaten the lives of people and can destroy their patrimony. Their destructive power is very great. The GPAE tries to reduce dangers in the favela, which have a complex architectural layout. There is the possibility of great risk when any bullet is fired. When brick houses are hit, when powerful weapons are fired, it can lead to irreparable losses.

Community policing was constructed in the collective imagination and among the police as something social. Many people do not think that this is police work; they think that police work is arresting and shooting. I have a very simple definition of community policing: It is the application of a methodology for resolving problems with the participation of society. It is nothing more than this. The police are not going to use guns; they are going to apply a police methodology to solve problems. I always see the police officer as an administrator of emotions. Therefore, it is important that we have a sufficiently consistent and objective methodology with respect to the use of force. Community policing is a threat to clientalistic politics. It opens new perspectives, opens the possibility that even [among people with] minimal levels of formal education, a consciousness is constructed inside a community in relation to what citizenship and the rights of a person are.

Question: Is community policing possible in the Alemão complex?
Carballo: Mathematically, there are not enough police officers for the GPAE in Alemão. There are not enough people. If we had enough people, I think yes, we could do community policing. It is a limited vision to say it cannot be done. It is a vision that says we have to buy more armored cars, more guns. There are certain things that I still do not understand. Why

doesn't Brazil try to have a democratic transition in the police organizations? We have had progressive governments to do this under [President] Cardoso and [President] Lula.

Question: Can you speak a little about recent Brazilian history and the consequences for the police?

Carballo: In the 1970s, many things happened. If we take the period from 1955 to 1975, Brazil changed with a velocity unequaled in world history. Brazil changed from a society with typically rural characteristics into an industrial society. This brought about great changes in the cities. The public power was not prepared either in terms of infrastructure or in terms of demand for services. People began to occupy spaces that, given the topography of Rio de Janeiro, which is different from that of of São Paulo or Buenos Aires, are difficult to access. Also, it was still a period of military dictatorship in 1975. The focus of police action was to search for subversives and to prohibit people discontented with the regime from demonstrating. This distanced the police from the daily life of ordinary people.

In the 1980s, we didn't take full advantages of our opportunities. Of course, there were advances, but on balance, Rio de Janeiro went backward while other states, such as Minas Gerais and some in the northeast, caught the bus. Today, the GPAE is in Minas Gerais. Today in São Paulo, training for the Military Police has a yearlong community-policing course. I think we are going backward in Rio. No other police have the reputation that we have. Children are dying—an absurd thing. We have militias. This also might occur in other states, but not as it does in Rio de Janeiro.

Question: Didn't the number of homicides fall in São Paulo?

Carballo: I do not know the number of homicides in São Paulo. It's a big mystery. What I do know is that here in Rio de Janeiro, we are beginning to discover some new things—no, not new things, but new information. Rio de Janeiro has an average of 3,600 to 4,000 cases of people who disappear each year. These cases are not computed as homicides. We have information that at least 70 percent of these cases are homicides. Considering that the number of disappeared are not included, and without counting "acts of resistance" caused as a consequence of police action, and of other types of violent deaths that are not counted as homicides, in reality we are saying that Rio de Janeiro has 10,000 or 11,000 homicides per year. That is a lot, but it does not appear in the statistics. We need a type of external monitoring. I think this would be very good for our governing class. Some indicators demonstrate that mortality rates for young men age fifteen to twenty-four in Rio de Janeiro are comparable to those of a society at war.

Question: How should we see the issue of police reform today?

Carballo: I think that, in the question of police instruction today, it's important that you have someone from within [the police] who speaks. But the change has to come from the society. If left to the politicians, the tendency would be to reproduce the same logics, the same schemes, and the changes would not take place. Then it's important to bring together the people who are on the inside and the organized society to increase awareness. All this investment that is being made in training, in improving the qualifications of the police, is a good initiative. It is a fully realistic view of the poor quality of police training. But while this is important, it is also public and notorious that it is done in vain. Why? It is what I call axiological conflict, a conflict of values, a practice that collides with a theoretical model. It's as if you might be trained to develop certain abilities, but in practice the institutional culture leads you to other behaviors. All that investment that was committed in the sense of providing professional preparation to exercise that activity well ceases to exist in practice. The practice is something else. What prevails in practice is the policy of confrontation, or the policy of beating people up. So why did you learn the principles of human rights and community policing if the practice is leading you in another direction? It seems that these are contradictory things.

Question: There have been several films about the police, especially *Elite Squad*, which seem to have had a great impact. Even political leaders recommend that we see *Elite Squad*.[10]

Carballo: I participated in a televised roundtable discussion with the director of *Elite Squad* [José Padilha] in São Paulo. In a certain way, I think the film recycles the Sebastian myth.[11] It's the idea that we need a savior and that the savior is Captain Nascimento. The population applauds the film. The setting now is one of distrust, of uncertainty and despair. I find that the film signals the failure of institutions, on the one hand, and, on the other, the figure of someone above good and evil who is going to redeem us.

Chapter 8

Voices of Government Officials

President Luis Inácio Lula da Silva:
A Discussion with Maria Helena Moreira Alves
and José Valentin Palacios, July 2008

L uis Inácio Lula da Silva was born into a poor family in the backlands of the Brazilian northeast in 1945. The region was known for periodic and devastating droughts, and Lula has often spoken about how, as a child, he watched a favorite goat die of thirst in his arms. At seven, he migrated with his family to São Paulo, making the journey in the open cargo area of a truck. He learned to read at ten. Lula worked as a machinist in São Paulo and emerged as a trade-union leader and public figure at a time when industrial workers in São Paulo were carrying out a series of strikes in the late 1970s. In 1980, he helped organize the Partido do Trabalhadores (Workers' Party) and became its leader. He ran for president three times (1989, 1994, 1998) before he was elected in 2002 and reelected in 2006. As president, Lula has overseen significant social advances for workers and poor Brazilians, as well as robust economic development that has benefited all classes. At the same time, he has assumed a role as an international leader. During his second term as president, his public approval ratings have been nothing short of phenomenal, continually hitting record highs of 70 percent and above.

Nevertheless, public security has posed a tremendous challenge. The Lula government invested heavily in the Federal Police during his first term (2003–2006). Beginning in his second term in 2007, the government created PRONASCI as a way for the federal government to partner with the states and municipalities to improve public security. Lula has consistently sought a fresh start in public security policy and debate and urged people to set aside discussion about who is to blame for failings in public security. He repeated this message while winding up a debate at the first National Conference of Public Security in Brasília in August 2009 and reminded those in attendance that "the police are not the enemy but a type of community guardian."

Maria Helena: Your first administration was dedicated to stabilizing the economy and reducing poverty. In an interview, President Fernando Henrique Cardoso told me that he handed the country over to you with inflation under control and that he thought your greatest challenge would be to solve the problem of public security and violence.

President Lula: He left me a completely bankrupt country, with a 17 percent rate of inflation. He left Brazil totally bankrupt. We didn't have a cent to import anything. We needed to make the greatest fiscal adjustment that a person could possibly imagine, and I did it, because I had enough political capital, but it was all very difficult despite being extremely necessary also to pay the enormous foreign debt and to set Brazil free of the IMF [International Monetary Fund]. I even felt a little annoyed with Fernando Henrique. But now, since the death of Dona Ruth [Cardoso's wife, who died in July 2008], when I was at the wake, I felt that I should try to speak with him. You know what happened? Present at that wake were so many people from the PSDB [Brazilian Social Democratic Party] and from the PT [Workers' Party] who have been friends during the past thirty years, so many people who fought together for democracy and now, in these last years, we've had a fratricidal quarrel. He complained that I didn't invite him to talk, to dinner. But he also didn't invite me, and he detests it when I compare my administration with his. So I decided that from now on, I'll only compare my two administrations, from 2003 forward.

Maria Helena: But this is what I want to do—compare administrations—because in my view, your first government had already left a mark on history as the administration that did the most to diminish social inequality and regional inequality. I am seeing a really great challenge for your second administration, principally with the perspective that I have of Rio de Janeiro, in the area of security. Do you think that your second administration can innovate in this area with programs such as PRONASCI?

Lula: Look, let me tell you something from the bottom of my heart: For me, PRONASCI is an extraordinary program to confront problems in the area of security. But in my opinion, in the case of Brazil, security is less a question of the police and more a question of the presence of the state in places where people need the state. When the Brazilian state, which was absent during centuries from the principal clusters of people in greatest need—be they the people of the northeast or people of the periphery in metropolitan regions—to the extent that the state was not present with health services, was not present with education, was not present with recreation, was not present from the perspective of improving the life of society, what happened is that this led people to absolute despair. It caused many people to fall into the hands of organized crime, of drug trafficking. This makes people violent, because imagine a person who watches the rich on television and sees so much corruption, and he's hungry and services are not there for him, the state is not there, the school for his child is the poorest. We are making an experiment together with PRONASCI—but not only with PRONASCI—to make a small revolution in the great Brazilian urban centers. When we decided to do PAC [Program for the Acceleration of Growth], we allocated 41 billion *reais* [approximately $20 billion in 2008] to urbanize the favelas and create basic sanitation infrastructure. This is permitting us to intervene in areas where the state was never present—for example, in the Alemão complex, Manguinhos, Rocinha, Pavão-Pavãozinho, among others. But we are not going to build a few little alleys. We're going to make better streets, better lighting, better houses and schools; places for small entrepreneurs; places to open a library or a police station or to give job training to young people. PRONASCI is present in all of this to train police in human rights and in citizenship, to complement the work of the community, to have a police presence in the community and not only for repression. I think that when the state is present body and soul in the poorest places of this country, with a policy of employment, with a policy of education, with a policy for public health, with a cultural policy, these people won't fall into the hands of organized crime anymore. You pass through a process of natural selection, with the people having options.

Look, Maria Helena, you are a social scientist, and you know the following: It's no small thing for a country to pass twenty years without growth, a country [that has gone] twenty years without generating jobs. Take the following data: In the first five months of this year [2008], we created more formal-sector jobs than during the entire first term of Fernando Henrique Cardoso. Civil construction spent twenty years only falling, only losing jobs. Shipbuilding in Rio de Janeiro in 1970 had 36,000 workers. In 2002, it had only 1,900, and today it has 40,000 again. The Brazilian auto industry was failing. Today, it hits record after record [in output]. All this—more basic sanitation infrastructure, more *bolsa família* [family grant program]. It's a group of social policies that are working, and, in having them, civil society perceives that people today have another outlook. But we are not going to manage to do everything. It's necessary to have another administration that dedicates four or eight more years to reinforcing all this so that you may dream about having a new generation ten or fifteen years from now truly living with dignity. That's our perspective, and this is my wish. You may put police in the city of Salvador, but if you don't have a policy for employment, a policy for youth, a policy for basic sanitation, the police are going to be beating up the poor. There are state interventions that can change the face of violence in Brazil.

José Valentin: Excuse the interruption. About the Alemão complex, I was working there in the community directly, and I wanted to say what people are feeling. I was strongly impressed when they spoke of constructing a *teleférico* (cablecar line) in the Alemão complex. I was a little bit worried, because the community is not accepting this. They say the cablecar line, hanging there, will become a target for gunfire. They want everything that you said: schools, health, basic sanitation, culture, jobs. But they object to the cablecar line's costing so much and being the main project, and on top of this, it is going to promote target practice.

Lula [*laughing*]: It's normal that they have this concern, because in the case of the cablecar line, the citizen thinks he is going to be up there suspended in the cablecar. But it's not going to be the open sky. He's going to be inside a cablecar. Let's put this in perspective. Look, one part of violence is true. The other part is that the Brazilian press, and especially television, transforms a fact of violence not only into information for society. In some cases, they transform it into a veritable soap opera. They spend days and days talking about the same thing. But let's see how it will work for poor people. With the cablecar line, people are going to save two hours that they spend today to get to the Rio subway. They are going to arrive in nineteen minutes. But they still don't know this. When you improve lighting, provide better transportation, give more opportunities, things begin to change. So it's necessary to have a group of measures, not only the teleférico.

Maria Helena: [Justice] Minister Tarso Genro raised an important question about the point at which the federal government can act or intervene in the states and municipalities. Up to what point can these programs really work if a state or a municipality resolves not to collaborate? Minister Tarso Genro even spoke of the need for a new federal pact. How do you see this?

Lula: There was a historical error in Brazil. There was no harmony among the federal government, the states, and the municipalities. There was no way for the federal government to do certain things in a municipality. For example, there is no way for the federal government to administer Volta Redonda. The one who has to administer Volta Redonda is the mayor, with our aid and the aid of the state government.

Maria Helena: Then what is the status of this idea that Minister Tarso Genro raised about a new federal pact? He suggested that there should be a new federal pact specifically with reference to the question of security, so that the federal, state, and municipal governments can work together in an integrated manner, without being boycotted by local political interests.

Lula: We are advancing a lot in the sense of integrated efforts with states and municipalities in various areas, not only in that of security. You remember how before I got here, the mayor wasn't welcome here. The mayors arrived here and were met by police dogs, even beaten. Since I was inaugurated, we have participated in the March of the Mayors every year. One year, eighteen [government] ministers and I went to the gathering. We participate in debates. I spoke; ministers spoke. The mayors come with lists of demands, and we spend the year seeing what we can do; the next year, we go there again to report on what we did, and they ask for more things; they give us another list of demands; there is more discussion. This is the new federal pact. It's not necessary to change the laws. It's necessary to have respect and really work together. It's important that people understand that it's not a question of the mayor coming here to ask for money. The important thing is that the mayor understands that he has here a federal institution that can treat him with dignity independent of the party he represents. César Maia [the mayor of Rio de Janeiro] can tell you all he does in opposition to my administration, but he has to admit that the city of Rio de Janeiro never received the money that it receives now in my administration, even being in opposition, and even using his blog to criticize me. Why does he receive money? Because I am not concerned with César Maia. I'm concerned with the people of Rio de Janeiro. And so it goes. Any mayor of the PSDB or PMDB [Brazilian Democratic Movement Party] or any party that you can imagine in Brazil is heard and heeded. Today, we have federal government participation in more than 5,200 municipalities in Brazil. The Territories of Citizenship is in my opinion the best program the left has had. Obviously, it is in an experimental phase, because it takes time to start a program, create a territory, create the designated localities, and start to function. But what is Territories of Citizenship? In the program, we have mapped the 2,000 poorest municipalities and organized them into territories. One territory might have twenty municipalities, while another has fifteen municipalities. You have a municipality that is the center. We have created managers of the territory in each municipality; each manager is chosen and elected by the community. We're going to bring all the public policies to the territories at once, and to do this, we have chosen the poorest municipalities and villages in Brazil. We are beginning with sixty territories, which gives us almost nine hundred municipalities. The coordinator of the program is the minister of agrarian development. I think that if it works out, we are really going to be able to arrive with materials and the presence of the state in places that, being isolated and poor, never could get the attention of the federal government and never had anything. If we put together various places, the involvement of the federal government becomes easier and improves public policies of health, education, development, employment, housing. And you know what else? We are working a lot in the agricultural area, which is the most problematic and poorest in Brazil. In the past six years [since 2002], we have already redistributed more than 35 million hectares of land. Do you know what this is? It's the whole of Chile.

José Valentin: This surprises me. Why, then, is the MST [Landless Movement] complaining so much that it doesn't have agrarian reform?

Lula: Just now, the MST doesn't know what to do. Look, it is no longer occupying land. It is occupying Monsanto, occupying Aracruz Celulose, stopping trains of the Vale do Rio Doce Company. But the truth is that we have already redistributed 35 million hectares of land, and we have already settled 509,000 families. Now they are angry with me because this year I stopped. This year I want them to produce. We just introduced the More Food program, because of the price inflation of food, and we are going to finance until 2010—70,000 tractors and other agricultural machines for family farming—with 25 billion *reais*. It's going to be integrated with the *bolsa família*, with the program of school lunches, with a guaranteed market, and also with a lowering of the price of food in general. Here everything is integrated.

Maria Helena: How are you also going to affect security and the integration of security programs?

Lula: Look, you cannot write on security thinking that it is only a police question. In fact, the police repress, and you have police violence, and you have to act to diminish that violence and change the pattern of police behavior. But most important, you have to treat security as a police question but principally in combination with the improvement of the lives of people. There's no way to make violence fall if the person has no way to survive.

Do your work on security, but do a chapter in order to innovate debate about security, because otherwise we're stuck in the classic discussion of security. First, who is to blame? Is it the federal government? Is it the state government? Is it the municipal government? You need to put more police on the street. The police are corrupt. This debate is fifty years old. It's worn out. We are going to continue having corrupt police until we have new generations educated in this country with another mentality. Even in the most advanced countries, you get tired of seeing situations with corrupt police. What is going to diminish the violence is good policing, more intelligence work, a police force that is more community-oriented, a police force that is closer to the population, with another professional preparation, another civil mentality. All this is correct. You can do all this. However, if you don't have food in people's mouths, if you don't have jobs, if you don't have education and good schools, there will be the possibility of people falling into criminal behavior.

So I think that your book about security should include the irresponsibility of the people who governed us, who allowed this country during the past fifty years to be what it was. When you were a little girl, Rocinha was a farm. When you were a little girl, the Alemão complex was a farm. Who let that become what it has become during the past fifty years? It happened because of extreme poverty, because of the carelessness of the people who governed us, because of the incredible irresponsibility of those who had the duty to make the state present and provide minimum good living conditions for people. All of them are [to blame], even those who say they are of the left. Let's begin with the carelessness. If you have ten houses occupying a poor site, you can intervene and construct houses that give people dignity in another place. But if you have twenty, a hundred, a thousand houses in places without physical safety, climbing the hills and even being washed down by the rains, then you have a social problem that you don't know how to fix anymore. I am thinking about how fifty years ago there was a farm, and how one could have made an urban project with adequate housing, with basic sanitation, with schools, with health clinics. I keep thinking about who were the irresponsible people who allowed people to live all these years under these terrible conditions without doing anything.

Maria Helena, for a long time I played soccer in the favela of Hiliópolis in São Paulo. At that time, we had more than forty soccer fields there. Who allowed that favela to grow when action could have been taken when the first person arrived, when the second person arrived? I am talking about that history of a total lack of state presence, of that irresponsibility that didn't do anything—didn't make decent housing, didn't provide education, didn't build a health clinic. And the politician went there, made a speech, and promised all this. I become indignant.[1]

I'm saying to people in the favelas that what we are doing now is a process of reparation. It is reparation on account of the irresponsibility of those who governed this country and allowed people to live badly. It was not necessarily the President of the Republic, it wasn't Getúlio [Vargas], because who is responsible is not only the mayor, the City Council member, the secretary of government, and the state governor. Governors have to induce the mayors to be responsible.[2] There was an accumulation of irresponsibility that we now are going to try to reverse by making interventions. I just went to Pernambuco [State] to launch a public work project in a place called the "Canal da Malária [Malaria Canal]." Look at that name: "Canal da Malária"! People live above the canal in houses on stilts. How is it that people were allowed to build houses there?

Maria Helena: Where is this?
Lula: In Pernambuco. The *palafitas*—we are now dismantling them, moving the people to secure areas without stagnant water full of mosquitos, with decent houses. How is it that people have been allowed to build houses on *palafitas* in this country?

Maria Helena: The same thing has happened in Rio. Maré still has palafita dwellings.
Lula: I think that in your book, you ought to analyze all this—the reasons for all of these subhuman conditions that end in this violence. With PAC and PRONASCI and other socially integrated programs, we want to change the violence by making this reparation.

Maria Helena: If you manage to do even a little of what you describe, it will go down in history as an integrated and innovative program in public security.
Lula: Look. I'm a Catholic. I believe strongly in God. I was very fearful of a second term [as president] because of the decline in motivation due to so many problems. And today I thank God that I have a second term, because this one is infinitely better than the first. You have no notion of the number of public works in this country. If you speak a half-hour with

Miriam Belchior, and she shows you all the public works under way, you are going to see that what we have is incredible.[3] Thank God, we managed to unshackle the country to make things happen. We have public works projects for airports, ports, roads, railroads. This also creates jobs.

Maria Helena: And public housing?

Lula: If you talk with the Federal Savings Bank (Caixa Econômica Federal) this year (2008), we are doing more than in the whole of my first term, because everyone has learned.[4]

Maria Helena: And you have more money?

Lula: It's not only because the government has more money. It's because the people have more money. If you don't have home buyers, you don't build houses and you don't have a home-building industry. You remember the invasion of housing projects in the 1970s and the beginning of the '80s? Why was that happening? Because the Federal Savings Bank was financing and the home builder was building, but [the houses] were unoccupied, and the people invaded [them]. See if you can find an empty housing project today. Things are happening in this country. Thanks to God, they are happening. You see that infant mortality in the northeast has fallen by 74 percent. There is food; the people are eating. And much more is still needed. I think we still need to consolidate economic stabilization, even though we have $200 billion in reserves. When could you have imagined this country would have this much? And the IMF is gone.

Maria Helena and José Valentin [*laughing*]: Of course. Now we can no longer go to the protests we liked so much, shouting, "IMF, Get out!"

Lula: Things are happening. Obviously, we don't have money to do everything we want, but just so you have an idea of what we are going to announce in public investments: This year, I am going to announce the building of four steel plants. And I have a refinery [that produces] 600,000 barrels [of oil] a day.

Maria Helena: Where will it be?

Lula: In Maranhão. I have one [refinery] that produces 200,000 barrels a day in Ceará. These alone represent investments of almost 160 billion *reais*, and they are going to create thousands of jobs in the poorest states of Brazil. Obviously, since this is going to create jobs, it's going to generate more income and give opportunities to greatly improve the lives of the poorest people. From time to time when I speak, I mention the example of a thirty-year-old man who is in jail today because he committed a crime, and how those responsible for transforming him into a thief go free. They were the ministers of economy and of planning, the politicians who never were concerned about him. They raised a generation without opportunities. An entire generation. Now we want to raise another generation. I'll give you an example in which I take pride: The first Brazilian technical school was created by President Nilo Peçanha in 1909 in the city of Campos de Guataquazes in Rio de Janeiro [State]. From 1909 to 2003, 140 technical schools were opened. When I arrived here, Paulo Renato, who was minister of education under Fernando Henrique Cardoso, had made a law taking responsibility for technical education away from the federal government. We changed this law. When I leave the presidency, in addition to the existing 140, we are going to have 214 more technical schools in the country.

Maria Helena: Not only in the big urban centers, but also in the interior?

Lula: Spread throughout the country. We are going to do in eight years—one and half times what was done between 1909 and 2002. You see the effort. We are building ten new federal universities; we are building forty-eight extension universities; we are building the Latin American University, with a Latin American curriculum, Latin American professors, and Latin American students. We are going to make in Ceará State the Africana University so that we can study Portuguese-speaking African countries. We created Pro-Uni which already has 400,000 students with scholarships in the universities.[5] Ask how many new universities Fernando Henrique created? He approved the São Francisco River Valley plan [to channel water], but we are going to carry it out. The country was abandoned. The country was left to its own devices.

Maria Helena: The city of Rio is still abandoned. The governors, the mayors, the state deputies, the city councilmen don't do anything, and so many are involved in successive scandals.

Lula: But the people of Rio also elect badly. It seems that they believe in Santa Claus. But we are hoping to make better investments. We are investing in a new petrochemical complex in Itaboraí.[6] Nine billion dollars of investment. [Governor] Cabral is a partner with us.

Maria Helena: But this policy of confrontation, do you agree with it?

Lula: You're speaking about the area of security. Let me say something to you. The police also are afraid. A police officer is not a superior being. In the case of Rio de Janeiro, many times the police have less powerful weapons that the bandidos. This is a fact.

Maria Helena: But if you're inside a Big Skull, you aren't afraid.

Lula: That's true. But you see how, when the bandidos' guns are displayed, they are more modern than the guns of the police. And they [the police] go into an area that they don't know. It was in that way that the United States was defeated in Vietnam. They went into unknown territory. There were those small, thin Vietnamese people in holes an armadillo could barely fit into. And they defeated the Americans. So it's important to work on the psychological side also. You have a police officer who is a human being, badly paid, badly prepared, who is as afraid to die as the bandido.

I think that in Rio de Janeiro, we have something special: Organized crime in Rio de Janeiro became an industry. It is an industry that employs many poor people, and the powerful people who command this industry are outside the favela. True barbarism takes place there. The police kill children; the army kills young people in Providencia Hill. So it's a question of community policing, the question of involving mothers, of having community social programs. There are no short-term solutions.

José Valentin: Excuse me, Mr. President. I am working in the community, and I am Chilean and, perhaps, more sensitive to violence [because it] reminds me of [the Chilean military dictator Augusto] Pinochet. For example, right now, at this time, you have to get rid of the Big Skull. This has to stop now, not in the long run, because the Big Skull enters, including going into schoolyards and firing in every direction. The problem, Mr. President, is that in the community one sees selective repression. For example, what happens in Penha in the Alemão complex doesn't happen in the hills in the Zona Sul, near the upper-class areas. The Big Skull doesn't invade Zona Sul favelas with guns firing. That would be unthinkable in Rocinha, because the bullets might reach [upper-class] São Conrado. But in Vila Cruzeiro, in Alemão, and in Penha, the Big Skull arrives, and the police start firing immediately. The police are full of fear, badly paid—all this I understand. But I don't understand how a person can open the gate to a schoolyard with a thousand small children and invade with the Big Skull and begin to fire from there at the hill. This is happening, Mr. President, and I would like to tell you personally about it, because we were present for many of these things. We thought about not speaking to you, because people are so afraid that they don't want us to say anything or to identify them because they fear reprisal—being persecuted or even murdered—and their families might also suffer. They do not want the schools where this happens to be identified. Look at their situation. After a schoolyard was invaded three times by the police, and with the Big Skull inside, the bandido chief demanded an explanation from the principal. "We never entered the school," the bandido chief said. "Why did you let the Big Skull come in?" But our concern, Mr. President, is that you should know what is happening directly, because we are working with the communities. We didn't find out from the newspapers or from an official entity. We learned from community members themselves because we went there.

Maria Helena: Are you going to talk about the bodies, José Valentin?

José Valentin: No, I'm going to talk first of the *corvo*, the knife designed with the point turned inward so it can be inserted into the lower part of the abdomen and pulled up to open the abdomen completely, exposing the intestines. In Chile, the *corvo* was used in Operation Condor. I was frightened when I heard people in Rio describe it, although they couldn't give it a name. They said it was being used in Rio communities by the BOPE. It's very serious that this may be happening in Rio de Janeiro . . . during a democratic government

Maria Helena: What is happening is very grave: summary executions, shootouts all the time, even the use of torture and the *corvo*. I think that perhaps [Governor] Cabral doesn't know. I'm sure that you don't know.

Lula: You should interview him. It's necessary that he be informed about this directly.

Maria Helena: I'm anxious to interview him. But I don't have access because I've been critical of this policy of confrontation.

Lula: He will meet with you. Of course, he'll meet with you. I'm going to give instructions for the Office of the President to schedule an interview for you with Cabral. He has to hear what you're telling me. It's very grave. Talk to Sérgio Cabral. It's very important.

Maria Helena: It's not possible that we struggled so much for democracy and for the rule of law so that the poorest people would suffer this type of terror. It's no good to say that security is for the long run. This has to stop now.

Lula: But it doesn't have a short-term solution.

Maria Helena: I asked people in the Office of the Secretary of Human Rights and the national secretary of security himself, and they said the same thing that I think: "The BOPE has to be abolished."

Lula: But if you abolish the BOPE, you're going to see that the population turns against the government.

Maria Helena: It won't.
Lula: It will.

José Valentin: The middle class and the upper class perhaps may turn against the government, but the poor won't.

Maria Helena: I bet they won't. If the government has courage to confront this violence against the poor directly, I bet that the population won't be against it, if and when they are better informed about what is happening.

Lula: You are speaking about the [Military Police], Maria Helena?

Maria Helena: No, about the BOPE. You saw how the BOPE is trained: "We're going to kill; we're going to steal your soul; we come to kill." Besides, Lula, I'm not alone in what I think. We had a meeting with the Nucleus of Studies of Violence at the University of São Paulo, and a major with the [Military Police] of São Paulo affected us deeply with what he said, "Do you want to know something? We were sending our people here in São Paulo to train with the BOPE of Rio de Janeiro. We stopped, because the training for the BOPE is so violent that we don't want our people from São Paulo to go to train there."

Lula: Did you see the film *Elite Squad*? Go see the film. It's all there. But I'll arrange for you to speak with Cabral. He has to know this.

Fernando Henrique Cardoso, Former President of Brazil (1995–2002): A Discussion with Maria Helena Moreira Alves, September 2007

Fernando Henrique Cardoso was elected to two terms as president of Brazil, serving from 1995 to 2002. He may be best known for launching the plan that ended decades of high inflation and gave Brazil a new currency, the *real*, in 1994 when he was minister of the treasury. As president, Cardoso, and his administration, not only kept inflation under control but also promoted social development, most memorably through a grant program to poor families that met a requirement to enroll their children in school. Although the political parties to which President Cardoso and President Lula belong have been fiercely competitive, there has been some continuity in policy between administrations, especially in striving to keep inflation low and advancing a social-development agenda. In this interview, conducted in 2007, Cardoso identifies several public security challenges that his government faced. The interview reveals some of the complexity of making public security policy, as well as the search for new ideas and practices in that area. Before he entered politics in the late 1970s, Cardoso had established himself as one of Brazil's leading sociologists, with a reputation that gave him international prominence in the field.

Fernando Henrique Cardoso: Regarding this issue of public security, to give you an idea of how disorganized Brazil was, we didn't understand the most elementary things [when I initially took office as president]. I'm going to give you an example: We had not defined white-collar crime. The idea of the crime of money laundering did not exist. In a globalized world of organized crime, money laundering, and drugs, we did not have the legal apparatus to act against this. The Brazilian Central Bank did not have the authority to report to the Federal Revenue Service what it knew. We had to establish mechanisms of control suited to the modern world. Inflation did not allow us to organize the state for many years. Everything was highly disorganized, and that includes public security. There was no program at the federal government level that would finance the improvement of state police forces, except the Penitentiary Organization Fund. We established a special fund to improve the operation of the state police forces. In my opinion, it was not properly used during my administration. I wanted to concentrate on the more dramatic cases so that we might have a type of "showcase," something well done so we could demonstrate that things can improve. But each of the governors—and public security is within their sphere—wanted some of the money. We created a fund, and the fund was dispersed. Later, we saw that the money was used basically to buy uniforms, tires, these things, and not police equipment.

However, we did manage to achieve some things. Specifically, two governors tried to bring about some change. One was Benedita [da Silva], governor of Rio de Janeiro.[7] The other one was Paulo Hartung, governor of Espirito Santo. My experience with Benedita is that she tried but did not manage to eliminate corruption in the Judiciary Police.[8] You've heard of examples of that corruption, like the prisoners are the ones who control the jails and so on. We tried to help by giving her money to jump start anti-corruption work. In Espirito Santo, we were successful. In Espirito Santo, a

good program of integration of the Federal Police with the local police, with
an integrated command, with a task force, dismantled a dangerous criminal
organization in which the boss was the president of the legislative assembly.
He's now in prison. There was contraband, drugs, violence, and the organization was dismantled through integrated police work.

Some things worked like that. However, there is the whole issue of
drugs. With drugs, we were greatly pressured by the Americans, who wanted
the army in control, just as they wanted in Colombia. They wanted to implement the Plan Colombia in Brazil, and we, being a democratic government,
were not about to accept this and never put it into effect.[9] Let me give you
an example of how difficult it is to control the flow of drugs into the country.
One day, I was taken to a flight control center and shown a radar screen on
which you could see all of the airplanes that were landing in Brazil. One can
see all of the planes that enter the country, legally as well as illegally. At the
time, at least ten illegal flights per day were landing. On the radar screen,
the controllers could see the air space through which the plane entered Brazil and where it landed. But look at the difficulty: We can't shoot down the
plane. There was no law that told us when we could shoot down a plane.
The air force intercepted the plane, but the pilot ignored the instructions.
He simply returned temporarily to his country. Approving a law for downing
a plane was very difficult.

Maria Helena: Was such a law ever passed?

Cardoso: Yes, it was, but it is a very complicated law. It's a law that
allows a plane to be shot down and people to be killed. But who is going to
give the order to shoot? A plane was shot down in Peru, and some Americans were killed. As a result, the U.S. government became nervous about
[Brazil enacting] a law to shoot down planes. Still, the law finally passed,
and we now have guidelines.

Maria Helena: The United States has passed a law to shoot down
planes as part of its legislation against terrorism.

Cardoso: Yes, but as far as I know, it has never been used. Getting
back to what I was saying about Brazil, it's difficult even to capture a plane
when it lands. For this to take place, the Federal Police, the Federal Revenue Service, and customs agents must be present. Those people generally
see planes that bring in drugs and that land in small airports in the interior
of São Paulo, Minas Gerais, or other places that are difficult to get to. Sometimes the places are so inaccessible that, although radar shows the plane
landing, there is no way to send troops in to capture it in time.

Let me add another important thing regarding public security. According to the Constitution, public security is not a federal responsibility. Instead, it is a state responsibility. The federal government can only supplement what the state government does. According to the Constitution, drugs, contraband, arms, and border defense are federal responsibilities. We established SENAD, the National Secretariat for Policies on Drugs. We asked General Alberto Mendes Cardoso to coordinate the work, and he was very much against the use of violence. Then the Federal Police turned against him and blocked SENAD's actions, insisting that it was only the Federal Police who could arrest suspects. SENAD was left without operational space in which to act. There are constitutional restrictions on carrying out anything. Finally, there are limitations on the public's understanding of the problem. You must make sure that the country participates in the process. That's the situation now, and that's not easily resolved unless you carry out an enormous public education campaign about the complexity of the problem.

Maria Helena: Didn't you also establish the Secretariat for Human Rights in your administration?

Cardoso: Yes. In the beginning, the Secretariat for Human Rights was housed within the Justice Ministry. Then, it became a secretariat with a cabinet rank and a minister. That set-up worked well. It featured a Human Rights Plan, and there was mobilization around it. We reviewed the issue of blacks in Brazil, women's issues, and the issue of juvenile delinquency. The whole human rights issue operated within the following reality: Brazil had a very negative record on human rights. We turned that around. The first action was accepting all decisions of international courts. We strongly supported the establishment of the International Penal Court, based in Rome. Another international tribunal that we supported was the court established to judge Pinochet, which is something new, because it means that one accepts that a country's sovereignty ends when certain types of crime are committed—in this case, genocide. It's not the country that can say yes or no; these are crimes against humanity. We supported this, and afterward it became operative. Later we supported "hearings" in which the United Nations sends special envoys. For example, Mary Anderson, who was the president of Ireland and, at the time, Secretary of Human Rights at the United Nations, came to Brazil for a hearing. We said, "Open the gates. Let them see everything." Before this, Brazil did not accept the entry of people from the United Nations or from the Organization of American States to conduct investigations. It was after this that we began to send the reports

that Brazil submits on the issue of blacks, women, and human rights violations. NGOs began to participate in the writing of these reports and even
traveled with government delegations. That was a difficult thing to do,
because it had not been done before, and our diplomatic establishment was
not accustomed to it.

Maria Helena: What about the security program that you implemented during your administration? Were NGOs consulted about it?

Cardoso: Yes, they were consulted, but everything was under government control. Consulting the NGOs does not mean that they decide. I think
that it is important to consult, but not to give up decision making.

Maria Helena: Did you ever think of establishing a Public Security
Force, like the National Security Force that Lula has put into effect?

Cardoso: No, I always had my doubts that this would be effective. It is,
in fact, a way to make the army do something that people want, but that the
army does not do. And the army is right. When Itamar Franco was president, and because of the Rio Conference,[10] a request was made to authorize
the army to occupy the favelas. But the problem is this: How are you going
to take the army out of the favelas? If the army goes in, everything calms
down. And afterward? Nothing changes. So I always had doubts that this
was the best road to follow.

There are cases when the army may intervene. For instance, we had a
time when we had high inflation, and at the same time we had problems in
the police force over salaries and so on. We had instances when the police
went on strike. We did have to send in the army to control things. And the
army can do this. However, according to the Constitution, the governor
must ask [for the army]. And in truth, when the army arrives, it stops the
strike. When the tanks arrive, everything stops. If it doesn't, there will be a
huge death toll, because the army is not trained for crowd control. Army
troops are not trained like regular police forces. The police infiltrate; they
first gather intelligence. They may do that well or badly, but they do it. They
develop suspects. It might be an imperfect operation, but they are not going
to kill everyone. They may kill innocent people, but not everyone. Soldiers
sent to repress kill everyone. They enter shooting. They don't know how to
operate any other way. I'm not trying to criticize anybody, because I know
that things are so dramatic now that the state thinks that it must do or prepare something because suddenly there might be a need. I do not want to
criticize Lula's government for what it has done. I'm only saying that using
the army is a dangerous thing. The army is a destructive force.

It's much more difficult to stop violence than to control inflation. My goal was to stop inflation. You can't do everything. I had to put the state in order. Lula's issue is violence. He wants to stop the violence and drug trafficking. Let's remember that the drug problem is not a local crime, limited to Brazil. It's an organized, global, difficult problem to deal with. We're looking at the globalization of crime. It's not just drugs. Everything has become global. Let's say a man wants a woman for sex. He goes online, describes the kind of woman he wants, and pays for her services. The central command for this service may be housed in Romania. Within forty-eight hours, the woman is at his doorstep. You want a new liver? You can order it the same way. The same thing happens if you want to adopt a baby. You read about this in the newspapers and are horrified. The worst aspect of all this is that these actions are carried out by a network of small and integrated, though not unified, groups scattered all over the world and using the Internet in a global way.

Right now the most serious problem is how drugs come into the United States. Drugs enter in myriad ways—in submarines, on airplanes, and through the borders. The fact that drugs come through the borders of the country means that there clearly is corruption among the police forces charged with guarding the borders. The large quantity of drugs that flows into the country cannot be coming only from the individuals who fool the police. There are other ways that perhaps are more dramatic and difficult to control. The guy who sells tomatoes to the United States is a businessman, but once in a while he may sneak a little package of drugs with his merchandise and earn a few more dollars. The separation between the legal and the illegal is a murky line. I'm describing this so that you can see that this is a very difficult issue to grapple with and may even be cultural.

Let's take Brazil as an example. I'll limit myself to the issue of violence. Either we establish a climate to resolve this by doing whatever is necessary because the problem is so bad, or we have no solution to the problem. We must have a national pact—above and beyond partisanship—and unleash an enormous national educational campaign, night and day, day and night. We have to decide on the measures that need to be taken and take them with enormous energy. It's not easy, by any means. Outside of that, what will happen? You're going to have violent repression and solve nothing. Most of all, we need to restrict the gray areas—for example, the young kid who is the drug carrier [avião]. He's not really a criminal, but he is part of the crime. So is the consumer. They form a network. We must break up that network. It has to do with a profound cultural change, with bringing about a change of attitude in the people. I think that we have to discuss even the decriminal-

ization of drugs, like marijuana. As the use of some drugs in the United
States decreases, organized crime increases their consumption in our countries. We have to unleash an educational campaign like we did with cigarettes. We have to use television, radio. We must make people ashamed of
using drugs and have drugs seen as antisocial. We have to change the culture completely. We have to stigmatize whoever is using drugs. It's not the
drug trafficker or the kid who's selling drugs that should concern us. It's the
user, the consumer. We never take on the user in Brazil. On the contrary,
the user is not now a criminal. This means that a guy gets into his car in
Copacabana, Leblon, and another rich neighborhood, goes to his drug sup-
plier, picks up his drugs, and returns home. He can even order drugs
through the Internet or by phone. This means that the focus in combating
drugs is wrong. Right now, it won't work for a governor or police chief to try
to solve this. It's not going to happen. What we need is an agreement for the
entire country.

Tarso Genro, Minister of Justice:
A Discussion with Maria Helena Moreira Alves
and José Valentin Palacios, July 2008

Tarso Fernando Herz Genro, who served as minister of justice from 2007
until 2010, is from the southernmost Brazilian state of Rio Grande do Sul.
He was twice elected mayor of the capital city, Porto Alegre (1992, 2000),
where he introduced the innovation of the participatory budget, in which citizens meet, consult, and debate to help choose municipal budget priorities.
President Lula named Tarso Genro minister of education in 2004 and minister of justice in 2007. He has a strong record in human rights, having worked
to stop torture in prisons, human trafficking, and child prostitution. His program for police and security reform has centered on the PRONASCI initiative, which he launched in Rio de Janeiro in 2007.

Maria Helena: First, can the federal government change the policy of
confrontation that Governor Sérgio Cabral is carrying out? Can it change
the training of the BOPE?

Minister Tarso Genro: This police operation model in Rio de Janeiro
is the model that was principally applied after the coup d'état of 1964,
where the form of police communication with the community is always
through violence and not dialogue, not through living in the community,
knowing the daily life of people in the community. In truth, what is

happening in Rio de Janeiro is the product of a certain type of learning process within the state itself. By this we mean that the state learned to use violence, learned to use repression, learned to separate the state from society. This happens in an extraordinarily negative form in public security. Then, how do you change this? It is necessary to change politically the federal pact among the federal government, the states, and the municipalities. It is not enough for the federal government to change its behavior. If we do not have a change in community culture at the base of society—a change in the repressive apparatus—this change is going to transform itself into impotence, and that impotence can exacerbate violence. So what are we proposing? We are proposing a radical change in the paradigm of public security in the country. It has to be accompanied by the governors, by their secretaries of public security and other institutions that are related to this, and it also has to be accompanied by the municipal governments that have more access to the daily life of people through crime-prevention policies. This is the model contemplated in PRONASCI. With reference to the police, we have to design a policy for training them so that they can accompany this institutional and cultural change.

Also, it is not enough only to substitute police weapons. If we only substitute the police weapons and do not work at the base of society to establish a new relationship, the consequence can be that the police may not want to enter the regions of greatest conflict; they may not want to enter regions of confrontation with organized crime, with the gangs that control a large part of the poorest regions of Rio de Janeiro. Thus, our proposal is a complete change of the paradigm whose effects will be gradual. They will not be immediate. For example, for the police of Rio de Janeiro, we are offering education immediately, and with funding, so they will receive an increase in salary while they are studying. Also, [we are offering] a plan for housing to take them out of areas where their families live under threat, outside the locales where they work, and combining them with policies of crime prevention that should be done by the municipalities and by the states according to the characteristics of each. This is a process of transition. We have to design a process of transition to another model of public security.

Maria Helena: But in the meantime, we have police who are using extreme violence, including torture, summary executions, and the disappearing of bodies. This is a great concern. The lawyers we have spoken to, including Leonardo de Souza Chaves, the under-solicitor general for human rights of Rio de Janeiro, said something that caught our attention: "Disappearance is very serious, because . . . [w]ithout a body, there is no crime.

Then impunity is guaranteed." At the same time, we have heard in the communities, "Everybody knows where they are buried. We know the location of the clandestine cemeteries but cannot get the authorities to come and search for the bodies." The Mothers of Acari we interviewed said that years ago they knew where their children were buried, but the authorities do not pay attention and do not come to search the places they indicate. I do not know if it would be possible for the federal government to do this, but the experience of Chile, Argentina, and in Central America has led to considerable success in the formation of commissions that search for the disappeared. If a body is found, a DNA exam is required to determine who it is. Then impunity can be ended and those who are possibly guilty can be tried. Is it possible to do this in Brazil? Is the minister of justice able to propose the creation of a commission to search for the disappeared?

Tarso Genro: It is not the prerogative of the minister of justice. He can make a political recommendation to create a congressional commission of inquiry to elucidate a given case. Since Brazil is nation with a federal system, there are strict limits on what we can do. I would say they are very restrictive of the powers of the federal government. In these cases, we can interfere, we can show the willingness to interfere at the request of the public prosecutor or a state governor. Now, what are the ways to do this? There are the Cabinets for the Integrated Management of Public Security (GGIS), where the Federal Police and even the federal highway police participate, and within which we can place at their disposal our system of intelligence, but not without the political willingness of the state government. If the state is unwilling, the federal government in truth does not have the right, unless it makes a federal intervention. That is something else. Making a federal intervention takes action by Congress, which has to vote. Also, in collaboration with Congress, [the federal government] can intervene in a given state if there is a serious request from an international institution with which Brazil has treaties that oblige the federal government to act with Congress.

But what we are sensing now in relation to the governor and the secretary of public security in Rio de Janeiro is that they want to change. They are rethinking this policy of confrontation. Right now, the entire machine is still in this negative position of police violence that you mentioned. What are we doing? We are intervening institutionally to hasten this change. Our group is already there through PRONASCI, through the National Secretary for Public Security, and they [the Rio de Janeiro authorities] have already redesigned their requests for resources. When they made this request for 44 million *reais* in resources, we redesigned all their requests. We included nonlethal equipment and weapons and funds to construct stations for community police.

Maria Helena: I would like to ask you about your experience as mayor in Porto Alegre that was very successful, including in this area.

Tarso Genro: In Porto Alegre, we brought about a profound change between the city government and the community. We instituted public participation in making law.[11] It was the city government working with the community and a process of real participation of the community in public administration that did not require the political commitment of the mayor. It did not depend on this. Participatory budgeting is a rule. What rule is it? In truth, it is a procedure negotiated by the city government with the organized community that we call the Norms of Contractual Public Law and that establishes the rules for participation. Sixteen popular councils were organized that summoned the local population to vote in large plenary sessions to choose the most important public works. We redesigned the political relationship with society, bringing participation into the making of great public decisions, in the investments that were made, in tax reform that the middle class did not want but where the population supported us, and in deciding how and where to make the investments. This improved the security of regions, and vandalism in public schools fell by 80 percent because the schools were seen not as belonging to the city but were revered by the community that helped to construct this new way to see and to do things.

Maria Helena: What about the police?

Tarso Genro: The police had little participation because the police were not an institution whose administration was integrated with the city government. The police obeyed the state government, the governor. But did policing improve? It improved because city lighting got better, the public squares were lighted at night, and the soccer fields had lights. The Military Brigade [Military Police in Rio Grande do Sul] is a local institution that established a relationship with the community as a result of living in the midst of it. This improved the pattern of city security and improved the life of individuals. The police were able to enter areas that were difficult to access to find a certain organized crime gang that was establishing itself. Before, the police did not have access. Evidently, they did this with the help of the city government. But there was no police project because the state government did not participate in what was happening in the city. It did not oppose it, but it also did not participate in an organic manner.

Maria Helena: Is this experience the basis of PRONASCI?

Tarso Genro: Yes, it is the basis of PRONASCI. It is the same concept. There are various projects that are only going to develop if you have the direct participation of organized society, such as the Mothers of Peace and all of the other prevention projects. All social organizations can participate: unions, neighborhood associations. Participation is voluntary. We have centered PRONASCI on two fundamental supports. Young people and mothers are the two fundamental supports in these areas—they are the ones who suffer the greatest violence. But PRONASCI depends on the work of integrated administration and the participation of the community.

Ricardo Brisolla Balestreri, National Secretary for Public Security: A Discussion with Maria Helena Moreira Alves and José Valentin Palacios, Brasília, July 2008

Ricardo Balestreri is a historian and an authority on public security, having studied the training of police in several countries. This helped prepare him to design PRONASCI, of which he was an important architect. He became national secretary for public security in 2008. He was also a well known human rights activist who had served as president of Amnesty International-Brazil and was active in the group Prevention of Torture in Brazil. His perspective is clearly in line with the idea adopted in PRONASCI that human rights and police work must be linked in public security. He began the interview by referring to the fatal shooting by police of three-year-old João Roberto Soares in 2008 as he rode beside his mother in a car the police mistook for a stolen vehicle. The event was widely condemned and interpreted as representing everything that was wrong with police work in Rio de Janeiro, where innocent people, even children, are continually made victims.

Secretary Balestreri: Regarding the case that is now in the newspapers, certainly [Governor Sérgio Cabral] is an honorable man, and Secretary [José Mariano] Beltrame also. They ought to be feeling consternation. It is not their fault. This case shows that a culture exists. Of course, if the victim were not a three-year-old white child, if it were not a murdered child—if it were, for example, three poor young black men from some community, no one would find what happened unusual. It would be recorded as an "act of resistance," or maybe "death in confrontation with the police," and their mothers would spend the rest of their lives trying to prove that their children were not bandidos but honest workers. But as it was a three-year-old white child, it caused difficulty.

Maria Helena: We have a case of an accusation in Acari by a father whose two-year-old son was killed by a member of the Military Police, and recorded as an "act of resistance." Two years old! The father is seeking an indictment and is being threatened.

Balestreri: In this case [of João Roberto Soares] being a white, middle-class three-year-old child, it will not do to register him as a drug trafficker.

Maria Helena: Ever since the time of the military regime (1964–1985), the Military Police have become ever more militarized, more and more heavily armed with weapons of war. And now we have this policy of confrontation by Governor Cabral and Secretary Beltrame. Can the Military Police interpret this as a green light to shoot as if they are at war?

Balestreri: I have good news. Here at the National Secretariat for Public Security, we are trying to change this. That case of the child could not have happened at a worse moment. Today, we are going to announce changes—for example, the program All Police in the University in collaboration with the Getúlio Vargas Foundation and other universities so that all police officers will attend university courses.

Maria Helena: But does this prevent them from killing people on the street?

Balestreri: No, but this is going to change the way of thinking. The project is national . . . and Rio de Janeiro is beginning to respond positively. We have two projects in Rio we are going to finance. One is All Police in the University and the other is Biometric Control of Arms. Today you take a gun, and tomorrow it is in the hands of the bandido. With this control, for example, the gun of the Military Police officer only enters the police arsenal and only leaves when he provides a fingerprint impression. We are going to know how many guns exist, where they are, who took them, and who is using them and where. This program is going to cost 17 million *reais,* which we are financing entirely.

Maria Helena: Are you going to be able to trace bullets? For example, if a person is killed, are you going to know by the bullet from which gun it was fired?

Balestreri: Of course, we're going to have a map. We are going to download the map on the computer that shows how many police there are, where they are, what arms they have, and this sort of thing. As to which gun a bullet came from, it's more complicated, but we are also working on this. These changes are new. They are being initiated by the federal government. Something else you are going to like to know is that SENASP (the National Secretariat for Public Security) has a new arms policy. To begin, we are against the ideology of war. People say, "We are at war. It's an undeclared civil war." This means the following: "If it's an undeclared civil war, in a war we kill or die. A car was mistaken for that of a bandido, and before anything was verified, a shootout took place, and an innocent person was killed—in this case, a child." For the police, this ideology signifies absolute loss of control. Then what is SENASP doing? To bring about public policy change, we are changing the type of arms that we are buying. This has to do with human rights. First, we are buying nonlethal weapons. For example, police training that indicates the police ought to have a gradual increase in the use of force will not count for anything if you only have weapons of war, heavy armaments. For example, if the police officer encounters someone who is drugged who threatens him with a knife, the officer is going to take his pistol and fire. So in addition to a pistol, he has to have a weapon that can contain, a weapon that produces an electric shock, a weapon that fires tear gas. He has to have a range of options before using a high-caliber automatic weapon. This is one thing. The other policy is against the use of high-caliber weapons. We know that the police have to be armed. We are not romantic about this. But the question is: Do the police need to make their rounds with weapons of war? No, because the police go where you have the whole of the population, the majority of whom are innocent, and having a weapon of war makes it easy to fire and to kill.

I'm going to translate this. We in the federal government are not going to pay for weapons of war for the states. We are not going to pay for machine guns, submachine guns, grenades, or automatic rifles, which are heavy-duty weapons for use in war. Then what are we paying for the police to have today? It is the carbine—that is, the 40-caliber rifle is the indicated police weapon in a situation of urban confrontation. What is the difference? In the favela, a shot from a high-powered rifle goes through two or three small houses, killing whoever is in the path and going through bodies. If he has a 40-caliber rifle, the police officer is democratically authorized to use it if there is no other way out. But the 40-caliber rifle, if used in a real confrontation, stops there. It does not pierce, does not go through one person to wound another, to wound innocent people. It does not go though walls and so forth. I only use this example to show that, through the control of weapons, the federal government can bring about an important reduction in fatalities, including in urban conflicts. It is a policy of human rights.

Maria Helena: Is Governor Cabral accepting this?

Balestreri: In part. We changed a request for a thousand high-powered rifles to five hundred 40-caliber rifles. I don't know if he is going to accept this and use them in Rio de Janeiro or not. But on the part of SENASP in Rio de Janeiro, as in the rest of Brazil, we are no longer accepting requests for war combat weapons. For our part, our money is in the first place for nonlethal weapons. In the second place, one needs weapons to confront organized crime, because with organized crime you cannot convert to the model of community policing. The "girl of our dreams" is the community police, but we know that's not possible when confronting organized crime. One cannot think about community policing in a place dominated by organized crime that will not change its posture because of this. There are different levels. For common crime, this thing that bothers the population—holdups, robbery, kidnappings—community policing works. What really reduces this? Is it the policy of confrontation? No. What really reduces this is what we call the neighborhood police. It's the police officer we knew in our childhood; we knew his name and surname, and he knew who we were and where we lived. It was this "Cosme and Damião" model that was abandoned in Brazil to imitate the American motorized police model of the 1960s and '70s. We have to return to the model of neighborhood police. This is the most important thing.

Second, there is another level, which is organized crime. With this there can be no discussion. You really need repression, a qualified form of repression. What do we call "qualified repression"? It is the gathering of intelligence and casing an area, not harming innocent people; it is taking care when using weapons of war, receiving specific training in their use, and employing them in situations only of confrontation with organized crime.

José Valentin: I would like to ask a question about the gun trade. How are you going to control the trafficking of weapons that come, for example, by sea and that is not organized from within the poor communities?

Balestreri: In this case, you have a discussion about the participation of the armed forces. We are having a discussion in Brazil about whether or not the armed forces ought to participate in public security. I'm not sectarian about this matter for the following reasons: The police do not have enough people to control either Brazil's borders, which are enormous, or the sea. For example, in the case of arms trafficking, the armed forces can participate in public security by taking care of the borders and the sea, but not by acting inside the poor communities.

Maria Helena: I want to return to the question of the Military Police. In Rio de Janeiro at least, the Military Police are very violent. The Big Skull terrifies the residents. The children especially that we have spoken to in the communities live in a state of panic. We've heard stories such as that of a grandmother who can no longer take her grandchild to the bank because when he sees an armed policeman, he begins to scream, "Grandma! Big Skull is here! He's going to kill us! Let's get away from here!" This is very real. So how far can the federal government intervene in the states and change this policy of confrontation and of war and change the training of the Military Police? You can make nonlethal weapons available for use in a range of situations, but the Military Police are trained to kill. When they use the Big Skull, for example, they arrive singing, "I'm going to take your soul, I'm going to get you, and I'm going to kill you." Are you going to change this behavior of the BOPE? Are you going to remove the most violent officers and bring in new people?

Balestreri: The federal government doesn't have legal power to change the system in the states. Under the legal federal system of Brazil, we cannot intervene at this time.

Maria Helena: Not even through the Cabinet for Integrated Management (GGI)?

Balestreri: No, not through the GGI or PRONASCI. It would strike at the constitutional principal of the federal division of power. What we can do, and we are doing more and more is to interfere through the initiation of public policies. As we have resources, and the states do not, we work with resources linking the policy of public security with the policy of human rights. For example, in the case of the program for the police to study in university, it is not simply to study. The curriculum has to emphasize human rights. We have at the national level a network of 66 institutions of higher education and 82 postgraduate courses in public security. This can also include the BOPE, changing the training a little. At the moment, we have 5,250 police students, municipal guards, and Fire Brigades of the Military Police in federal government courses, a yearlong course meeting the standards of the Ministry of Education and Culture. You can see how this is revolutionary. We only accept a curriculum that has at least four parts. First, the issue of gender. This includes not just the question of the rights of women, but also the question of the culture of violence of men against

women. Second, all courses also have to treat the question of homophobia
that is a very serious problem in Brazil. It's a serious question of persecution
and assassination since Brazil is one of the places where homosexuals are
most murdered. Third, all courses must study the question of racial equality,
of respect for and promotion of the question of rights for racial minorities.
Fourth, all courses must consider the question of age-based rights, of children, adolescents, and the aged. In this way, no police officer, civil or military, municipal guard, or fireman is going to do courses without studying
human rights.

Maria Helena: But here we enter the question of the Big Skull.

Balestreri: But there are two tasks with a given time in which to realize them. You have to work on changing the culture in the so called superstructure, and you also have to work on changing the infrastructure in the
question of weapons. The Federal government works on the superstructure
through education. When it educates police officers, it creates a group, a
critical mass for cultural resistance. When you work through this question
of culture, you are creating an anti-hegemonic group within the corporation.
Or at least, another group with another vision.

Maria Helena: What are you doing with those that are already inside
the corporation and were only trained to use force to kill and spread terror?

Balestreri: Let's become specific. At the federal level, we are creating
another force, the National Force for Public Security that has a different
training and vision. We are creating with it a special group that is not the
BOPE. It is the BEPE or the Special Battalion for Rapid Deployment. This
battalion will have 550 men and women coming from all states in the country, and they are going to be in a barracks here in the Federal District.
These men and women are going to receive the best training in special operations, and the best equipment on the planet. This training is entirely based
on this principle that the use of force has to coexist with a civilizing vision.
At the end of the year we are going to have these men and women from all
over Brazil trained in the defense of life, and not attacking life. At the end,
we are going to return to the states a group specially prepared to engage in a
process that we call "positive contamination" because it's a group highly
trained in special operations, technologically advanced from the point of
view of equipment but with a correct philosophy.

Maria Helena: But then you are going to have a different group inside
each corporation. Excuse me for insisting so much on this, but how are you

going to be able really to change the policy of security to this vision? For
example, when they get into a Big Skull, are they going to stop shooting at
everything as has been done?

Balestreri: Allow me to state how we at the federal level can act. We
have a limit, and I am not going to provide a demagogic answer. This is a
federalized country and within federal democracy there are limits as to how
we can act inside each state in the federation. To provide a concrete example, what can we do about the Big Skull. We received a request to buy 200
Big Skulls. We said, "No." Our federal government money will not be used
to buy the Big Skull. And they said, "But this armored car is considered a
necessity for the police throughout the world. The United Nations also has
armored cars." Our answer: "But the UN uses them differently."

The armored car can be used in one way or another. It is not used to go
into a community shooting. It is only used for the protection of police in
order for them to reach areas of operation. This is the position that the federal government can have. We are not going to approve any request for the
purchase of Big Skulls unless you can demonstrate that you are going to use
them in a different way, with a civilizing vision. We cannot go into the state
of Rio de Janeiro, and impose on them how they are going to use their
armored vehicles. We can only impose the idea that with our money there
will not be armored vehicles unless they change how they are used.

Maria Helena: Can you, as the federal government, use laws, for
example, that define torture? For example, can you intervene if there is a situation of large-scale police violence, of murders, of torture?

Balestreri: Yes, there are laws that can federalize crimes that are
considered heinous and in violation of human rights. But, you know how
Brazilian justice is. You have to prove that such a crime took place. Also,
what I am trying to say is that the public security forces in Brazil won't
change overnight. They will change with the implementation of effective
public policies. And the federal government today has very effective public policies. Here, we don't approve any project which goes against human
rights or increases police brutality. We are inflexible on this issue. And
large funds for public security in Brazil are here. We only approve projects which will reduce brutality and will respect human rights. You know
the power of money. Money changes practices. And we are using that
power to bring about change. This is the element we can use to change
the culture of Brazilian public security. I am confident that a policy like
that of Minister Tarso Genro will bring about different practices in
another two years.

Maria Helena: Then, in the case of torture, of an action classified as torture, the federal government can intervene?

Balestreri: No, federal justice cannot intervene. The federal government is limited by the federal pact. What I can say is the following: if you are the governor of a state and ask for machine guns, we are not going to finance the purchase of machine guns because they are arms for war and cannot be used in an urban environment. In two or three years you're going to learn that to coexist with me and with the money that I have you're going to have to come up with another system. Now, I can't say "Governor, you must change your system." The federal executive cannot give orders to the state executives. However, the power of money is great and can effect changes. If I receive a serious complaint of torture or extreme violence, I have to intervene in the case so that the Secretariat for Human Rights, and the public prosecutor will take notice so that action by federal justice will be set into motion.

Maria Helena: And how does the Cabinet for Integrated Administration work?

Balestreri: The Cabinet for Integrated Administration may advise and help to develop a policy with a different vision. But I cannot order the dissolution of the BOPE, for example. No one at the federal government level has the right to intervene in the police operations of the states. For that to happen, we would have to approve a new federal pact in the area of security, and have the country united on the issue of public security. Like the United States with its Patriot Act, where, in certain cases, the federal government has the right to intervene directly in the states, creating thereby a country united on questions of national security where part of the federal constitution is suspended.

That's a problem for international human rights organizations to understand. The states get all of their funding from the federal government. And the federal government must adhere to strict limits and within the present federal system of Brazil, the federal government can only use its financial power to bring about certain public security policies. But it cannot order or intervene directly. Let me give you a concrete example in an instance of international condemnation such as "the federal government must stop torture in the police stations of Brazil." That's very good, but it has no concrete consequence. The federal government does not have control over police stations or the police forces of any state. The federal government has no control over the state Military Police forces. No authority. Unless you count moral authority or the authority inherent in the granting of federal resources.

Maria Helena: You're making this change very quietly.

Balestreri: Yes, but it is a very significant change. I am certain that within the next two years we're going to begin to see a change of vision and conduct in the states.

Maria Helena: And this change already began with Minister Márcio Thomaz Bastos?[12]

Balestreri: Yes, in a quieter manner. Let us just say that Minister Tarso Genro has a bolder vision about this issue. The PRONASCI was created with this vision, that of complementing a policy of prevention with a policy of more restricted repression. But consider this, the most important thing for us is the following: we have to change the model followed by the police in Brazil. The police must cease following the reactive, invasive model that you are describing, a predominantly invasive one. The model must change to one that requires even in special operations that the police operate according to the law and, more than the law, with ethics and morality. Then, the most important issue is that police cannot be predominantly reactive or invasive. The predominant model for the police to follow is that of the neighborhood police officer with all the present day technology.

Do you know the police in Copacabana? Where do you go to get help from a police officer? You would have to go to the barracks where the police are militarized. Take my own home state of Rio Grande do Sul. There, we didn't speak of Cosme and Damião. For us, it was Peter and Paul. I remember that my parents would say that "we have to control our police forces." And "control" meant our nation taking control of its police forces.

What happened in Brazil was a kind of kidnapping of the police by the state. Today, the state must turn the police over to the nation, to our citizenry. The dictatorship did away with any notion of neighborhood police forces. What happened in Brazil from 1964 on, and especially after 1968, with the worsening of the coup, is that all of those models of neighborhood police forces were eliminated. All of the previous experiences, including that of Cosme and Damião and other models of neighborhood police forces were forbidden. The police forces were quartered in barracks, placed in vehicles circulating the entire day and the Military Police, under the command of the army, was used only as a force for repression. The Civil Police, instead of being an investigative organization, became a kind of office to register incidents, totally distanced from the population, and we ended up having an absent police force. You don't know who is your police force, don't know where to find them or speak to them. If you have to register an incident at the police station, you know that you may possibly be doubly victimized. You were already victimized by the criminal, and now you are going to be victimized by the police force. With rare exceptions, most people did not think of the police as being theirs. It stopped belonging to the citizenry and passed into the hands of the state. So we have this mission before us. We must return the police force to the people. And how are we going to do that? By creating a policing model, the neighborhood police force. If we can create in Rio de Janeiro a model of neighborhood police, the people themselves will begin to change their view of the police force and its mission.

A short while ago, we approved a 55 million *real* fund for public security in Rio de Janeiro, but we have one demand. "Take note of this," we said, "the federal government will only disburse these funds to you if you present a project for neighborhood policing in the Alemão complex. We no longer want a police model that only enters the Alemão complex shooting, that leaves shooting only to come back shooting again. What we want in the Alemão complex is a police force that stays, coexists, and dialogues with the people there. It is a demand of ours, the federal government. You're asking for 55 million and you'll receive it if you submit a project for neighborhood police. A police contingent that will live with and be permanently with those people." We made the suggestion and the Rio government accepted, and that's why I find that this is indicative of a change that can come.

Paulo de Tarso Vannuchi, Minister and Special Secretary for Human Rights: A Discussion with Maria Helena Moreira Alves and José Valentin Palacios, Brasília, June 2008

Paulo de Tarso Vannuchi has been a consultant to political parties, trade unions, and social movements and was a political coordinator in Lula's campaigns for president. He was also a political prisoner in São Paulo from 1971 to 1976, during the military dictatorship, and signed a report to the Brazilian Bar Association that identified types of torture carried out in military detention centers and named torturers. He was appointed special secretary for human rights in 2003. He identifies the human rights movement in Brazil as largely having originated during the military dictatorship period of 1964–1985 and points to the challenge of incorporating human rights values into police work. He also describes an official visit as secretary for human rights to the favela of Providencia in 2008, in which he was taken to the chief of the local drug gang to explain his presence. Vannuchi has been a critic of the policy of confrontation.

Maria Helena: There is a lot of fear of the police in the communities of Rio de Janeiro. Incredible things are taking place, including accusations that the BOPE has been using a curved knife and eviscerating people. What is the federal government—specifically, the Office of the Secretary for Human Rights—doing to address this situation?

Secretary Vannuchi: What the federal government is doing you are going to get principally from [Justice] Minister Tarso Genro and from [National Secretary for Public Security Ricardo] Balestreri. My focus, which I think is important, is human rights. It may not be as important for the content of your research, but I think you might break the ice with the theme of how human rights emerged during the military regime—first, because they did, and because it's a great paradox. Before 1964, people were not speaking about human rights. I don't know if this was so because this period saw the marked presence of the communist tradition in the social, labor union, and opposition movements and because the Soviet Union had not yet signed the Declaration of Human Rights of 1948 because it contained the article that said every person had the right to property, alone or in association with others.

Because of the violence of the military against opposition of every type during the military regime, a human rights consciousness was born. It began with the Catholic church. Afterward, it spread through the social movements and outside the church. When the military regime ended—we can say in 1985—this authoritarian debris remained until the new Constitution was promulgated in 1988. That's twenty years. Twenty years constructing a new political mentality against almost five centuries, because the historical Brazilian mentality is slaveocratic. Institutional violence by the state has been a permanent feature from the earliest construction of the state, with torture considered normal, and the killing of slaves and Indians, and two dictatorships during the twentieth century. Also, we came out of the dictatorship with the vision that the police are the enemy. What was specific to the military regime also carried over to our human rights movement. After the transition to democracy, there was no effort either to move closer to the police or to transform the police.

What we had was this: Franco Montoro won the gubernatorial election in São Paulo in 1983. Since 1983, there have been courses in human rights for the police. But it was only one component: The professor gave the class from 7:00 to 10:00. At 10:00, the next class was offered, "Suppression of Crime by the Police." What was this class on suppression of crime by the police teaching? That if you have a car with three black men in it, you have to stop it, because statistically it has been established that the men are criminals, and you cannot ask them to show documents from inside the car, because an officer who did this was shot in the forehead. So with gun drawn, you have to order them to get out of the car with their arms raised, and if you feel some trepidation, you start kicking them. So everything that had been taught about human rights from 7:00 to 10:00 was annulled after 10:00. We were training a police force that was not modified during the military regime and basically continued with the same training. Now, in Lula's government we have a great chance with PRONASCI. PRONASCI started in our Institute of Citizenship that was born in 1990 when the presidential campaign of 1989 showed all of us, and others close to Lula's campaign, "Look, you are going to be President."[13]

Beginning in 1990, in the Institute of Citizenship we concentrated on the elaboration of public policies in a pluralistic manner. We were going to bring in other parties, and especially other social segments, because we began to think that when the hour comes that we elect the president, he is not going to be president only of the working class, and he is not going to be president only of the Workers' Party (PT). We worked on one program after another. The first three were agrarian reform, agricultural policy and food security. They were the first programs that had density. That is, we began to make a realistic analysis, and not a wish list, so that we could say where we would get the money, what law had to be changed in those three areas, and so forth. After came a program for education, for housing, Zero Hunger, and in 2001 during the power blackouts we launched the program for energy "Electric Energy for Brazil" with Dilma Rousseff as coordinator.[14] At the end of 2001 and the beginning of 2002, we did "Public Security for Brazil."

The turnaround in public security is not a problem just for the police. It is for the police, but it's for the state as a whole, with education, health, and so forth; dialogue between the police force and the community; a proposal to create municipal guards, to municipalize security to the extent possible in order to have a police force close to the community, a return of the "Cosme and Damião" police officer. This construction involved a new network of education and postgraduate training of the police in human rights. We must rethink what public security is.

Constitutionally, the system of public security is given to the states. The idea of constructing a single system of public security involves an innovation, but it cannot be a federalization of the Santiago type against the rest of Chile, of Buenos Aires against the rest of Argentina. Brazil has to incorporate the federal idea. It's a very large country; there are too many geographical differences, differences in climate, and differences in culture for us to try to mount a centralized system in Brasília that is going to work. This dialogue is very thorny. It's been thorny with Governor Sérgio Cabral, even though Secretary Beltrame practically had been indicated for the position by us here. I am in a delicate situation in human rights. Why? Because of the option that Sérgio Cabral took that he calls the "policy of confrontation." It goes against the general spirit of what we launched at the Institute of Citizenship, and when we launched it, we made it a national matter here in Brasília. The minister of justice in the government of Fernando Henrique Cardoso, Aloisio Nunes Ferreira, accepted the document and said, "This is the most serious study ever made in Brazil with respect to public security."[15] It was a remarkable moment in the life of the republic. An adversary, on the eve of an election, recognized the importance of this vision.

We have to reconstruct the theme of human rights at the national level. Today, human rights for the poor is a curse word impregnated with the idea of defending bandidos. [Paulo] Maluf hammered on this at the end of the military regime.[16] He managed to fix this idea in the public mind. We have to reconstruct the correct conception that human rights are a good thing and not something bad. Brazil has a mental block with respect to human rights. Sérgio Cabral made a mistake in choosing this policy of confrontation. He sent me a message saying that I had to understand that he was working with public opinion, and that the public was giving 80 percent approval to this policy of confrontation. But I don't want to quarrel with him. This is not in my area, since I'm from the federal government. But then the first, the second news of deaths in the Alemão complex arrived. The third time, we had to investigate with an independent expert. I called on Pedro Montenegro, coordinator of Combat against Torture, who is from Alagoas, and he took two more experts from the Medical Legal Institute of Rio Grande do Sul to bring expertise from outside the Rio de Janeiro State. Pedro said, "Let's disinter the bodies." I decided against this because it does great violence to exhume bodies after a week. I said that we should make an expert technical determination based on the medical report. We also had photos of the cadavers, one of them scorched with gunpowder, and this only happens when bullets are fired at ten centimeters. Two had bullets in the back of the head, with a downward trajectory, and [the police report] called it death in combat. Death in combat usually means that a person was shot while running away, but being shot in the neck is contrary to the recommendation of proportional use of force, which orders that [the police] fire at the legs, buttocks, or other nonlethal region. The police academy teaches this. When you have a descending bullet trajectory in the back of the neck, it is more likely that the person had surrendered, was on his knees, or thrown on the ground.

If I wanted, I could have had ten minutes to talk about the events in the Alemão complex on *Jornal Nacional* [*National Journal*, a nightly news broadcast], but I did not do anything of the sort. I telephoned the Brazilian Bar Association and Beltrame and said, "We are delivering the independent report." Beltrame went to the press and said it was absurd. He was against me. I phoned him and said, "This is not the way you deal with these matters. You have a report. I have another. Let's get a third." I always have this weapon: an international report written by an expert. This was reflected in the treatment given to Philip Alston, the United Nations Rapporteur for Extrajudicial, Summary, or Arbitrary Executions. He came here. I received him. I explained to him the Brazilian government's position on human rights. It was the policy we had before the Lula government, and we reinforced it. What is that position? We are not hiding our problems, and for each demonstrated problem, we show policies that are under way to overcome this. And what happened? Philip Alston travels. He comes here, after he goes to Rio de Janeiro, to São Paulo, and to Recife. The only friction is in Rio. His encounter with Beltrame and others was tense. When Alston announced his position about what was happening, there was a lot of friction.

Maria Helena: One Military Police officer gave him a toy Big Skull as a present.

Vannuchi: Yes, he gave a Big Skull as a present, and Beltrame went over his head to the press. President Lula, on a flight with me and after having finished lunching with Cabral, said, "It would be good if you respond to the United Nations report." I said, "Mr. President, the United Nations report is correct." I explained to him, and he agreed. Yes, this problem exists. We have death squads in Brazil. We have seven states with this problem.

But returning to Rio: For a long time, organized crime has killed people, cut open their bodies, and thrown them in the ocean. This thing of the knife [the *corvo*] used by the BOPE is cause for worry. The Military Police probably also do it, the militia also. With so much coastline in Rio, it's very difficult to find the bodies. It's a waste of time to search for bodies. I did not know about this thing of the curved knife. It's something classic. You open the abdomen, remove the intestines, and the bodies sink. It is a horrific situation. Now I'm thinking that I've been at this for two and half years and have had conversations with the CESeC [Center for the Study of Public Safety and Citizenship], with Julita Lembruger, with Rubem César Fernandes [director of the NGO Viva Rio] that the hour has arrived to give our discourse a mantra, to emphasize everywhere public security and human rights as a first priority. If we do not do this, we are going to lose the debate.

The episode of Providencia Hill was extraordinarily grave in that, within six months of the army's presence, contamination [of the army] by organized crime, by the drug traffickers, took place. I went to Providencia Hill to converse with the mothers, with the Federal Police, and with the army commander.[17] I went with Rubem César Fernandes. When we were at the Residents' Association to speak with the mothers, a man from the Red Command arrived and said to one of Rubem César's advisers, "Look, the chief ordered you to come up. Right now!" He practically put us under arrest. The two of us were taken to the headquarters of the Red Command. We were placed us in a small room, and the chief asked, "What's your business here?" They said to him, "No, he's clean. He's the secretary of human rights who came to speak with the mothers of the dead boys." And [the chief] said, "OK, then it's fine. Let them speak. You can let them go." So I think that it's important that you put in your book that the situation is not only police violence, as it was in the time of the military dictatorship. A very grave situation exists of loss of territory, loss of government control, including national control, in certain areas to organized crime groups that are in command and go beyond the authority of the nation's government. This is very grave. It's very difficult to combat this. What Brazil needs today is research that shows and denounces the use of the curved knife by the BOPE, but that also does not avoid showing the seriousness of the control of territories by organized crime, because otherwise no one is going to understand, for example, the position of Sérgio Cabral.

Maria Helena: In spite of all this, I do not understand the position of Sérgio Cabral. There is no explanation for entering a poor community shooting indiscriminately from a Big Skull inside schoolyards and killing so many people and without catching the true chiefs of organized crime that everyone knows do not live in the favelas.

Vannuchi: I understand what he thinks. He thinks this way: "In a policy of confrontation, I'm going to have 10 percent of intellectuals against [me] and 80 percent of the people are going to be in favor." But it is mistaken thinking, because the 10 percent who are against are in the right with international laws and national laws, and sooner or later they are going to influence public opinion, and it will change. Public opinion will turn against this policy of confrontation and death unless the incidents of mugging, kidnapping, and armed robbery really begin to fall rapidly. But in this sense, the policy of confrontation is not efficient. For all the indices for Rio de Janeiro, not one is getting better. I think that Cabral is going to begin to think about another option, and in this sense Balestreri is going to be able to influence and to build something with PRONASCI.

Sérgio Cabral, Governor of the State of Rio de Janeiro: A Discussion with Maria Helena Moreira Alves and Philip Evanson, July 2008

Governor Sérgio Cabral is the son of a much loved Rio de Janeiro journalist and writer of the same name. The younger Cabral also began as a journalist but soon focused on politics. In 1990, at age twenty-seven, he was elected a Rio state representative, and in 1995 he became president of the Rio de Janeiro State Assembly. In 2002, he was elected to the Federal Senate. In 2006, Cabral won a runoff election to become governor of Rio de Janeiro State. He has been praised for fiscal responsibility and improvements in the administration of state government. He has also strongly supported the policy of confronting drug gang bandidos and has characterized the conflict between drug gangs and the police as a war. His critics argue that the policy leads to unnecessary loss of life while criminal groups continue at full strength. However, Cabral believes that a hardline policy toward bandidos has public support. The policy of confrontation has sometimes put Cabral at odds with President Lula's ministers who prioritize human rights and less violent and better-trained police. Nevertheless, Cabral and Lula remain political allies, and the governor can answer his critics by saying that Rio de Janeiro was awarded the 2016 Olympic Games despite widespread reports of crime and violence. Like Lula, Cabral blames past government leniency that allowed people to occupy land in a disorganized, unplanned manner for the problems in the favelas.

Maria Helena: To formulate the plan for public security for the present government, did you consult with the police and civil society organizations?

Governor Cabral: I spent about a hundred hours bent over my plan for governing in 2006, and I sought to hear the most diverse segments of the population—the most diverse possible. For example, in the area of security, I heard the Police Union, I heard Viva Rio, I heard Afro Reggae, I heard the police leadership: In short, I heard all groups, which strengthened my convictions as someone who was active in the public life of the state as a legislator and as president of the State Assembly. My relationship with the population is very strong. I was the state deputy who received the most votes in Rio de Janeiro in 1994. I was the senator who received the largest number of votes in the history of Rio, and now, as governor, I had 60 percent of the runoff vote. I know the people and the community leaders. I am absolutely certain that in the matter of security, we have to consider other areas that have an interface with security, and that the absence of these services constitutes enormous violence against the population. The violence is not only a police officer who may corrupt himself through illicit dealings, or a police officer who is truculent with the honest citizen, but is also the absence of a school, a hospital, or water and sewage infrastructure.

In the area of security, I knew that we had to bring in someone absolutely immune to this history [of the police], but who at the same time knows the history. For this reason, I chose Beltrame, because he is absolutely immune and, at the same time, from the inside, because until he took his position as secretary of public security, he was the chief of operations of the Federal Police in support of Rio de Janeiro. He was an inspector of the Federal Police for more than twenty years, and he has an arsenal of information on the Rio de Janeiro underworld, as much on white-collar crime as on street-corner crime.

What is most important is that for the first time in Rio de Janeiro, the governor is giving the secretary of security a completely free hand in choosing his team. In the eighteen months I have been governor, I have never involved myself in choosing security deputies. I did not even get into the matter of Military Police promotions or in choosing the chief of the Civil Police or any officer. These are all decisions for Beltrame to make. Besides, it is a democratic principle, and it makes a big difference. For example, one of the scenes from the film *Elite Squad* shows a deputy negotiating with the secretary over a position. This practice ended in our government. It does not exist. It's an important principle of police autonomy.

Another important principle is to re-equip the police, not only with information technology, but also in other areas. In this matter, one more scene shown in *Elite Squad* no longer exists in our government: the one showing how government vehicles are maintained. They change a carburetor here, do something else there, always negotiating with what is illicit. For the city of Rio de Janeiro, we bought new vehicles and we have outsourced the maintenance work. The Military Police cannot have in their hands an activity that consumes the time of hundreds of police officers and leaves few cars operational.

Maria Helena: And the Big Skull? Are you going to eliminate the Big Skull?

Cabral: We are buying other types of armored cars that are important in the sustaining police operations. Unfortunately, we face a situation in Rio de Janeiro that is the fruit of a distortion. That is, my generation is post-amnesty [1979], after the end of the dictatorship. In Rio de Janeiro, during the post-dictatorship period, there was an enormous and false dichotomy between "law and order" and "human rights." It was as if law and order and human rights could not live together. Then there was leniency on the part of public authorities, a permissiveness that was absolutely brutal for the city. This vision took control of the city, which permitted the disorderly occupation of urban land, meaning that the favelas grew to irresponsible sizes.

Maria Helena: You mean that people concerned with human rights did not control this growth?

Cabral: They did not control; they did not prevent the disorderly occupation; they did not establish rules of civilization that any state with a democratic rule of law requires. The moment that poor communities are permitted to grow but are not provided with water, sewerage infrastructure, schools, jobs, a culture of poverty is installed and, at the same time, the demand for drugs undeniably grows. Let's establish a point to sell drugs here, and let's sell drugs. Organized crime has grown greatly in the past twenty years. If we may make a comparison, you will see that New York is a city that votes for Democrats for representative, senator, even president but votes for Republicans for mayor. The Republicans understand that it is necessary to have absolute conditions of law and order. Everyone has the right to demonstrate, but meanwhile law and order are absolutely guaranteed.

Maria Helena: But there is a difference, if you'll permit my saying so. A New York politician would never think of sending police into the streets of Harlem like the BOPE goes into the communities firing guns and playing, "I'm going to get you, I'm going to kill you, I'm going to leave bodies on the ground, I'm going to take your soul." Never. It is unthinkable for any governor [of New York] to go into Harlem, for example, in this way where you have the same problems in terms of drugs or organized crime that we have.

Cabral: No, they do not have the same problems, and yes, the police have been sent in.

Maria Helena: But they don't enter firing guns randomly with the Big Skull.

Cabral: No, of course not.

Maria Helena: Is it possible to have a policy of confronting directly, as you are doing, and simultaneously respecting the human and civil rights of the residents? Is this possible in the context of Rio de Janeiro?

Cabral: To cite another First World city, I'm not Napoléon III, and we are not in nineteenth-century Paris.

Maria Helena [*laughing*]: We hope we're not.

Cabral: Rio is not Paris, and we don't have Baron Haussmann.[18] Napoléon III said, "We need to open Paris," and he called Baron Hauss- mann, who opened the streets. Paris of that epoch was entirely the Latin Quarter. Haussmann designed the city that we have in Paris.

Maria Helena: I don't see how this applies to Rio de Janeiro.

Cabral [*rising out of his chair to make a point*]: My thesis is we have the fruit of this irresponsibility of making the city in this way, of allowing growth without planning, without any infrastructure. What we have today is a need to enter the modern world—in logistics, in the physical part, in accessibility. The communities are inaccessible not only to the police, but to postal delivery, to firefighters, to trash collectors. In Rio das Pedras, dozens of shacks were on fire, and the firemen were not able to enter and reach them. Accessibility is not guaranteed, contrary to Harlem. The tension increases dramatically when you go into a community to which you do not have access. You are a police officer, and you enter alleys and paths, not knowing where the bullets are coming from. You see a kid wearing Bermuda shorts walking through an alley—a decent, honest kid—and behind him you see a kid wearing Bermuda shorts and carrying an automatic rifle ready to fire. There are many little alleys. The physical logic of the communities is absolutely adverse to police authority and extremely helpful to the bandido, to organized crime. However, it is also helpful to the unscrupulous police officer, because there he can do his business with the drug traffickers with- out anyone seeing. Or even for parallel activity by police or former police officers, who when they are off duty can oversee business deals, kill a half- dozen drug traffickers, take control of the area, of the community. So he goes there, puts a bullet in the head of one, kills another, and everything is in order. You do not have any more drug dealers. Instead, distribution of gas is with him, cable TV hookup is with him, transportation is with him. They [unscrupulous police and former police officers] were strengthening this parallel power in the communities and today their armed power is very great.[19] What is our vision? Again, it is not only the combating, the confronting. Our security perspective is much broader.

Maria Helena: It is, but you have said publicly that combating comes first, that it's necessary "to retake territories."

Cabral: Exactly, but that is not all. I'm going to give you an example. Today, the bus companies in partnership with the [Rio state] secretary of labor are training 2,000 drivers because there is a demand for bus drivers, who have full social-security rights at a salary of 1,200 *reais* a month. Because we have to deal with alternative transportation, we had to provide rules for alternative transportation.[20] We asked for bids, and we separated the wheat from the chaff. A part of the system of alternative transportation is controlled by the drug traffickers or by the militias.

Maria Helena: What is being planned with PAC in the favelas? It's integrated with PRONASCI, isn't it?

Cabral: Yes, but PAC is the big thing. PRONASCI is a very important complement. PRONASCI already began with us with the training of our police. We now have about 5,000 police receiving the PRONASCI scholarship, and we are going to reach 20,000 who take these courses and are remunerated. They earn up to 1,900 *reias,* and earn 400 *reias* more a month as a course scholarship, which helps them a lot. It's a partnership with Justice Minister Tarso Genro. But in the PAC, we are spending 450 million *reais*. And what are we doing there? Making streets, avenues, public squares, libraries, schools, health clinics, transporation. . . .

Maria Helena: Is this where the cablecar line comes in?

Cabral: Yes. As I observed in Colombia, in Medellín. Secretary of Security Beltrame and I went to Medellín, and we sent a team to Medellín. It is a city with half the population living in favelas. We have a fifth of our population in favelas, but, at the same time, the economy of Rio de Janeiro is the size of Colombia's. We learned a lot when we were there. We even met King Juan Carlos and Queen Sophia of Spain, who were then inaugurating a beautiful library. What, then, was the work there? There was a hardline conservative federal government under [President Álvaro] Uribe and a progressive mayor. The two were from different parties acting in opposition to each other but working together, each doing his part. When you enter a favela in Medellín, you take a cablecar to the top and see the shacks. And they are shacks—nothing is made of mortar. The people there do not have a third of the goods that people of Rocinha have in their homes. But there you see a community without fear—with a police presence, but without fear. How is it that they reached this point?

Maria Helena: Are you also making places to live, houses?
Cabral: Yes, inside the community. Just so you can have an idea, in Manguinhos, the fruit of this disorderly favela growth, the deterioration of some suburban areas is fantastic. At one time, the communities had sidewalks, houses with porches. Penha and Iraja had excellent houses. What happened? The factories were closed, and the businesses left. In the Manguinhos complex and in Bomsucesso, where we are going to spend 350 million *reais,* a big part of this investment in the communities will be spent retaking areas. In the Alemão and Manguinhos complexes, and in Bomsucesso, there are enormous areas that were factories and are now abandoned and where people live in subhuman conditions. We are going to reclaim these, make good dwellings and places for public use such as plazas and recreation areas. We are reclaiming the areas around these communities and abandoned buildings. At an army base in Manguinhos, an attractive place attached to the community, for example, we are building a theater and a school, and there are also going to be houses.

What is the difficulty? It is the day to day. We are running the train at high speed. We have to switch the train's cars—upgrade the police, recycle the police, combat illicit thinking within the police, develop and reward good police—while the train is running at a high velocity. To give you an idea, a month ago the headline on a Sunday edition of O *Globo* was, "Homicide Falls in Rio de Janeiro." I spoke with people, but they weren't very enthusiastic. We still have a lot to do. I don't have illusions. I know that it's going to take a long time to improve things, including changing the mentality of the police.

We have the case of the child João Roberto [Soares]. You have some disconnected people who are saying, "This is the policy of the governor who gives the order to shoot." It's not acceptable to dress me in the clothing of someone who orders the police to fire at innocent people—not even at people who might be bandidos. The logic was that they were bandidos. The police did not fire knowing that a mother and two children were in the car. They fired because they thought they were doing something right, that there were bandidos inside. Which was absolutely wrong. In the language of war, when you confront your enemy, you disarm him and take him prisoner. You don't immediately kill without knowing. What happened was a massacre.

Maria Helena: From what I've seen in your statements to the press, it seems that you and Secretary Beltrame believe that nothing can be done without first reoccupying territory. You believe that it's necessary first to surround with a police operation, as was done in the Alemão complex.

Cabral: No! We are going ahead with many projects in the Alemão complex—in Rocinha, Pavão-Pavãozinho. The projects are going forward. It is a moving experience because you can see that, in spite of everything, we are opening workshop schools in these communities. Today more than 5,000 people are being trained in these workshop schools opened by the Residents' Associations. Our approach is to use the maximum possible number of local workers in these projects because they are large-scale projects that generate many jobs. I went to inaugurate the workshop school in the Alemão complex, and it was an emotional experience. Today, many people, including older women, are learning carpentry and other things, becoming qualified so that contractors will hire them for construction work.

Philip: What is happening to people in organized crime? Are they abandoning this?

Cabral: I believe that they are intractable. They are not lying low. They are trying as hard as they can to maintain their economic activity, which is drug trafficking. But without firing a shot, we seized fifteen tons of marijuana and cocaine in various communities, and we are seizing many guns. We are disarming the drug traffickers.

Maria Helena: Then can one think that it is going to be less necessary to undertake police mega-operations as PAC and PRONASCI work advance?

Cabral: Yes, but we are also combating militias, as you can see from the newspapers. We are arresting them and combating illegality. A City Council member from my party is under arrest, and there are police under arrest. Since this book is going to be an international publication, I want to say that I have already spoken with many international leaders, including those at a seminar at the Council of the Americas, in which I said—and had already said publicly—that we have to review our drug laws. The fact is that people consume drugs. Drugs exist in the world, and every year have more power. What logic is this? I've been saying this publicly. We have to review the issue of legalizing drugs. It's an international discussion.

Philip: You said that Brazil can take the lead in this.

Cabral: Yes, I said that Brazil can take the lead in the discussion in the United Nations and the Organization of American States. It's a discussion that has to be taken to the First World countries. The U.S. government has to raise the subject, has to provoke this discussion.

Philip: But the present U.S. government thinks that it is successful in combating drugs.

Cabral: Which isn't true.

Philip: Do you have a program to fight organized crime?

Cabral: This plan requires investment in intelligence. Today, we have upgraded information technology that allows us to monitor telephone conversations and other things. We have to work together with the Office of the Public Prosecutor. We have destroyed many things of organized crime and the militias by using this equipment. This work permits us to arrest some organized crime leaders without firing a single shot. But we also take firm, decisive action in these communities because part of our strategy is to weaken organized crime through confrontation. Confrontation is serious, because if you go into one of these communities, you can be shot, because there is a strongly armed little army that shoots when it sees a police officer. This is a situation opposite to what it ought to be. When a police officer is in Laranjeiras, he isn't shot.[21] But when he goes up the hill into Alemão, he is fired on. When he goes into Rocinha, he is fired on. This cannot be part of the landscape of Rio de Janeiro. It is within this framework that we are also acting.

The other part of the strategy that is also very important concerns qualifications. PRONASCI brings a training program in citizenship to these communities; it also brings job and police training. It is evident that our police are frightened. We have to create a program that psychologically trains police in a way that is permanent, because the police officer who is dealing with a middle-class woman in the Zona Sul is the same officer who, ten minutes later, can be using an automatic rifle to confront a crazy guy who has just snorted cocaine and who is shooting at him and the community. The true story of the stray bullet is mainly about someone who has been doing drugs, who shoots a gun without thinking about hitting an innocent person. He shoots without aiming because he is not prepared to use guns— we are talking about unprepared kids, kids using hallucinogenic drugs, who have the most powerful guns available. From this fact comes our decision to use the armored cars and armored helicopters. They are necessary.

Philip: Don't you think that the police may be under too much pressure? They receive training in how to deal with citizens, but with so much pressure day after day, they may throw aside the training manual and think about their own lives, their own survival.

Cabral: No. An orientation is given by the secretary of security, and it is evident that if police do not follow this orientation, they can commit errors. One order is: No one enters a community without a planned and well-thought-out action, something that is not altogether clear to the public. The actions that we are undertaking are planned.

Maria Helena: This is being done now, because before it was not this way?

Cabral: I have contacts with community leaders, respected people from the community movements. They say to me, "Governor, you are not wrong. You have not made a mistake. Do not stop these operations." I have never met here at the palace door a group from the Residents' Associations who came to complain. In that famous operation of surrounding the Alemão complex, where more than a thousand men were used, not even a mother came here to complain about the death of her child. Not one. I'm not saying that in an operation such as that one, as well as it was planned, there are not enormous risks. Because of the layout of the favela, there is an enormous risk of committing an error. For example, in an operation in which a helicopter was used in the favela of Corea, and this is even on YouTube, an automatic rifle was fired into the favela, and it is evident that it was fired from a laje. A child died there, and it is evident that it was drug traffickers who fired the gun. There were no police officers in the area. But I don't want to exempt the police from blame. Besides, a news report yesterday in O *Globo* made a comparison between Recife and Rio. The police there kill many people. Here I say, the governor likes the poor. The governor here in Rio de Janeiro does not want to engage in social slaughter. The governor here speaks about social inclusion.

Maria Helena: Then you are not in favor of what Colonel Marcus Jardim stated: that the Military Police is the best social insecticide? It was a police officer—Jardim—who said this.

Cabral: An absolutely unfortunate statement. Of course, I'm not in favor of this. Throughout my public life, I have been identified with the most humble. I have only legislated for the most humble members of our society. I was the one who made the law providing bus passes for the elderly and for students, the laws that provide incentives for culture. The upbringing that my father gave me is the struggle on behalf of the poor. I want these people to have decent living conditions, to be free of this evil, of this disease, because if it is bad for the whole of society, for them, it is much worse. We have a program for the communities: the program of health clinics open twenty-four hours. It's necessary to open small clinics for rapid care. Rio de Janeiro has received aid from the Ministry of Health for rapid-care clinics. They are clinics with observation beds that provide rapid care. They are open twenty-four hours a day and integrated with services of mobile and rapid care. The idea began in Rio de Janeiro. During one year of these clinics' existence, 99.7 percent of those who were admitted were successfully treated in the rapid care clinics. This means 600,000 people receiving care. There were seven clinics. It's a structure of 1,000 square feet. . . . By the end of the year, we are going to open more in order to reach twenty rapid-care clinics. If you go there, you are going to receive the care that your health plan provides. The clinics are in poor communities. This is a way to attend to the population well, isn't it? This is what citizenship is.

In education, we have a most serious situation. Our teachers have not received salary adjustments in twelve years. In the past year, we gave an adjustment; this year, we are also going to give one. We are doing teacher training. In the state we are responsible for all middle-school education. But beyond middle school, due to the fragility of the municipal governments, the state has 600,000 students in elementary education through the ninth year of school.

Maria Helena: Are you able to inspect the PAC projects? How are you going to inspect and audit them and also inspect the work of PRONASCI with the NGOs?

Cabral: We work very little with NGOs, but we have an office for the administration of projects that inspects all of the projects. In education, we have to train teachers and increase access to middle-school education. We are buying private schools to turn them into public schools. For example, we bought the Santa Teresa Swiss School, which has a swimming pool, a theater, and so forth. We bought it to transform it into a public school because it's important to provide young people with good schools so they can have opportunities. But don't ask me to produce miracles. We have to punish police that were violent, but we have to work in the social and health areas. The third front is the economic agenda, which is going very well. Rio de Janeiro has 100 billion *reais* invested in the petrochemical industry. Lula has invested more in technical schools. There are dozens of technical schools to prepare young people for the new investments. We are renovating schools, such as the one in Niteroi for the shipping sector, where we are spending 10 million [*reais*] on renovation.

Philip: PAC and PRONASCI represent a new relationship between the federal government and the state government. How is the Cabinet of Integrated Administration working?

Cabral: We are working together very well, and we have met every week. We took various ideas from São Paulo—for example, the outsourcing of vehicle maintenance for the Military Police. In relation to your question, when I spoke with the president, I relied heavily on what was happening in São Paulo, in Minas Gerais, in Espirito Santo in presenting our plans. Our relationship with the federal government is very good and is being translated into large investments. But the position of the president is also very important. For example, with regard to security, following the election in 2006 and a week before I was sworn in, organized crime set a bus on fire, killing seventeen people. The president, while speaking at my swearing in, took the initiative to say that he was going to help Rio de Janeiro combat this barbarism. The next day, with Justice Minister Márcio Thomaz Bastos, we established the Cabinet of Integrated Administration with the principles under which it operates. I said that I needed help. We identified twelve drug-trafficking leaders, the twelve chiefs, and we needed to transfer them out of Rio. It took place within the hour. The armed forces came and took away the twelve. We also have an important partnership with the National Security Force. From the beginning of my government, the NSF has collaborated with us.

We have to revive Rio de Janeiro—not the old Rio, but Rio for the twenty-first century. We have a positive agenda with the federal government, including the campaign to bring the Olympic Games here. It's Rio with quality of life; the people deserve to live in peace and with dignity. We spent 350 million *reais* on new trains to improve urban service. We are expanding the subway system. All of this is being done in partnership with the federal government and with the international sector. Today we have international credits for investments. But everything is very difficult, and I don't have illusions.

Maria Helena: But everything seems contradictory. Ricardo Balestreri told us that, as national secretary for public security, he was only paying for nonlethal weapons. Are you going to apply to this program?

Cabral: I think that in urban operations they can be used. There they are important. It also depends on the operation in the favela, on where we are and who we are confronting. Then what did Beltrame say? "From now on, all police operations in the favelas will be organized and planned. All police who enter favelas separate from these operations will be punished."

Entering separate from these operations? This sort of thing might even be considered a militia. If it is happening against the order of the secretary of public security, something strange and wrong is happening. Quite possibly, it is really a corrupt police officer, or even perhaps a militia. We have to be very careful not to radicalize criticism. In my thinking, the police cannot turn into a "Geni," because if people turn radically against the police, we won't be able to do anything.[22]

Maria Helena: But for the police not to turn into a Geni, the faith of the population in the police, especially the poor population, will have to be restored. But speaking of serious accusations, you said that no mother came to the palace to complain to the governor. I know many mothers in poor communities, and a poor mother does not have the courage to approach the governor. A mother from the middle class might, but a poor mother will not. Then will this channel be open?

Cabral: Of course, it's open.

Maria Helena: Where can a poor mother go to reach the governor? Where can she present a serious accusation of police violence?

Cabral: The Residents' Associations could be a conduit. But she can come directly here through our press office. And another thing is the change in the BOPE. Last week, I made a speech to the BOPE telling them they had to change. I can guarantee you that this thing of playing that song, "We are going to eat your liver and kill people," has stopped in my government. I went to the BOPE and said this. I don't want this. In truth, the degree of aggressiveness of the Military Police begins with their training. And the relationship among them even in the hierarchy has to be more fraternal. It is the same with the communities. There is a tremendous degree of stress, and we really have to change this in our police.

Conclusion

Brazil is clearly a nation immersed in contradictions. On the one hand, important advances have been made in reducing poverty and advancing social rights, which provides greater opportunities to those who historically have been excluded. In 2009, the important Statute of Racial Equality became law and could prove a landmark in dealing with racially based social exclusion. On the other hand, human rights have been lost in certain areas due to the actions of criminal groups, state agents, or both. It is not acceptable for officials to say that continued operations by police in the favelas, with daily counts of anonymous dead people who are always called "bandidos," are necessary to wrest territory from the control of criminal gangs. These gangs exist, and conflicts between them take place and make the right to life for residents in affected communities fragile. However, acknowledging the existence of gang conflicts cannot be allowed to provide a blank check to the state government to enter communities shooting randomly from the Big Skull vehicles, and even from helicopters, wounding and killing people. As of 2010, such events were part of the daily news in Rio de Janeiro.

Brazilian Solutions

What are the solutions? Some possible solutions are included in the federal government's innovative PRONASCI program. Others require a constitutional amendment, such as the proposal by United Nations Special Rapporteur Philip Alston that the Military Police be abolished and replaced with a newly created civil police force trained to serve, not to repress or kill, citizens. Other reforms that would deal with the serious problems of drug crime, white-collar crime, money laundering, and acts of terrorism, such as the burning of buses, may require another constitutional amendment redefining the responsibilities of each branch of government and the division of power between the federal government and state governments. Justice Minister Tarso Genro's opinion is that a "new federative pact" is required so that public security can be dealt with jointly by federal, state, and municipal governments. PRONASCI has included a version of this federative pact in requiring each state that makes an agreement with PRONASCI to form a Cabinet of Integrated Administration that includes representatives of the federal, state, and municipal governments to select and oversee PRONASCI projects. However, PRONASCI, with all of its promise, is still only the program of President Lula and his administration. To carry through the intended reforms, it must have continuity by becoming a permanent part of the Brazilian state's agenda, independent of political parties in power and supported after 2010 by a new president leading a new administration.

Clearly, real public safety must include zero tolerance of government abuse of police power. The Constitution of 1988, like modern democratic constitutions everywhere, guarantees the safety of all citizens. Therefore, the state must be primordially concerned with *enforcing obedience to this already existing legislation,* which includes such citizenship rights as the right to life itself, to be considered innocent until proved guilty within the judicial system, to come and go freely within a community, to be free of entry into the home by police without a warrant issued by a judge, and to not be subjected to cruel treatment or torture by state agents. There is also the obligation to preserve the scene of a crime and provide complete access to forensic experts, which becomes all the more important when the possibility exists that the crime was committed by agents of the state in the course of their official duties. It is also against the law for police officers to remove bodies, cause them to disappear, or affirm that those who died were criminals killed in acts of resistance. Solutions for protecting the human rights of citizens can be said already to exist in the 1988 Constitution, which marked the transition from military dictatorship to democracy, and in other good laws, and they need to be followed strictly by agents of the state, with procedures put in place to monitor, investigate, and punish criminal behavior by state agents.[1]

Solutions Recommended from outside Brazil

Solutions to bad public security conditions also have come in recommendations from outside Brazil. Since the 1990s, international organizations such as Amnesty International and Human Rights Watch have issued numerous reports attesting to large-scale human rights violations in Brazil that continue largely unchecked despite all of the unfavorable attention they engender. These reports helped to bring about the fact-finding mission to Brazil in 2007 by Special Rapporteur Alston. His report, issued in 2008, has raised human rights violations to a new level of scrutiny and opened Brazil to possible United Nations sanctions, because Brazil has signed several international treaties that commit it to protecting human rights. Alston's report makes specific recommendations in different areas and can be considered a platform on which to build real solutions to preserve human rights and specific constitutional rights of all citizens.[2]

These recommendations identify key areas where public security actors have failed to protect human rights. For example, in criminal procedure, the report recommends eliminating the statute of limitations for intentional crimes against life and the practice of allowing individuals convicted of murder to remain at liberty while appealing their verdicts, as is common in Brazil. Convicted murderers' right to remain at liberty facilitates the intimidation of witnesses and produces a sense of impunity. An effective program of witness protection is only in a first phase in Brazil, and poor people feel intimidated. The report notes complaints about the Big Skull armored vehicles; it recommends that videocameras and audio recorders be placed inside and that monitoring be done in cooperation with the community. The report recommends abolishing the Military Police, which is certain to be strongly resisted by state governors for whom the Military Police consitute an army under their command. It would also be fiercely resisted by the police themselves. The main criticism of the Military Police is they are trained as soldiers for combat in war, with urban warfare techniques and even the use of lethal weapons of war. They are trained to demolish obstacles, invade homes, and kill enemies. Because of this training, the Military Police cannot be seen as a reliable force for protecting human rights. Alston's report recognizes the seriousness of the PRONASCI program but notes that it does not go far enough in tying state funding to compliance "with measures aimed at reducing the incidence of extrajudicial executions by police."[3]

Nor has another reform been institutionalized: the police *ouvidoria* (ombudsperson). Laws on the books provide for ombudspersons, but they do not make the position independent. Current ombudspersons do not have their own resources to conduct investigations or hire staff independent of the police who can prepare dossiers for prosecutors. Further, there are no independent ombudspersons who are not connected to the state police structure, such as a prosecutor from another state or even a public security authority from another country. Other countries have tried such methods. Perhaps the best-known example was the appointment in 1999 of Nuala Patricia O'Loan of Ireland to be the first police ombudsperson in Northern Ireland and whose work became important in the peace process between Catholics and Protestants in Northern Ireland.

The Alston report emphasizes the importance of transparency and accountability in police work. After all, the police are also citizens, and their professional responsibility is to protect and aid other citizens. Police expect to be respected by citizens, just as citizens expect to have the respect of police. However, the police, especially the Military Police, have long operated in a closed world of public denial, contesting critics, and having limited dialogue with the public at large. Their superiors—namely, state governors and their secretaries of public security—have tended to follow suit. The report raises serious issues that require open discussion and dialogue, such as police impunity, control of police firearms, establishing independent units for internal police investigation with ample resources, the inviolability of forensic evidence, and increasing police salaries. It recommends:

1. In each state, the secretariat of public security should establish a reliable specialized unit to investigate and prosecute police involvement in militias and extermination groups.

2. Off-duty police should under no circumstances be permitted to work for private security firms. To facilitate such changes, police should be paid significantly higher salaries.

3. Systems for tracking the use of firearms should be established in all states, and where some procedures already exist, they must be improved, and the government must ensure they are followed. The weapons and the quantity of ammunition provided to each policeman should be recorded, and every bullet should be regularly accounted for. Every instance in which a police officer fires his or her weapon should be investigated by internal affairs and recorded in a database. This database should be accessible to Offices of Police Ombudspersons and used by police chiefs and commanders to identify police who need closer supervision.

4. The current practice of classifying police killings as "acts of resistance" or "resistance followed by death" provides carte

blanche for killing by police and must be abolished. Without prejudicing the outcome of criminal trials, such killings should be included in each state's homicide statistics.

5. The National Secretariat for Human Rights should keep a detailed database of human rights violations by police.

6. The integrity of work by the internal affairs services of the police should be ensured by (1) establishing a separate career path for those who work in internal affairs; (2) establishing clear procedures and time limits for investigations; and (3) making all information regarding investigations and recommended disciplinary sanctions freely accessible to Offices of Police Ombudspersons.

7. In cases that involve killings by police and other allegations of serious abuse, internal affairs services should publicly provide information on the status of individual cases, including the measures recommended to police chiefs and commanders.

8. Police under investigation for crimes that constitute extrajudicial executions should be removed from active duty.

9. Offices of Police Ombudpersons, as they exist in most states, should be reformed so they are better able to provide external oversight.

10. The routine failure of police to preserve crime scenes must end; should problems persist, the Office of the Public Prosecutor should use its authority to exercise external control of the police to ensure the integrity of its prosecutions.

11. Hospitals should be required to report to police precincts and police internal affairs units all cases in which the police bring a deceased criminal suspect to a hospital.

12. State Institutes of Forensic Medicine should be made fully independent from secretariats for public security, and expert staff should receive employment guarantees that ensure the impartiality of their investigations. Additional resources and technical training should also be provided.

Most democratic countries, having made multiple attempts to deal with problems that were similar or comparable to those that make public security a leading issue today in Brazil, are now following these recommendations. In all reforms that have been successful, the issue of *external* and *independent* control of the police has been crucial to contain and root out police corruption and violence. Finally, the Alston report concludes that the federal government of Brazil must ensure that the report is sent to all officials, at all levels, and that it become one of the responsibilities of the federal Secretariat of Human Rights to ensure compliance with the recommendations of the United Nations by all branches of government. Even though the Constitution of Brazil mandates a division of the responsibilities of federal, state, and municipal authorities on matters related to public safety, it is nonetheless the obligation of the federal government to carry out the recommendations of the United Nations contained in the report. The fact that Brazil has signed international treaties that deal with many of the issues raised in the report supersedes the internal impediments to federal interference in the states and municipalities when there is clear evidence of serious violations of human rights and international law.

Notes

INTRODUCTION

1. Alves 2007; Fortes 2008, 35–40; United Nations Human Rights Council 2008, 13–26.
2. The icon on the armored vehicle is a *caveira*, meaning skull or death's head; hence, the name *caveirão*, or Big Skull.
3. Amora, Motta, Pontes, et al. 2008; Zaluar 2007.
4. Alves 2007; Fortes 2008, 35–40.

CHAPTER 1

1. Another recent form of popular transportation run by small private entrepreneurs who are not necessarily connected either to drugs or to militias is the *moto-taxi* (motorcycle taxi). Entrepreneurs in the favela of Rocinha have pioneered these small companies that provide fast transportation up and down the streets and tight alleys of this community of almost 100,000 inhabitants. It is a wild rollercoaster-like ride on the back of a moto-taxi up and down the crowded alleys, with sudden turns to avoid running over people or crashing. Rocinha's entrepreneurs were quick to grasp the potential of tourism in this and other adventures in the hills of Rio's most famous favela. Several agencies organize guided tours of Rocinha with the right to visit the local "Academicos da Rocinha" samba school. The tour can include lunch at one of the local restaurants that specializes in Brazilian food.
2. As of early 2011, the period of low economic growth appears to have ended. Plans to host World Cup soccer matches in 2014 and the Summer Olympic Games in 2016 and large investments in deep-water oil drilling and the petrochemical industry have raised expectations for Rio de Janeiro, which led all Brazilian states in new job creation at the end of 2010.

3. Center for the Study of Public Safety and Citizenship 2008.

4. Amora 2007.

5. Holston 2008, 307; Lembruger 2006.

6. See Vieira 1994 for a review of *The Broken City.*

7. Souza e Silva 2003; see also Souza e Silva and Barbosa 2005.

8. See Perlman 1976; also Perlman 2010 for Janice Perlman's views on the Rio de Janeiro favelas three decades after publishing the pioneering *Myth of Marginality.*

9. Arias 2006, 63–64.

10. Amora, Motta, Pontes, et al. 2008.

11. Ibid. (August 28), 17.

12. The police do not consider the decentralized drug gangs organized crime. The gangs may control territories, but they do not engage in money laundering or accumulate and invest capital, as do the militias, which, for example, acquire real estate (Conde 2009).

CHAPTER 2

1. Zaluar 2007, 12.

2. Antônio Vicente Mendes Macial (1830–1897), better known to his followers and in history as Antônio Conselheiro (Anthony the Counselor), led a movement of utopian Christians in the backlands of Bahia, where he founded a holy city in the small settlement of Canudos in 1893. Authorities first in Bahia and then in the national capital, Rio de Janeiro, came to view Canudos as a threat to the newly established republic, especially when Antônio Conselheiro's followers defeated a series of military forces sent against them. The Brazilian Army, directed by the minister of war, finally prevailed in 1897 in a war of annihilation against Canudos. The story of this war is memorably told in Euclides da Cunha, *Os Sertões* (1902), available in English in the classic translation by Samuel Putnam as *Rebellion in the Backlands* (1944). *Os Sertões* has been called Brazil's greatest book.

3. Zaluar 2007, 12.

4. See French 2009.

5. Luz 2008.

6. "Subnormal agglomerations" are defined as more than fifty dwelling units arrayed in a "disordered and dense" layout on land that belongs to someone else and that lacks essential services. This definition, favored by the United Nations Human Settlements Program and accepted by the Brazilian Institute of Geography and Statistics, hardly applies to long-established favelas, with their small brick homes supplied with running water, electricity, and sewerage systems, although land-ownership rights of the occupants may not be fully established in law.

7. The Lei do Ventre Livre (Free Birth Law) passed by the Brazilian Parliament on September 28, 1871, declared free from that date forward all children born of enslaved mothers, thereby condemning slavery to extinction. That an infant might emerge from the womb already a bandit—a sort of *lei do ventre bandido* (law of the bandit womb)—condemns the favela as a nursery of bandits and serves to justify a rhetoric of sterilizing men and women and killing young men.

8. Levitt and Dubner 2005.

9. Freire 2007; Soares 2007.

10. Luz 2008.

11. Cited in Amora, Motta, Pontes, et al. 2008 (August 30), 22.

12. Institute of Applied Economic Research 2008.

13. Ministry of External Relations 1966, 125.

14. Quoted in *Jornal do Brasil*, July 12, 1991, 1.

15. Center for the Study of Public Safety and Citizenship 2008.

16. United Nations Human Rights Council 2008, 2.

17. Cruz and Batitucci 2007, 11–24, 51–104.

CHAPTER 3

1. Colonel Ubiratan Ângelo was the commandant of the Rio de Janeiro State Military Police in 2007–2008 and a strong supporter of community policing.

2. Tim Lopes was a journalist with *O Globo* investigating crime in the Alemão complex. He was kidnapped and brutally murdered while on this assignment.

3. This is a reference to Governors Anthony Garotinho (1999–2002) and Rosinha Garotinho (2003–2006).

4. Getúlio Vargas Hospital is a state hospital that serves people in the Zona Norte, which includes areas occupied by the Alemão complex.

5. Operation Condor dates from the era of national security state dictatorships in Argentina, Bolivia, Brazil, Chile, Paraguay, and Uruguay in the 1970s and early 1980s, when these countries' military-intelligence forces, supported by the United States, collaborated in a program to eliminate individuals considered subversive through kidnapping, torture, and assassination. An estimated 50,000 people were killed, and 30,000 disappeared in what has been called a "common market of death." For futher details and the history of Operation Condor, see Dinges 2004.

6. An X-9 is an informant or a snitch.

7. New Holland is one of the favelas in the Maré complex.

8. The police officer investigated and charged with the crime was murdered under unexplained circumstances while awaiting trial in February 2010.

CHAPTER 4

1. The Brazilian answer to Mattel Corporation's popular Barbie doll in the United States. Estrela dolls are now collector's items.

CHAPTER 5

1. "Brizola na cabeça," which can also be translated as "High on Brizola" or "Brizola at the Head of the Ticket." Leonel Brizola (1922–2004) was a nationalist-populist political leader who achieved the distinction of being elected governor of two different Brazilian states, once in Rio Grande do Sul (1958), and twice in Rio de Janeiro (1982, 1990). He was forced into exile by the military dictatorship of 1964–1979. In the 1982 election in Rio de Janeiro, the Brizola campaign distributed tens of thousands of paper visors with the "Brizola na cabeça" campaign slogan printed on them.

CHAPTER 6

1. The DOI-CODI (Department of Information Operations–Center for Internal Defense Operation) was a feared political police force during the military dictatorship from 1964 until it was effectively disbanded in 1985 with the end of the dictatorship and political repression.

2. Soares, Moura, and Afonso 2009.

3. See the interview with Ricardo Brisolla Balestreri in this volume.

4. In the film *Quasi dois irmãos* (Almost Two Brothers [2004]), this myth becomes part of the story line, though by the end of the film, the common criminals' understanding of a corrupt world reality has prevailed over the revolutionary vision of the political prisoners of the left.

5. See the inteview with José Mariano Beltrame in this volume.

6. *Extra* Debate 2008, 1, 12–13.

7. "Os Ricos Querem Paz para Continuar Ricos. Nós Queremos Paz para Continuar Vivos."

8. Gomide 2007.

9. Caruso, Moraes, and Pinto 2005.

10. Lembruger, Musemeci, and Cano 2003, 148.

11. Military Police of Rio de Janeiro State and Viva Rio 2006.

12. Lembruger, Musemeci, and Cano 2003, 60–89.

13. Stress lines between the Military Police and the Civil Police are discussed in Soares 2002, which provides a detailed and fascinating narrative of an ill-fated effort to implement public security reform in Rio in 1999–2000.

14. In 2009, Military Police salaries in Rio de Janeiro ranged from roughly $2,500 per month in take-home pay for a full colonel—the highest rank—to $750 for a corporal and $500 for a soldier (Sousa 2009).

15. Lembruger, Musemeci, and Cano 2003, 43.

16. Conde 2009.

17. Lemle 2007a.

18. A summary of research on police deaths for the state of Rio de Janeiro between 2000 and 2006 states that the rate of violent deaths for police was 3.6 times greater than that for the male population of Rio de Janeiro, and 13.6 times greater than that for the general population of Brazil (Lemle 2007b). Lembruger, Musemeci, and Cano (2003) conducted extensive interviews with police that identify and record their complaints and provide their diagnosis of the disorder that is institutionalized in police work. The police themselves are victims of perverse professional socialization, low salaries, and poor training even as many deviate from the rules of good police work, break laws, and make victims of citizens.

19. In a statement to the large-circulation weekly newsmagazine *Veja* in 1996, General Cerqueira described the program as an effort to stimulate "productivity in the administration of human resources of police institutions. Just as in the private sector, we are giving pecuniary rewards and promotion for bravery in an effort to give incentives to the police" (quoted in "A Morte às nossa portas" 1996).

20. Soares (2000) provides a compelling narrative and reflections on this reform

effort. For the genesis of the program during the 1998 gubernatorial campaign, see Garotinho and Soares 1998.

21. Fernandes 2008; see also the interview with Antônio Carlos Carballo Blanco in this volume.

22. The Cardoso government's 2000 Plano Nacional de Segurança Pública (National Plan for Public Security) has been derided for substituting language for a program with goals, but it did lead to the creation of the SENASP and to the budgeting of federal money to be spent on public security in the states. On the Cardoso government's plan, see Bailey and Dammert 2006, 24–43.

23. Arias 2006, 64–65. Three years later, in 2008, a community leader described the area controlled by the League of Justice militia in the Zona Norte to us. "When you go and look at the League of Justice, you have the police, politician, municipal councilman, state deputies, and death squads. You have it all there" (see the interview with Carlinhos Costa in this volume).

24. Quoted in *O Globo*, July 25, 2008, 3.

25. However, Article 144, sec. 2, of the 1988 Constitution does assign repression of drug trafficking to the Federal Police, which might open the door to more direct Federal Police actions in states against drug traffickers should a state government find such police work beyond its ability.

26. The Conferencia Nacional de Segurança Pública (National Conference on Public Security) was held in Brasília on August 27–30, 2009. President Lula addressed the conference, saying that public security was everyone's "responsibility" and urging people to stop trying to assign blame for failings in public security, especially on the police, who are not the "enemy, but a type of guardian of the community."

CHAPTER 7

1. The Escola Superior de Guerra was established in 1949 to provide courses for Brazilian military and civilians on national security issues broadly defined.

2. Beltrame seems to identify "central" areas as those in the hilly terrain near middle-class and upper-class residential neighborhoods, including the picture-postcard tourist areas of Rio de Janeiro, as contrasted with the "periphery" of the Baixada Fluminense.

3. The Rio Card is an electronic pass for public transportation provided by employers in Rio de Janeiro. It is also available to students and to people who are older than sixty-five.

4. This is a reference to deaths caused when Military Police mistakenly killed innocent people while pursuing presumed bandidos in stolen automobiles.

5. In 2009, the Rio de Janeiro state legislature approved a law to raise the number of Military Police on active duty from 40,000 to 60,000. These numbers for the state of Rio, with slightly more than 15 million people, compare very favorably with São Paulo's 93,000 Military Police for a population of 41 million.

6. Beltrame is referring to the motorized launch *Bateau Mouche* that, overloaded with people, sank in Guanabara Bay on New Year's Eve of 1989. Of the 153 aboard, 55 died.

7. In establishing UPPs since 2009, the police have come to adopt the practice of notifying communities beforehand that a UPP will be entering so that drug traffickers can leave or make other arrangements that will not involve armed resistence to the police. Elsewhere, in communities without UPPs, unannounced police actions in pursuit of traffickers, guns, and drugs continue, with innocent people wounded and killed.

8. In 2007, British police killed the Brazilian João Carlos Meneses on a London subway car, mistaking him for a terrorist.

9. Espaço Criança Esperança is a collaborative project of the state government of Rio de Janeiro, the NGO Viva Rio, and UNESCO to make sports and other activities with artistic and educational aims available to children and adolescents in the favleas of Cantagalo and Pavão-Pavãozinho.

10. *Elite Squad* takes the point of view of the police in their war with bandidos in Rio de Janeiro. The elite squad itself is the BOPE, whose members are trained with rigor and required to meet standards that include the requirement to remain free of the corrupt, criminal behavior commonly thought to be practiced by many members of the Military Police. The film portrays a badly organized, inward-looking police force striving for self-sufficiency, with officers assigned to repair police cars whose condition is so poor that they should be scrapped and other officers working as cooks in Military Police battalions, two practices that have been ended by Governor Sérgio Cabral. The film shows the BOPE as a crack police force, the one Military Police battalion that knows how to combat and eliminate bandidos in Rio de Janeiro, and that is feared by them. However, conflicting views of the BOPE exist, especially among residents of the favelas, as can be seen in the interviews in this book. The film also has been controversial because it seems to approve of the harsh and violent activities of the BOPE in the communities. Although *Elite Squad* appears to have made a tremendous impact in Brazil—and certainly on some political leaders we interviewed—it is filmed fiction in the tradition of realism, not a documentary film.

11. Sebastianism, which has a long history in Portugal and Brazil, is the belief that a redeemer will appear in difficult times. It is linked to the fate of Portugal's King Sebastian (1557–1578), who disappeared during an ill-conceived invasion of Morocco in 1578 without leaving an heir, which in turn led to the period of the Babylonian Captivity in Portuguese history (1580–1640), when the kings of Spain were also the kings of Portugal.

CHAPTER 8

1. In 2009, a few months after this interview, Lula offered another view, stating publicly that he understood how politicians seeking votes might encourage the poor to occupy land, leading to further growth of favelas, and how later it made sense that politicians seeking votes would be reluctant to condemn the occupations.

2. Gétulio Vargas was the iconic president of Brazil in 1930–1945 and 1951–1954. A nationalist and populist politician and statesman, Vargas was removed from power by the military in 1945. Rather than be removed by the military a second time, in 1954, he committed suicide.

3. Miriam Belchior was an important staff member of the Casa Civil (Civil

Household) of the president that coordinates domestic policy. In 2010, Belchior was named executive-secretary of the PAC.

4. The Federal Savings Bank, or Caixa Econômica Federal, is a large public bank that provides mortgages and other banking services.

5. Pro-Uni is the University for All Program that provides partial or complete scholarships for students from low-income families who have completed secondary education and taken the national exam for secondary education and who are attending private institutions of higher education. Pro-Uni was created to help reach the goal of the National Education Plan of 2000 to have 30 percent of all eligible individuals between eighteen and twenty-four attending institutions of higher education.

6. Itaboraí is a municipality in Rio de Janeiro State.

7. Benedita da Silva was elected vice-governor of Rio de Janeiro in 1998 and succeeded Anthony Garotinho as governor in 2002, when Garotinho resigned to run for president of Brazil.

8. Judiciary Police are members of the Civil Police who investigate a crime and prepare reports of their findings that are then turned over to the criminal courts.

9. The Plan Colombia originated with Colombian President Andres Pestrana in 1998, who requested international aid for social and economic development that would provide alternatives to the illegal drug-trafficking economy while the government negotiated peace with the Revolutionary Armed Forces of Colombia (FARC) guerrillas. The U.S. contribution was an aid package that earmarked nearly 80 percent of its funds for the Colombian police and military.

10. The Rio Conference, held in 1992, was an international conference on the environment in which heads of state participated.

11. Participatory budgeting began in Porto Alegre in Rio Grande do Sul State in 1989. It brings ordinary citizens into the process of prioritizing budget allocations through annual neighborhood, regional, and city assemblies.

12. Márcio Thomaz Bastos was the minister of justice from 2003 to 2006 during the first Lula administration.

13. Lula finished second in the presidential election of 1989, losing the runoff election to Fernando Collor.

14. The Zero Hunger program to provide food security for all Brazilians was a main theme of Lula's successful presidential campaign of 2002 and found support in all social classes. Dilma Rousseff became Lula's anointed candidate to succeed him as president in 2011.

15. Aloisio Nunes Ferreira was the minister of justice in 2001–2002.

16. Paulo Maluf is a former governor of São Paulo and former mayor of the city of São Paulo. He was the military regime's candidate for president in 1985. Maluf was defeated by Tancredo Neves, who died before he could be sworn in. Neves's vice-presidential runningmate, José Sarney, served as president from 1985 to 1989.

17. The army was sent to the Providencia Hill favela in the center of Rio de Janeiro in 2008 to make it safe for PAC public works projects. However, soldiers turned three young male residents over to members of a drug-gang faction in a nearby favela, who tortured and murdered them. The mothers Vannuchi visited were those of the murdered youths. A strong public reaction followed, forcing withdrawal of the army unit from Providencia Hill.

18. Baron Georges-Eugène Haussmann (1809–1891) was charged by Napoléon III with the task of rebuilding Paris, which included replacing the narrow streets and congested neighborhoods of the medieval city with broad boulevards and parks, giving Paris its modern layout.

19. When using the terms "parallel activity" and "parallel power," Cabral is clearly referring to the actions and growing threat of militias composed of police and former police who establish themselves as organized crime groups in various favela communities.

20. "Alternative transportation" refers to the vans that circulate in large numbers, competing with local buses and that go where buses do not have routes. Vans cost less than buses and often take passengers to their homes, but many are viewed as under the control of militias.

21. Laranjeiras is a middle-class and upper-class area in Rio de Janeiro.

22. "Geni" is a reference to lyrics to a song in Chico Buarque de Holanda's *Opera do Malandro* (1978), a Brazilian updating of the eighteenth-century *Beggars' Opera* about everyone turning against an individual who is then beaten, spat on, and stoned—in effect, a figure of derision.

CONCLUSION

1. In late 2009, the Lula government issued the National Plan for Human Rights 3, the third such plan since 1996. The plan adhered to established international norms in human rights and public security work. It identified objectives such as combating torture and investigating *homicidas* when agents of the state were involved. The state was to gather and publish data on all such cases and investigate each and every case with the help of an enlarged and better-trained group of experts in forensic medicine. However, the plan was limited to public security agents of the national government such as the Federal Police. For the state and municipal governments, the plan was only a long list of recommendations, not required guidelines to follow. Included was the recommendation that armored vehicles such as the Big Skulls not be used to intimidate people or violate their human rights and that expressions such as "acts of resistance" and "resistance followed by death" no longer be used in police records. Despite its limitations, human rights NGOs throughout Brazil strongly supported the plan, noting that it reinforced Brazil's commitment to international law in defense of human rights derived from treaties the country had signed (see President of Brazil's Special Secretariat for Human Rights 2009).

2. For the Alston recommendations, see United Nations Human Rights Council 2008, 42–49.

3. Ibid., 43.

Glossary

Ação Comunitária do Brasil Rio de Janeiro (Community Action of Brazil in Rio de Janeiro): NGO founded in 1967 by businessmen and businesswomen who did not agree with the violent removal of favelas in Rio de Janeiro.

Amigos dos Amigos: Friends of Friends, a drug-trafficking syndicate in Rio de Janeiro.

baile funk: Funk dance.

bairro nobre: Middle- or upper-class neighborhood of Rio de Janeiro.

bairros Africanos: Nineteenth-century African-Brazilian communities.

Baixada Fluminense: Flatlands area that includes sixteen different municipalities north and west of Rio de Janeiro.

bandido: Bandit; in this book, a member of a crime group.

boca de fumo: Literally, "smoking mouth"; a point of sale for drugs.

bolsa família: Federal family grant program in which more than 11 million low-income families were enrolled as of 2009. Families enroll through municipal governments.

BOPE: Batalhão de Operações Policiais Especiais (Special Operations Police Battalion).

Brizolão: Popular name for a CIEP (Centro Integrado de Educaçao Públic), a public school named after Governor Leonel Brizola whose administrations imagined and built the schools.

Candomblé: Afro-Brazilian religion.

capoeira: Brazilian martial art.

carioca: Resident of the city of Rio de Janeiro.

caveirão: "Big Skull," a large armored vehicle used by BOPE units. It is named for the skull-and-crossbones logo emblazoned on it.

CEASM: Centro de Estudos e Ações Solidárias de Maré (Center for Studies and Actions for Solidarity in Maré), an NGO with educational and cultural projects for the people of the Maré complex of favelas.

CEDAE: Rio de Janeiro state company for water and sewerage.

centro social: Social center; in this book, used in the sense of centers in favelas financed by public funds made available to politicians.

CESeC: Centro de Estudos de Segurança Pública e Cidadania (Center for the Study of Public Safety and Citizenship), Candido Mendes University, Rio de Janeiro.

chacina: Police massacre.

CIEP: Centro Integrado de Educação Pública (Integrated Public School Center).

Civil Police: State police force charged with investigating crimes.

Comando Vermelho: Red Command, the largest of the criminal drug-trafficking syndicates in Rio de Janeiro.

COMLURB: Companhia Municipal de Limpeza Urbana (Municipal Urban Cleaning Company). Trash-collecting and street-cleaning public service of Rio de Janeiro, with work done by men and women in orange uniforms.

dono do morro: "Owner of the hill" or crime boss of a particular favela.

escola de samba: Samba school. Community cultural organization that prepares a dancing opera theater in which thousands participate for the annual Carnival; a main reason for Rio de Janeiro's reputation as a city of happy people.

favela: Densely populated, self-built community of mostly low-income people, usually imagined in Rio de Janeiro as occupying hills, and often a main theater of conflict between bandidos and the police.

fazenda: Large farm, plantation. Owners of *fazendas* and their families have traditionally dominated rural Brazil economically, socially, and politically.

Federal Police: Police force of the federal government.

FETRANSPOR: Federação das Empresas do Transporte das Passageiros do Estado do Rio de Janeiro (Federation of Passenger Transport of the State of Rio de Janeiro).

Fire Brigades of the Military Police: Corpo de Bombeiros da Policia Militar; the firemen are militarized.

fuzil: Rifle. In present-day Brazil, a high-powered automatic rifle that fires projectiles and tracer bullets that can perforate bodies and pentrate cement.

GGI: Gabinete de Gestao Integrada (Cabinet for Integrated Administration). Also, GGIM (Cabinet for Integrated Municipal Administration) and GGIS (Cabinet for the Integrated Administration of Public Security).

GPAE: Grupamento de Policiamento em Áreas Especiais (Police Group in Special Areas). Community policing units created in 2000.

IDDH: Instituto dos Defensores de Direitos Humanos (Institute of Defenders of Human Rights).

Igreja Universal do Reino de Deus: Universal Church of the Kingdom of God.

Imagens do Povo: Images of the People, a school of photography since 2004 of the Observatório de Favelas.

INA: The unreliable submachine gun that took its name from Indústria Nacional de Armas (National Industry of Arms), the company that manufactured it.

IPEA: Instituto de Pesquisa Econômica Aplicada (Institute of Applied Economic Research).

ISER: Instituto de Estudos da Religião (Institute of Studies of Religion); has sponsored important research on public security in Rio de Janeiro.

laje: Cement slab often built as a top floor of houses in favelas and that serve for social gatherings, cookouts, and children's playgrounds.

League of Justice: The strongest of Rio de Janeiro mafia-style militias.

Macumba: Afro-Brazilian religion.

Military Police: Policia Militar, the state police force that patrols streets and neighborhoods. Charged with maintaining order.

MST: Movimento Sem Terra (Landless Movement). Social movement of landless rural people who occupy land and seek transfer of it to them under agrarian reform law.

mutirão: Collective effort to help an individual or community complete a task.

NGO: Nongovernmental organization.

nordestinos: Residents and workers who migrated from the Brazilian northeast to other areas of Brazil.

NSF: National Security Force (Força Nacional de Segurança), a shortened version of National Public Security Force, a militarized national police force comprising members of the Military Police and Fire Brigades of the Military Police from different states and available for service in states at the request of state governors.

OAB: Ordem dos Advogados do Brasil (Brazilian Bar Association).

Observatório de Favelas: Observatory of the Favelas; an NGO committed to providing educational and job-training opportunities for residents of favelas in Rio de Janeiro.

PAC: Programa de Aceleração do Crescimento (Program for the Acceleration of Economic Growth).

PDT: Partido Democrático Trabalhista (Democratic Labor Party).

PMDB: Partido do Movimento Democrático Brasileiro (Brazilian Democratic Movement Party).

Projecto Uerê: NGO that works with street children and low-income children in favelas. "Uerê" literally means "the spirit of a child."

PRONASCI: Programa Nacional de Segurança Pública com Cidadania (National Program of Public Security with Citizenship).

PSDB: Partido da Social Democracia Brasileira (Brazilian Social Democratic Party).

PT: Partido dos Trabalhadores (Workers' Party).

real (reais): Brazilian currency since 1994.

Rede Latino-Americana de Policiais e Sociedade Civil (Latin American Network of Police and Civil Society): Organization created in 2006 with contributions by research centers, NGOs, and police organizations from ten Latin American countries, including Argentina, Brazil, Chile, Colombia, Mexico, Peru, and Venezuela.

samba enredo: Theme song and lyrics that tell the story that a samba school represents during its Carnival dancing theater display.

Sambódramo: Outdoor structure designed by Oscar Niemeyer to accommodate spectators who watch the parade of samba schools during Carnival in Rio de Janeiro.

SENASP: Secretaria Nacional de Segurança Pùblica (National Secretariat for Public Security).

telecurso: Distance-learning course that allows Brazilians to complete elementary and secondary education.

Terceiro Comando Puro: Pure Third Command, a drug-trafficking syndicate in Rio de Janeiro

traficante: Drug trafficker.

Umbanda: Afro-Brazilian religion.

UPP: Unidade de Polícia Pacificadora (Police Pacification Unit).

vereador(a): City Council representative.

Viva Rio: NGO based in Rio de Janeiro.

Zona Norte: Northern Zone; a socially and economically heterogeneous area of metropolitan Rio de Janeiro.

Zona Oeste: Western Zone; an area that includes more than half of the districts of the city of Rio de Janeiro.

Zona Sul: Southern Zone; area dominated by middle-class and upper-class neighborhoods, including Botafogo, Copacabana, Flamengo, Gloria, Ipanema, Leblon, Leme, and São Conrado.

References

References in this list that are not cited in either the text or the notes were consulted for general information during the research for this book.

Alves, Maria Helena Moreira. 1984. *State and Opposition in Military Brazil.* Austin: University of Texas Press.

———. 2007. "A Guerra no Complexo de Alemão e Penha: Segurança pública ou geno- cidio?" Available online at http://www.redecontraviolencia.org/Artigos/143.html.

Amora, Dimmi. 2007 "Czar da drogas. Um general diante da guerra de vez." January 7. Available online at http://www.oglobo.globo.com/rio/ancelmo/reporterdecrime/ default.asp?palavra=dimmi+amora.

Amora, Dimmi, Cláudio Motta, Fernanda Pontes, Carla Rocha, and Selma Schmidt. 2008. "Favela $.A." *O Globo,* August 24–September 1.

Amorim, Carlos. 1993. *Comando Vermelho: A história secreta do crime organizado.* Rio de Janeiro: Editora Record.

Amnesty International. 2005. "'They Come in Shooting': Policing Socially Excluded Neighborhoods." Report no. 109/025/2005, December.

Anderson, Jon Lee. 2009. "Gangland: Life in the Favelas of Rio de Janeiro." *New Yorker,* October 5, 46–57.

Arias, Enrique Desmond. 2006. *Drugs and Democracy in Rio de Janeiro.* Chapel Hill: University of North Carolina Press.

Azevedo, Leonardo da Silva Petronilha. 2006. "A política de direitos humanos no Rio de Janeiro: Ouvidoria da polícia e correjadoria geral unificada—Estrategias de controle social no estado democráctico de direito (1999–2006)." Master's thesis, Universidade Federal Fluminense, Niteroi.

Bailey, John, and Lucía Dammert. 2006. *Public Security and Police Reform in the Americas*. Pittsburgh: University of Pittsburgh Press.

Balestreri, Ricardo Brisolla. 2003. *Direitos humanos: Coisa de polícia*, 3rd ed. Porto Alegre: Centro de Assessoramento e Programa de Educação para a Cidadania.

Bandeira, Antônio Rangel, and Josephine Bourgois. 2006. *Firearms: Protection or Risk?* Trans. Jessica Galeira. Rio de Janeiro: Parliamentary Forum on Small Arms and Light Weapons.

Barcellos, Caco. 1987. *Rota 66: A história da polícia que mata*. Rio de Janeiro: Editora Globo.

———. 2003. *Abusado: O dono do morro Dona Marta*. Rio de Janeiro: Editora Record.

Barros, Antonio Jorge. 2007. "Reflexões sobre a nossa guerra em particular." June 13. Available online at http://www.oglobo.globo.com/rio/ancelmo/reporterdecrime/default.asp?.

Bill, M. V., and Celso Athayde. 2006. *Falcão: Meninos do tráfico*. Rio de Janeiro: Editora Objetiva.

Cano, Ignacio. 1997. "The Use of Lethal Force by Police in Rio de Janeiro." Rio de Janeiro: Instituto de Estudos da Religião.

———. 1998 "Racial Bias in Lethal Police Action in Brazil." Rio de Janeiro: Instituto de Estudos da Religião.

Caruso, Haydée Glória Cruz, Luciane Patricio Braga de Moraes, and Nalayne Mendonça Pinto. 2005. *Polícia militar do estado do Rio de Janeiro: Da escola de formação à prática policial*. Available online at http://www.comunidadesegura.org.br/.../policiaestadoesociedadepraticasesabereslatinoamericanos.pdf.

Carvalho, José Murilo de. 2004. *Cidadania no Brasil. O longo caminho*, 5th ed. Rio de Janeiro: Editora Civilização Brasileira.

Cavallaro, James. 1997. *Police Brutality in Urban Brazil*. New York: Human Rights Watch.

Center for the Study of Public Safety and Citizenship. 2008. "Estado do Rio de Janeiro: Numero e taxa de homicidios dolosos registrado pela policia civil por regiões, 1990–2007." Available online at http://www.ucamcesec.com.br/arquivos/estatisticas/evol2007_p01.xls.

Cezar, Paulo Bastos. 2002. "Evolução da população das favelas na cidade do Rio de Janeiro: Uma reflexão sobre os dados mais recentes." Coleção Estudos Cariocas, no. 2002020. Rio de Janeiro: Instituto Municipal de Urbanismo Pereira Passos.

Chevigny, Paul. 1995. *The Edge of the Knife: Police Violence in the Americas*. New York: New Press.

Conde, Miguel. 2009. "Rodrigo Pimentel, roteirista do 'Tropa de Elite,' diz que e preciso transformar a PM do Rio." *O Globo Online*, May 12. Available online at http://oglobo.globo.com/rio/mat/2009/05/12/rodrigo-pimental-roteirista-do-trapa-de-elite-diz-que-preciso-transformar-pm-do-rio-755839134,asp.

Cruz, Marcus Vinicius Gonçalves da, and Eduardo Cerqueira Batitucci, organizers. 2007. *Homícidios no Brasil*. Rio de Janeiro: Fundação Getúlio Vargas.

Dinges, John. 2004. *The Condor Years: How Pinochet and His Allies Brought Terrorism to Three Continents*. London: New Press.

Dowdney, Luke. 2003. *Children of the Drug Trade*. Rio de Janeiro: 7 Letras.

Extra Debate. 2008. "Beltrame: Políca do Rio não vai mais usar fuzil." *Extra*, July 30, pp. 1, 12–13.

Fernandes, Rubem César, coordinator. 2005. *Brasil: As armas e as vítimas*. Rio de Janeiro: 7 Letras. (Also available in English at http://www.vivario.org.br.)

———. 2008. "Controlar a violencia armada: Notas sobre o trabalho do Vivo Rio." Paper presented at Viva Rio seminar, Resende, July 25–26.

Fortes, Rafael, organizer. 2008. *Segurança pública, direitos humanos e violência*. Rio de Janeiro: Editora Multifoco.

Freire, Aluizio. 2007. "Cabral defende aborto contra violência no Rio de Janeiro." Globo.com. Available online at http://g1.globo.com.

French, Jan Hoffman. 2009. *Legalizing Identities: Becoming Black or Indian in Brazil's Northeast*. Chapel Hill: University of North Carolina Press.

Garotinho, Anthony, and Luiz Eduardo Soares. 1998. *Violencia e criminalidade no estado do Rio de Janeiro: Diagnóstico e propostas para uma política democrática de segurança pública*. Rio de Janeiro: Hama Editora.

Gay, Robert. 1994. *Popular Organization and Democracy in Rio de Janeiro: A Tale of Two Favelas*. Philadelphia: Temple University Press.

———. 2005. *Lucia: Testimonies of a Brazilian Drug Dealer's Woman*. Philadelphia: Temple University Press.

Goldstein, Donna. 2003. *Laughter Out of Place: Race, Class, Violence, and Sexuality in Rio Shantytowns*. Berkeley: University of California Press.

Gomide, Rafael. 2007. "Policia do Rio mata 41 civis para cada policial morto." *Folha de São Paulo*, July 16. Available online at http://www.ucamcesec.com.br/md_part_texto.php:cod_proj=30.

Holloway, Thomas H. 1993. *Policing Rio de Janeiro: Repression and Resistance in a 19th-Century City*. Stanford, Calif.: Stanford University Press.

Holston, James. 2008. *Insurgent Citizenship: Disjunctions of Democracy and Modernity in Brazil*. Princeton, N.J.: Princeton University Press.

Human Rights Watch/Americas. 1994. *Final Justice: Police and Death Squad Homicides of Adolescents in Brazil*. New York: Human Rights Watch.

———. 1999. *Brazil Slow on Human Rights Reform*. New York: Human Rights Watch.

Institute of Applied Economic Research. 2008. "Desigualdades raciais, racismo e políticas públicas: 120 anos apos a abolição." Available online at http://www.ipea.gov.br/sites/000/2/pdf/08_05_13_120anosAbolicao/coletiva.pdf.

Kant de Lima, Roberto. 1986. "Legal Theory and Judicial Practice: Paradoxes of Police Work in Rio de Janeiro City." Ph.D. diss., Harvard University, Cambridge, Massachusetts.

Leeds, Elizabeth. 1996. "Cocaine and Parallel Politics in the Brazilian Urban Periphery: Constraints on Local-Level Democratization." *Latin American Research Review* 31 (no. 3): 47–83.

Lembruger, Julita. 1998. *Cemiterios dos vivos: Análise sociologica de uma prisão de mulheres,* 2nd ed. Rio de Janeiro: Editora Forense.

———. 2006. "Segurança publica é responsabilidade de todo(as)." *Forum de Entidades*

Nacionais de Direitos Humanos. Available online at http://www.direitos.org.br/index.php.

Lembruger, Julita, Leonarda Musemeci, and Ignacio Cano. 2003. *Quem vigia os vigias? Um estudo sobre controle externo da polícia no Brasil.* Rio de Janeiro: Editora Record.

Lemle, Marina. 2007a. "Mercenários inconscientes?" *Comunidade Segura.* Available online at http://www.comunidadesegura.org/pt-br/node/35660.

———. 2007b. "Muito mais polícias morrem em folga." *Comunidade Segura.* Available online at http://www.comunidadesegura.org/pt-br/node/35688////pt_priv.

Levitt, Steven, and Stephen Dubner. 2005. *Freakonomics: A Rogue Economist Explores the Hidden Side of Everything.* New York: Harper Collins.

Luz, Hélio. 2008. "A Favela é a Senzala do século XXI." Available online at http://politicaetica.com/2009/10/21/a-favela-e-a-senzala-do-seculo-xxi.

Mereola, Ediane. 2008. "Rio é motivo de orgulho para 73% dos cariocas," *O Globo,* March 28. Available online at http://oglobo.globo/Rio/riocomovamos/mat/2008/07/31/rio_motivo_de_orgulho_para_73_dos_cariocas_547499021.asp.

Military Police of Rio de Janeiro State and Viva Rio. 2006. "A Polícia que queremos." Available online at http://www.comunidadesegura.org/en/node/495.

Ministry of External Relations. 1966. *Brazil 1966.* Brasília: Ministry of External Relations.

"A Morte às nossa portas." 1996. *Veja,* August 21, 1996. Available online at http://veja.abril.com.br/arquivo_veja/capa_21081996.shtml.

Perleman, Janice E. 1976. *The Myth of Marginality.* Berkeley: University of California Press.

———. 2010. *Favela: Four Decades of Living on the Edge of Rio de Janeiro.* New York: Oxford University Press.

President of Brazil's Special Secretariat for Human Rights. 2009. *Programa Nacional de Direitos Humanos (PNDH—3).* Brasília: Secretaria de Direitos Humanos/Presidência da Republica.

Ramos, Silvia, and Leonarda Musumeci. 2005. *Elemento suspeito: Abordagem policial e discriminção na cidade de Rio de Janeiro.* Coleção Segurança e Cidadania, no. 2. Rio de Janeiro: Editora Civilização Brasileira.

Ramos, Silvia, and Anabela Paiva. 2007. *Media e violência: Novas tendencias na cobrança de criminalidade e segurança no Brasil.* Rio de Janeiro: Centro de Estudos de Segurança Pública e Cidadania, Instituto Universitário de Pesquisas do Rio de Janeiro, and Secretaria de Direitos Humanos e União Européia.

Sapori, Luís Flávio. 2007. *Segurança pública no Brasil: Desafios e perspectivas.* Rio de Janeiro: Fundação Getúlio Vargas.

Sento-Sé, João Trajano, coordinator. 2006. *Prevenção da violencia: O Papel das cidades.* Coleção Segurança e Cidadania, no. 3. Rio de Janeiro: Editora Civilização Brasileira and Centro de Estudos de Segurança Pública e Cidadania.

Soares, Barbara Musumeci, Tatiana Moura, and Carlo Afonso, organizers. 2009. *Autos de resistencia: Relatos de familiaraes de vítimas de violência armada.* Rio de Janeiro: 7 Letras.

Soares, Barbara Musumeci, and Leonarda Musumeci. 2005. *Mulheres policiais: Presença feminima na polícia militar do Rio de Janeiro.* Coleção Segurança e Cidadania, 1.

Rio de Janeiro: Editora Civilização Brasileira and Centro de Estudos de Segurança Pública e Cidadania.

Soares, Glaucio Ary Dillon. 2008. *Não matarás: Desenvolvimento, desigualdade e homicidios.* Rio de Janeiro: Fundação Getúlio Vargas.

Soares, Glaucio Ary Dillon, Dayse Miranda, and Doriam Borges. 2007. *As vitimas ocultas da violència na ciade do Rio de Janeiro.* Rio de Janeiro: Editora Civilização Brasileira and Centro de Estudos de Segurança Pública e Cidadania.

Soares, Luiz Eduardo. 2000. *Meu casaco de general.* São Paulo: Companhia das Letras.

Soares, Luiz Eduardo, M. V. Bill, and Celso Athayde. 2005. *Cabeça de Porco.* Rio de Janeiro: Editora Objetiva.

———. 2006. *Segurança tem saída.* Rio de Janeiro: Sextante.

Soares, Ronaldo. 2007. "Entrevista: José Mariano Beltrame" *Veja 2032,* October 31. Available online at http://www.veja.com.br/311007/entrevista.shtml.

Sousa, Alexander de. 2009. "Quanto ganha um políca militar do Rio de Janeiro." Available online at http://concurso,depolicia.com/2009/02/01/salarios-pmerj-quanto-ganha-um-policial-militar-do-Rio-de-Janeiro.

Souza e Silva, Jailson de. 2003. "Adeus 'Cidade Partida.'" Observatorio de Favelas website. Available online at http://www.observatoriodefavelas.org.

Souza e Silva, Jailson de, and Jorge Luis Barbosa. 2005. *Favela: Alegria e dor na cidade.* Rio de Janeiro: Rio Senac.

United Nations Human Rights Council. 2008. "Report of the Special Rapporteur on Extrajudicial, Summary, or Arbitrary Executions Mr. Philip Alston on His Mission to Brazil (4–14 November 2007)." Available online at http://www2.ohchr.org/English/issues/executions/docs/A_HRC_11_2_ADD_2_ English.pdf.

Vale, Sandra Cristina Dias do. 2007. "Viva Rio: Uma organização para os novos tempos." Master's thesis, Rio de Janeiro, Centro de Pesquisa e Documentação de História Contemporânea do Brasil.

Ventura, Zuenir. 1994. *Cidade Partida.* São Paulo: Schwartz.

Vieira, Gustavo. 1994. "Paz entre bárbaros." *Jornal do Brasil,* August 26. Available online at http://literal.terra.com.br/zuenir_ventura_biblio/sobre_ele/imprensa/04paz_entre_barbaros.shmtl?bio.

Zaluar, Alba. 1994. *Condominio do diabo.* Rio de Janeiro: Editora Revan.

———. 2007. "The Case of Rio de Janeiro, Brazil." In *Global Report on Human Settlements 2007: Conditions and Trends,* United National Human Settlements Program. Available at online at http://www.ims.uerj.br/nupevi/thecaseofrio.pdf.

Zaluar, Alba, and Marcos Alvito, eds. 1998. *Um século de favela.* Rio de Janeiro: Fundação Getúlio Vargas.

NEWSPAPERS

O Dia
Extra
Folha de São Paulo
O Globo
Jornal do Brasil

HUMAN RIGHTS AND COMMUNITY WEB SITES

Americas Watch (http://www.hrw.org/en/americas)
Amnesty International (http://www.amnesty.org)
Global Justice (http://www.globaljusticnow.org)
Observatório de Favelas (http://wwws.observatoriodefavelas.org.br)
Rede de Comunidades e Movimentos Contra a Violencia (http://www.redecontra violencia.org)
Viva Rio (http://www.vivario.org.br)

FILMS

Elite Squad [Tropa de Elite], dir. José Padilha. Universal Pictures, 2007.
Noticias de uma guerra particular, dir. Katia Lund and João Moreira. Sales, Coleção-videofilmes, 1999.
Quasi dois irmãos, dir. Lúcia Murat. Imovision, 2004.

Index